ROSS HODDINOTT

Welcome...

"The world is a beautiful place and few know that better than the dedicated outdoor photographer. Exploring the diversity of locations and life on our planet surely must rank as one of the most desirable pastimes. The UK, despite its relatively small size, is blessed with appealing photo opportunities that could keep most photographers busy for a lifetime. From stunning scenics to captivating wildlife and beautiful flowers, there's no shortage of subjects to cover. Of course, this barely scratches the surface of the wonders that await those of us who are lucky enough to travel abroad. But regardless of where you may live, this *Essential Guide to Outdoor Photography* aims to provide advice and inspiration to passionate outdoor photographers looking to take their best ever images.

"Our team of experts provide in-depth advice on the three core interests: wildlife, nature and landscapes, as well as other challenging areas of outdoor photography, including night and architecture. This guide also features major sections dedicated to filters and essential kit. We trust it helps you develop your photo skills and passion for photography and leads to your best ever outdoor images. All the best!"

DANIEL LEZANO, EDITOR

Meet our outdoor photography experts

Our experts are regular contributors to *Digital SLR Photography*, the UK's fastest-growing photo magazine. For expert advice and inspiration to help improve your photo skills, pick up the latest issue, on sale the second Tuesday of every month. For more information, visit: www.digitalslrphoto.com

MARK BAUER

Former teacher Mark is now one of the UK's leading landscape photographers and an expert on Dorset's Jurassic coastline and the New Forest.

www.markbauerphotography.com

ROSS HODDINOTT

Ross is an award-winning photographer with many years of experience capturing the diverse beauty of the Britain's landscapes and wildlife.

www.rosshoddinott.co.uk

HELEN DIXON

Helen is living the dream, having given up a full-time job to become a professional landscape photographer. She is one of the UK's brightest talents.

www.helendixonphotography.co.uk

LEE FROST

A pro for two decades, Lee Frost's one of the best-known names in the UK photography business, with 20 books to his name and worldwide image sales.

www.leefrost.co.uk

HELEN DIXON

The Essential Guide to Outdoor Photography

Produced by *Digital SLR Photography* at:
6 Swan Court, Cygnet Park,
Peterborough, Cambs PE7 8GX
Phone: 01733 567401. Fax 01733 352650
Email: enquiries@digitalslrphoto.com
Online: www.digitalslrphoto.com

Editorial

To contact editorial phone: 01733 567401
Editor **Daniel Lezano**
daniel_lezano@dennis.co.uk
Art Editor **Luke Marsh**
luke_marsh@dennis.co.uk
Designer **Luke Medler**
luke_medler@dennis.co.uk
Editorial Co-ordinator **Jo Lezano**
jo_lezano@dennis.co.uk
Editorial contributors: Mark Bauer, Helen Dixon, Lee Frost, Ross Hoddinott, Rebecca McKie, Paul Ward & Robin Williams

Advertising & Production

Display & Classifield Sales: 0207 907 6651
Advertising Sales **Guy Scott-Wilson**
guy_scott-wilson@dennis.co.uk
Sales Executive **Joshua Rouse**
joshua_rouse@dennis.co.uk
Production Controller **Dan Stark**
dan_stark@dennis.co.uk

Publishing & Marketing

NICKY BAKER DIGITAL PRODUCTION MANAGER
DHARMESH MISTRY BOOKAZINE MANAGER
ROBIN RYAN PRODUCTION DIRECTOR
JULIAN LLOYD-EVANS MD OF ADVERTISING
DAVID BARKER NEWSTRADE DIRECTOR
BRETT REYNOLDS CHIEF OPERATING OFFICER
IAN LEGGETT GROUP FINANCE DIRECTOR
JAMES TYE CHIEF EXECUTIVE
FELIX DENNIS CHAIRMAN

For licensing contact Hannah Heagney on +44 (0)20 7907 6134 or email hannah_heagney@dennis.co.uk
For syndication contact Anj Dosaj-Halai on +44 (0)20 7907 6132 or email Anj_Dosaj-Halai@dennis.co.uk

The paper used within this Magbook is produced from sustainable fibre, manufactured by mills with a valid chain of custody.
The Essential Guide to Outdoor Photography ISBN 1-907779-92-2
Printed by Benham Goodhead Print (BGP)

CONTENTS

THE ESSENTIAL GUIDE TO OUTDOOR PHOTOGRAPHY

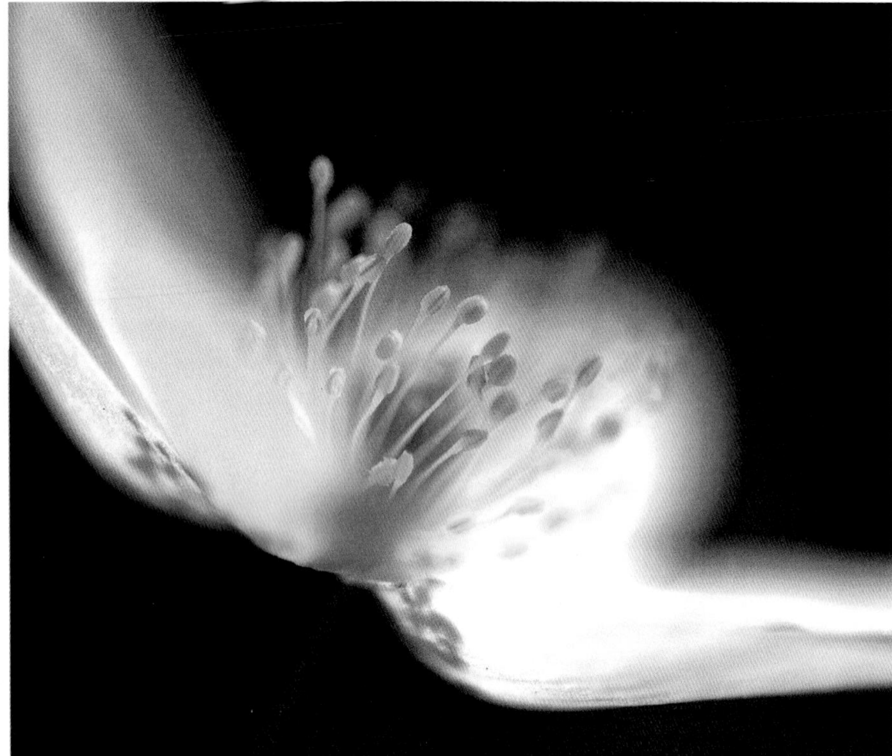

TURN TO PAGE 148 TO FIND OUT ABOUT OUR FANTASTIC SUBSCRIPTION OFFERS

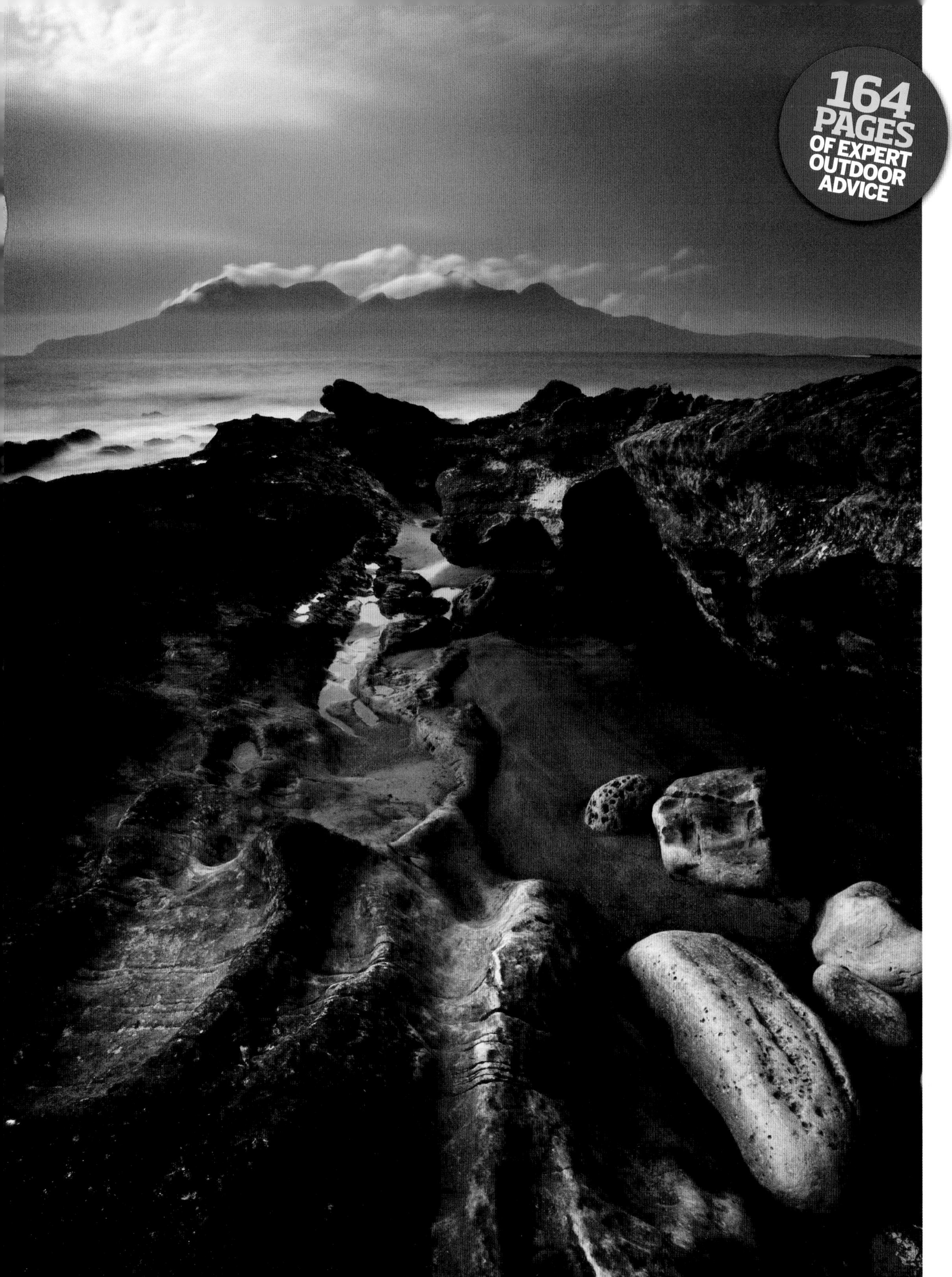
164
PAGES
OF EXPERT
OUTDOOR
ADVICE

Aperture-priority: Your mode of choice

So what is it that makes the aperture-priority mode more useful than any of the other exposure modes? When and why should you use it? Read on, and all will be revealed

Aperture-priority gets its name because it allows you to decide which aperture (f/number) you want to use to take a photograph, while the camera automatically sets a shutter speed, based on light levels, to achieve the correct exposure. In other words, it lets you prioritise the aperture selection, and it chooses the shutter speed accordingly.

As the lens aperture is the most influential factor over the depth-of-field (the zone of sharp focus) in a photograph, aperture-priority mode is the most practical choice of shooting mode if you are photographing a subject or situation in which control over depth-of-field is important.

Landscape photography is a good example. Generally, when shooting landscapes, you'll want to make sure your depth-of-field is broad enough to record the whole scene in sharp focus, from the immediate foreground to infinity, which means that you'll need to set a small aperture, such as f/11. Aperture-priority mode lets you do that easily, because you have to actively set the required aperture.

When shooting wildlife or portraits, the opposite tends to apply – you want shallow depth-of-field, so that your subject is recorded in sharp focus but the background is thrown out of focus. That means making sure you take the picture at a wide aperture such as f/4 or f/2.8, which again is easy when shooting in aperture-priority mode because it's you and not the camera who decides which aperture to use.

That said, you can still control which aperture is set using other exposure modes, but it just requires a slightly different (and longer) way of working. In shutter-priority (S or Tv) mode, for example, all you need to do is change the shutter speed until the camera sets the aperture you want. Similarly, in program mode, you can use the program shift function to change the aperture and shutter combination that the camera has set until you get the right aperture.

Where aperture-priority triumphs over these alternative modes is that once you've set a particular aperture, the camera won't change it, even if light levels change. Instead, the shutter speed adjusts to maintain the correct exposure. This wouldn't be the case if you set the camera to shutter-priority mode – if light levels change, your DSLR automatically adjusts the aperture to maintain correct exposure, giving the shutter speed priority, so your control over the depth-of-field is diminished. Similarly, in program mode, the camera would change the aperture/shutter speed combination in response to changing light.

Aperture-priority is also a handy mode to set for general use, when you're just wandering around, shooting anything that takes your fancy, whether it's architecture, details or abstracts. Depth-of-field requirements will vary depending on the shot – one minute you need lots of it, the next, as little as possible – but this can be quickly altered with the flick of the camera's input dial, and the viewfinder display will keep you fully informed of exactly which aperture (and corresponding shutter speed) you're using.

ROSS HODDINOTT

THE EFFECT OF APERTURES With depth-of-field having such an effect on the final image, it's no surprise that many experienced photographers rate aperture-priority as their favourite mode. These two shots show how different apertures can produce very different results.

Setting aperture-priority on your DSLR

Choosing aperture-priority mode is simple – all you need to do is turn your exposure dial (or in some cases push the exposure mode button) and select A or Av. Your DSLR will then be set to aperture-priority mode and all you need to do is rotate the small input dial (found either on the handgrip or on the top-right corner of the rear of your camera) to change your aperture. If you lightly depress the shutter button to activate the exposure system, you can keep a check on the shutter speed the camera has selected.

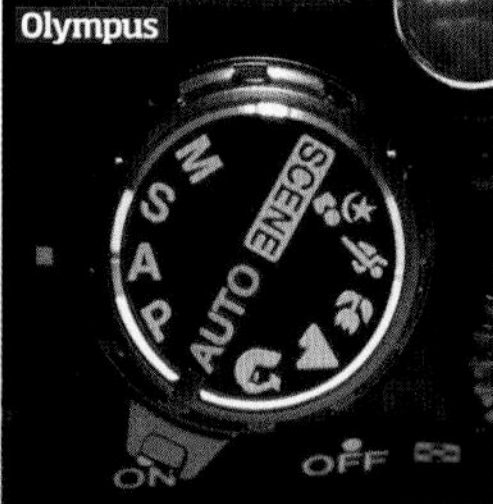

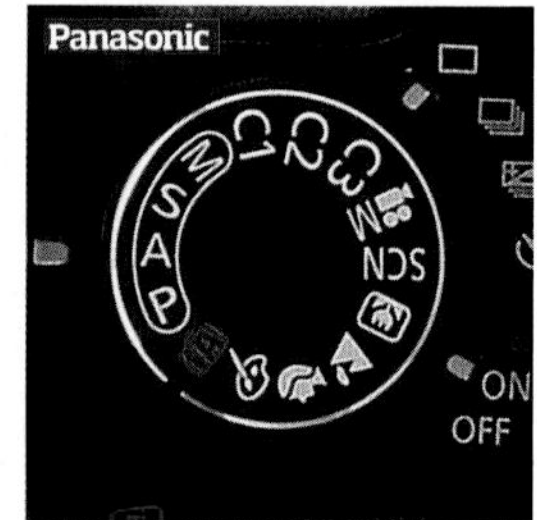

How other exposure modes work

We've already established that in aperture-priority mode, you set the desired aperture and the camera sets the accompanying shutter speed to give the correct exposure. Here's a quick rundown of how the other modes work.

Full-auto Mode

The camera sets the shutter speed and aperture to achieve correct exposure and you can't change the combination to use a specific aperture or shutter speed.

Program Mode

Works in a similar way to full auto, but you can usually alter the aperture/shutter speed combination if you need to use a specific aperture or shutter speed.

Shutter-Priority

You set a shutter speed and your DSLR sets the appropriate aperture. If light levels change, the same shutter speed is used and the aperture changed.

Metered Manual

You manually set both the aperture and shutter speed independently of each other, so neither changes unless you adjust them, even if light levels fall or rise.

Scene Modes

These program modes are tailored to suit a specific subject, with various camera functions like the AF, flash and exposure systems set accordingly.

Image: f/22

Aperture-priority allows landscape photographers to control how much of the scene is sharply in focus.

MARK BAUER

Aperture-priority 'tools'

Once you get used to shooting in aperture-priority, you'll discover that your camera has several functions that can help you get the best from this mode

ALTHOUGH APERTURE-PRIORITY is a practical and versatile exposure mode, it must still be used with care and it can only work within the limitations imposed by your camera's other features. For example, if you're using a small aperture such as f/16 or f/22 to maximise depth-of-field, there's a danger that the shutter speed set by the camera will be too slow to shoot handheld without risking camera shake. Even worse, when shooting in low light, such as at at dawn or at dusk, the shutter speed required to maintain a correct exposure at a small aperture may be outside the automated range offered by the camera, so if you go ahead and shoot, the picture will be underexposed. Similarly, if you're shooting at a wide aperture such as f/2.8 or f/4 in really bright conditions, there's a danger that even if the camera sets its fastest shutter speed, it could still be too slow, in which case overexposure would result. A flashing shutter speed in the viewfinder or LCD panel usually alerts you to these problems. The question is, what can you then do to overcome them?

Use a tripod

If you regularly shoot at small apertures to maximise depth-of-field, it would make sense to mount your camera on a sturdy tripod. That way, even if the shutter speed set by the camera is slower than about 1/30sec, you won't have to worry about camera shake ruining your shots. Image stabilisation does give you some leeway, making it possible to hand-hold your camera at slower shutter speed than normal, but only by a few stops! A sturdy tripod is therefore essential if ultimate quality is your goal – which is why all serious outdoor photographers use one most of the time.

Checking the depth-of-field

Using aperture-priority mode can help you to control depth-of-field, but how can you tell if the aperture you've set gives the depth-of-field you require? One solution is to use the camera's depth-of-field preview. This is activated by pressing a button (usually found on the front of the camera, near the lens release button or beside the on/off switch surrounding the shutter button). This stops the lens down to the aperture (f/number) you've selected. The only problem is that if you've selected a small aperture, the viewfinder image becomes dark when the aperture closes down. Use this facility with LiveView and the camera adjusts screen brightness. Canon users can change apertures and check the depth-of-field instantly using LiveView. If your camera is an older version that lacks the preview facility or LiveView, take a shot and magnify the image to check sharpness.

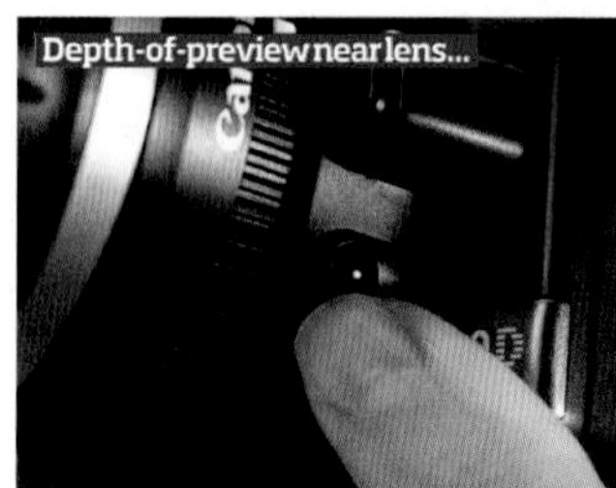

Depth-of-preview near lens...

Or by the shutter button

Switch to the Bulb setting

If you're shooting in low light and the required exposure time is outside the camera's range, instead of increasing the ISO, try selecting the camera's Bulb mode (B), using a remote release to hold the shutter open manually (more advanced remotes allow you to set time values). This allows you to maintain the original aperture, keep the ISO low for optimum image quality, and achieve the correct exposure.

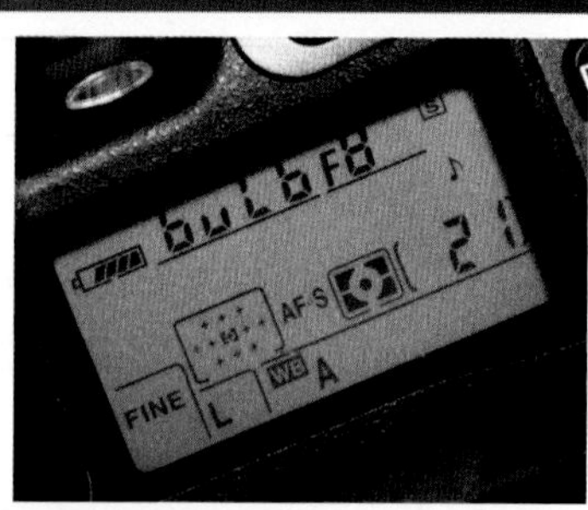

ISTOCK PHOTO

Adjust the ISO rating

If you find yourself without a camera support, a quick and easy way to avoid slow shutter speeds and camera shake when handholding is to increase the ISO rating to help raise the shutter speed. For example, if you're shooting at ISO 100 and the camera sets a shutter speed of 1/15sec (too slow to safely handhold), by increasing the ISO to 400, the shutter speed will be increased to 1/60sec, which is manageable. Similarly, if the long exposure warning flashes when shooting in low light, to show that the longest exposure time isn't slow enough, you can increase the ISO to increase the exposure and bring it within the camera's range. Of course, this is always going to be a trade-off, because the higher the ISO, the more image quality falls, so always shoot at the lowest ISO you can get away with; and rather than increase it to allow a faster shutter speed, mount your DSLR on a tripod. Just remember to reset the ISO back to its usual lower setting when you're done!

Raw file correction

If your camera cannot give you as fast or slow a shutter speed as your aperture requires, you could try shooting in Raw format and correcting the under- or overexposure in post-production. Raw files carry more image information than JPEGs, and are not processed in-camera, so they allow you to get away with a certain amount of exposure error. However, if the highlights are blown or it's grossly underexposed and the shadows block-up, the shot will not be salvageable, but it's worth a try if all else fails!

ROSS HODDINOTT

Use a Neutral Density filter

If your camera's top shutter speed isn't fast enough to achieve correct exposure when shooting at a wide aperture, the solution is to put a Neutral Density (ND) filter on your lens. ND filters are designed to reduce the amount of light entering the lens, without causing colour changes. They come in various densities to give you increased control – a 0.3ND reduces light by one stop, a 0.6ND reduces by two stops, a 0.9ND by three stops and a 1.2ND by four stops. These are the most popular strengths, though specialist ND filters are also available up to ten-stops. By placing an ND filter on the lens, it will reduce the amount of light reaching the sensor and the camera will be forced to set a slower shutter speed. This can also be used to achieve slow shutter speeds in bright conditions, for blurring movement.

Exposure compensation

If your metering produces an under- or overexposed result while shooting in aperture-priority mode, using exposure compensation allows you to quickly increase or decrease the shutter speed

Aperture-priority: Shooting nature

Ross Hoddinott explains how this shooting mode helps him capture great nature shots

WHEN PHOTOGRAPHING NATURE, one of the keys to success is being able to select the most appropriate exposure settings with speed and efficiency. For example, when shooting flighty birds or insects, you cannot afford to waste valuable time by pressing too many buttons and twiddling dials – otherwise, your subject might move or scurry away before you've had time to release the camera's shutter. For this reason, whichever exposure mode you select is vitally important...

Nature photography often involves using specialist optics, such as a long telephoto or macro lens. At such high levels of magnification, depth-of-field is often limited. Arguably, this makes aperture selection more important when shooting nature than with any other type of subject. When you photograph nature using one of your camera's fully automatic modes, you are allowing the camera to dictate the amount of depth-of-field for you. Therefore, the results can be very different from what you were aiming for. To avoid disappointment, don't rely on a program mode – instead, take control of your settings. Aperture-priority is the best choice in most shooting situations, regardless of whether you are a beginner or an experienced pro. It allows you to manually select the most appropriate f/number for the subject. For example, if you require a large depth-of-field to maximise back-to-front sharpness, which is useful when shooting flower close-ups, for instance, set a small aperture of f/16 or f/22. In contrast, if you require a shallow depth-of-field, to throw distracting foreground and background vegetation out of focus, or to draw attention to your point of focus, opt for a larger aperture, like f/4 or f/5.6. Aperture-priority allows nature photographers the level of control they require. Even in situations where a fast shutter speed is needed to freeze fast action, such as when photographing a bird in flight, aperture-priority remains a highly useful mode. This is because when you select the widest aperture, you're also setting the fastest shutter speed available.

1 I noticed this tiny mushroom growing on a tree stump and thought it would make a nice close-up. I liked the moss growing nearby, so I chose an angle from which I could include it in the frame. With my DSLR on a tripod, I composed the shot and, with the help of a Plamp, positioned a small reflector nearby to illuminate the fungus' gills.

2 I wanted to take a picture where the fungus and moss were both sharp. Set to full auto, my DSLR chose the maximum aperture to give the fastest available shutter speed. The resulting depth-of-field proved far too shallow. When focused on the moss, the fungus behind is badly out of focus.

3 Still using the full auto mode, I adjusted the focus so that the AF locked on to the cap of the mushroom, but now the clump of moss was completely out of focus. In fact, at such a large aperture, even the stem of the fungus wasn't sharp. It proved that I needed to change the mode.

4 I decided to try the close-up mode and found the camera could still only 'guess' at the effect I was trying to achieve. It opted for a small aperture to generate a large depth-of-field. Whilst the mushroom and moss are sharp, too much of the background is showing, which proves distracting.

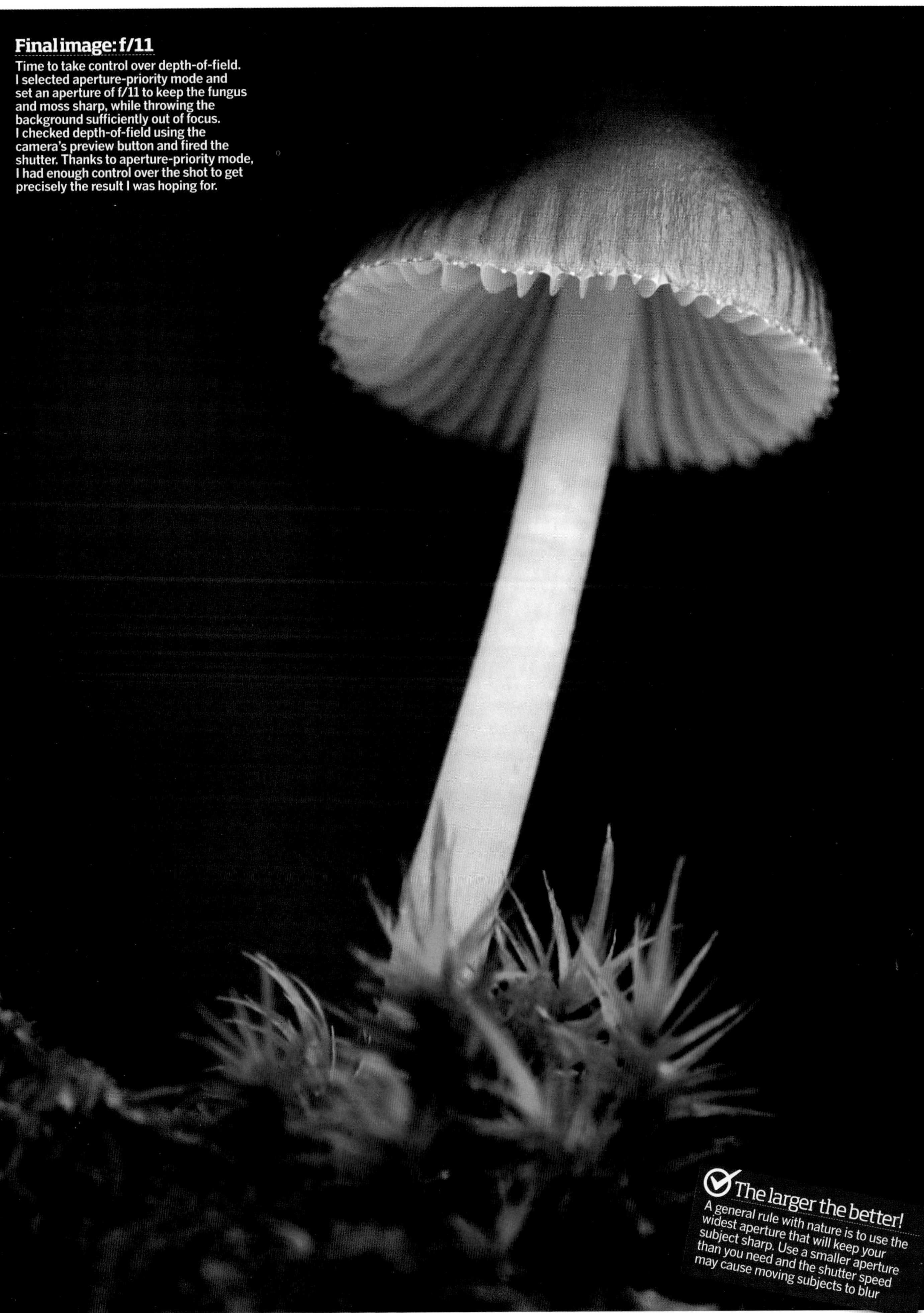

Final image: f/11

Time to take control over depth-of-field. I selected aperture-priority mode and set an aperture of f/11 to keep the fungus and moss sharp, while throwing the background sufficiently out of focus. I checked depth-of-field using the camera's preview button and fired the shutter. Thanks to aperture-priority mode, I had enough control over the shot to get precisely the result I was hoping for.

The larger the better!

A general rule with nature is to use the widest aperture that will keep your subject sharp. Use a smaller aperture than you need and the shutter speed may cause moving subjects to blur

Aperture-priority & landscapes

Landscape specialist Lee Frost shows why aperture-priority is the most practical exposure mode to use when shooting scenics

ONE OF THE FUNDAMENTALS of successful landscape photography is being able to control and assess depth-of-field to ensure that the image is sharp from front-to-back.

Aperture-priority mode helps you to achieve this, not only by forcing you to think about which aperture to set, but also by making sure that once it is set, that aperture won't change if light levels fluctuate or if you put filters on the lens. If the exposure has to be adjusted when shooting in aperture-priority mode, the camera does it by changing the shutter speed, so that the aperture remains constant. This is vitally important, because achieving extensive depth-of-field is not just about aperture selection, but also focusing distance, and a careful balancing act between the two is required to ensure the best possible results. You could take every picture at f/22 with the lens set to infinity and most wide-angle shots would be sharp from front to back. Unfortunately, this simple approach won't always work – so you're not going to get the best results. Wide-angles and zooms tend to give their worst optical performance when at minimum aperture and their best around f/11, so ideally you should shoot as close to f/11 as you can to achieve optimum optical quality, and focus the lens at a distance that maximises depth-of-field at that aperture.

My favourite technique is based around something known as hyperfocal focusing, which involves focusing on a point known as the hyperfocal distance, where depth-of-field is maximised for the aperture in use. Lenses used to feature a hyperfocal distance scale on the barrel but virtually none do today. There is an equation for calculating hyperfocal distance for any lens and aperture, so in true *Blue Peter* fashion, I did just that and created a hyperfocal distance chart, which you can copy and refer to when you're on location. The distances in metres (m) represent the hyperfocal distances for each focal length and aperture. If you focus your lens on that distance and set the corresponding aperture, depth-of-field will extend from half the hyperfocal distance to infinity. So, if you're shooting at 24mm and f/11, focus on a point 1.5m away and depth-of-field will extend from 0.75m (half the hyperfocal distance) to infinity – which is more than enough depth-of-field in most situations.

Aperture-priority & multi-zone metering

Before finally 'going digital' back in the spring of 2008, I'd spent 20 years shooting with film cameras that had no internal metering, so I used a handheld spot meter to determine correct exposure – which then had to be manually set on the camera. Thankfully, those days are long gone. Digital cameras have fantastic integral metering systems that are capable of producing perfectly exposed images in all but the most demanding situations, so I can't see the point in making my life more complicated than it needs to be. These days my digital SLR is set to aperture-priority mode and multi-zone metering and generally stays that way. Combined with the feedback provided by the camera's preview image and the image histogram, I've got all I need to ensure I get perfect exposures in any shooting situation. The same applies to you.

	Hyperfocal Distance Chart for focal lengths from 16mm to 200mm								
	16mm	20mm	24mm	28mm	35mm	50mm	70mm	100mm	200mm
f/8	1.0m	1.4m	2.0m	2.8m	4.2m	8.5m	17m	35m	140m
f/11	0.75m	1.0m	1.5m	2.0m	3.0m	6.3m	12.3m	25m	100m
f/16	0.5m	0.7m	1.0m	1.4m	2.1m	4.3m	8.5m	17.5m	70m
f/22	0.35m	0.5m	0.7m	1.0m	1.5m	3.1m	6.2m	12.5m	50m
f/32	0.25m	0.35m	0.5m	0.7m	1.0m	2.2m	4.2m	8.5m	35m

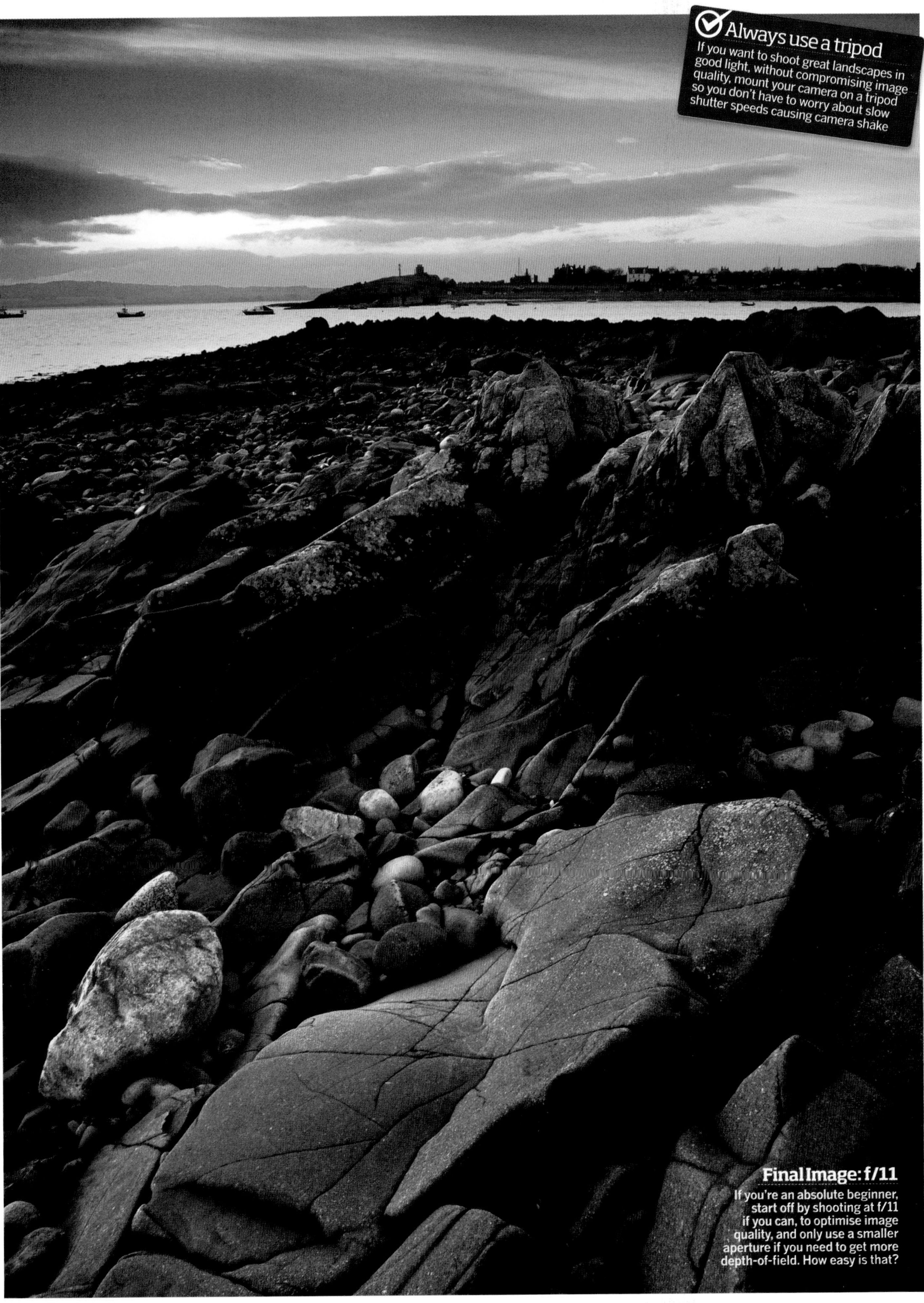

Always use a tripod

If you want to shoot great landscapes in good light, without compromising image quality, mount your camera on a tripod so you don't have to worry about slow shutter speeds causing camera shake

Final Image: f/11

If you're an absolute beginner, start off by shooting at f/11 if you can, to optimise image quality, and only use a smaller aperture if you need to get more depth-of-field. How easy is that?

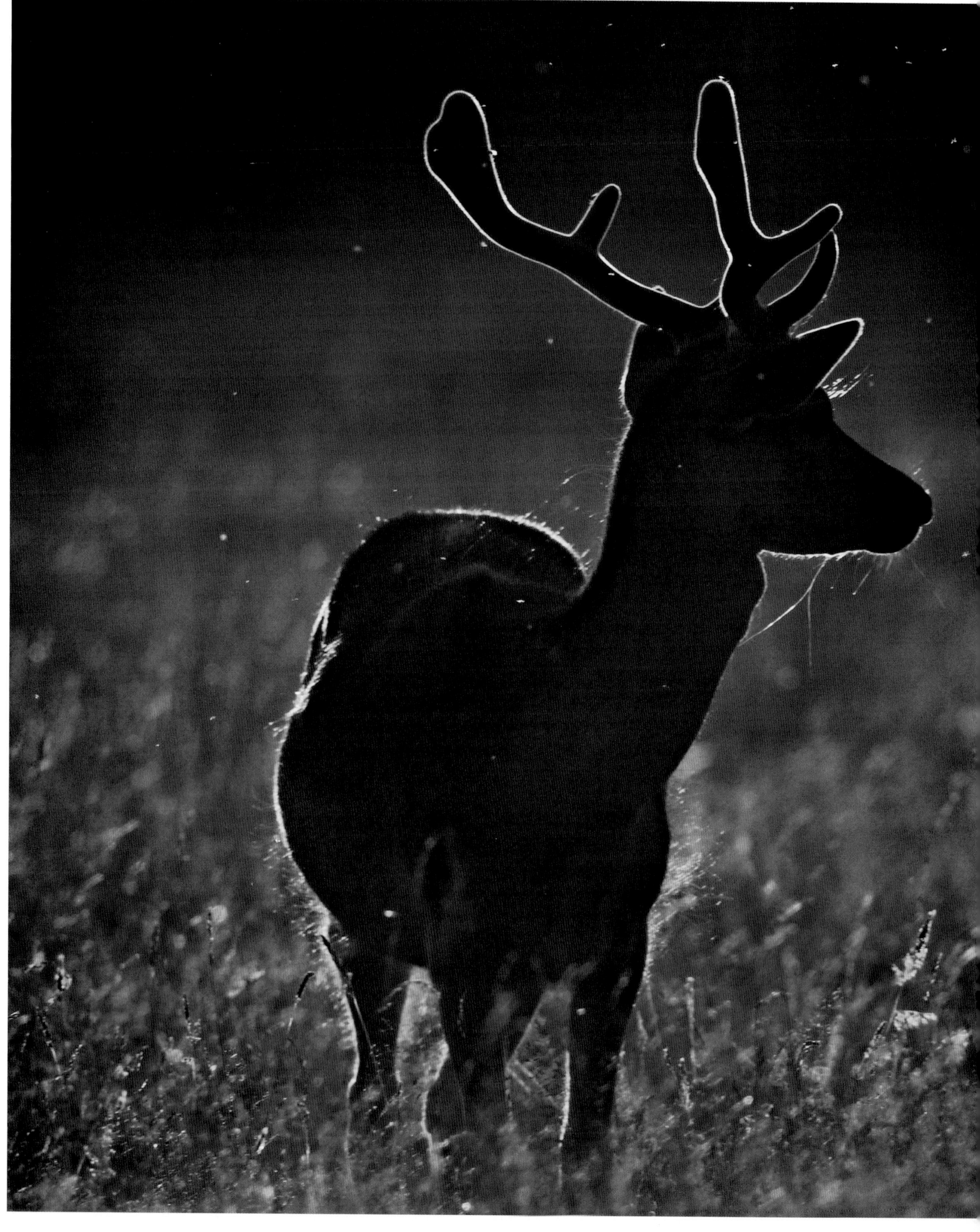

PAUL BUNYARD

WILDLIFE

The majority of digital camera owners will want to try their hand at wildlife photography at some point, but its reputation for specialist gear and remote locations can prove discouraging. We show the would-be nature photographer that you don't necessarily need to go on safari or buy long, pricey telephotos to capture great images. As well as provide an expert insight into wildlife, we offer simple ideas and practical techniques to help you shoot stunning wildlife images

NO MATTER WHERE YOU LIVE, there is a great diversity and wealth of natural history. Whether your location – urban, rural or coastal – you will never be far from natural subjects to capture on camera. Before you begin taking pictures, you first need to locate your subject. Being a good natural history photographer doesn't rely on your skills with a camera alone; it also depends on your knowledge. Having a good understanding of the subject's diet, habitat, behaviour and life cycle will prove hugely beneficial when trying to take pictures. This knowledge will help you locate wildlife and prevent wasting time. Use the internet to research good wildlife locations in your region. You will no doubt be aware of some already – maybe parks, heaths, woodlands or a local reservoir. However, every county has its hidden gems, so spens some time on the internet researching your local area.

Photographing truly wild animals is challenging. They are naturally timid, so often require the use of a hide and a long telezoom. You might have to invest hours of time and patience just to achieve a handful of usable images. For this reason, it is better to begin by photographing garden or parkland wildlife, which can often be 'stalked' slowly on foot. Remember to always work within the capabilities of your kit and be realistic when selecting subjects to shoot. For example, if your longest lens is 70mm, there is little point trying to photograph a buzzard flying high above you. Instead, look for wildlife that will allow you to get within range, or attach a close-up filter and photograph smaller subjects, like amphibians.

Practically any lens can be used to photograph wildlife – so don't be deterred if you're new to digital photography or have a limited budget. Wide-angle and standard optics can be used to capture animals within their environments; whilst telezooms, upwards of 200mm, are better for isolating your subject from its surroundings or shooting frame-filling portraits. A macro lens, or close-up filter is ideal for macro, while a teleconverter will extend the pulling power of your telezoom. Owners of DSLRs with an APS-C sensor (that's the vast majority of us!) will have the magnification of their lenses increased still further – useful for distant birds and mammals.

Regarding camera settings, there is no secret formula guaranteed to produce the best result. How you set up your camera depends on a number of variables, including the subject, its behaviour, available light, the lens attached and the type of image you wish to create. However, it is worthwhile always working in Raw + JPEG whenever possible. As well as being able to change the White Balance, Raw files have greater exposure latitude compared to JPEG – so if you do make an exposure error, it can often be corrected on your computer. This is particularly reassuring when photographing nature, as you will rarely have the time or luxury of being able to review images via playback – or check histograms – between frames.

Wildlife rarely keeps still for long, so it's usually best to use the fastest workable shutter speed. To do this, you may have to set a fast ISO rating. The slight increase in digital noise this generates is preferable to images suffering from subject blur. You will frequently shoot at maximum aperture, so depth-of-field is shallow. Whilst this is useful for reducing distractions in the background, it also means your focusing will need to be accurate to keep the subject acceptably sharp.

One last thing... wildlife photography can prove frustrating. It is a challenging discipline that often demands great patience – there is no point trying to pretend otherwise. Be prepared to see your subject move, fly or run away just as you are about to release the shutter. But persevere and you'll be rewarded with some great wildlife shots.

Wildlife: Get geared up!

Contrary to popular belief, you don't always need long, costly telephoto lenses to photograph wildlife. Optics boasting a fast maximum aperture may be the choice of professionals, but beginners – and photographers on a budget – can still achieve excellent results even with a basic digital camera outfit

Telephoto lenses

If you want to capture frame-filling portraits of mammals and birds, a telephoto or telezoom is a must. Opt for a focal length of around 300-400mm – anything less requires you getting too near to your subject, increasing the risk of scaring it away. 55-200mm telezooms are common and are ideal, as when used with an APS-C sensor, they have an effective focal length of 75-300mm. Most manufacturers offer good quality options at budget prices among their range. They normally have a maximum aperture of f/5.6 at the longest end. This will prove fast enough in most shooting situations – other than in low light. However, lenses with built-in image stabilisation are becoming more common, and cheaper, and offer the ability to shoot in low-light conditions and still get sharp images. Another advantage of using a telezoom is that, despite their focal range, they are surprisingly compact and lightweight, making them easy to use handheld.

Teleconverters

Teleconverters are placed between the SLR and lens and magnify the lens's focal length by the converter's strength – typically either 1.4x or 2x. For example, a 300mm lens will become a 420mm with a 1.4x converter, or 600mm with a 2x. They don't affect the lens's minimum focusing distance and prove a compact and inexpensive way to extend your lens's reach. However, they do reduce the amount of light reaching the sensor by either one stop (1.4x) or two stops (2x). This will lengthen shutter speeds, problematic if you need a fast speed to freeze subject movement. Converters can also reduce image quality, although if you buy a good quality brand, this will be negligible. Finally, it is worth noting that some optics are incompatible with teleconverters – so read the lens's instruction booklet prior to buying or attaching one.

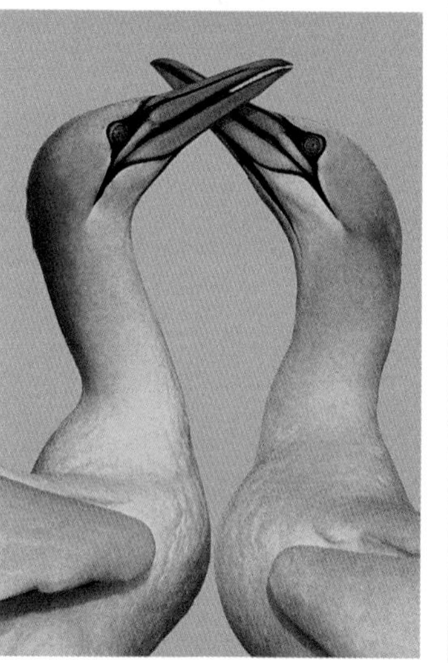

GUY EDWARDES

Getting close-up

To photograph small animals, like insects, amphibians and reptiles, you will require a close-up attachment. A dedicated macro lens has a reproduction ratio of 1:1 (life-size) and is optically superior to some other attachments, like close-up filters. Opt for a focal length around 100mm, as this will allow you to keep a reasonable distance from your subject, minimising disturbance, yet fill the frame. Alternatively, buy an extension tube – or set. Like teleconverters, they fit between the lens and camera but are hollow, with no optical components, and work by simply extending the lens away from the sensor, decreasing the minimum focusing distance. They are best combined with a short focal length lens and are available in varying strengths.

ROSS HODDINOTT

Wildlife accessories

HIDE: Many of the best wildlife images are the result of careful planning, patience and the aid of a hide. Positioned close to a breeding site or feeding station, a hide will conceal your whereabouts and movements, allowing you to take pictures without causing disturbance. It is best to introduce a hide gradually – moving it closer to where you expect to photograph your subject over the course of several days. By doing so, the wildlife can slowly get accustomed to seeing it around. Compact, collapsible versions are available from www.wildlifewatchingsupplies.co.uk or www.stealth-gear.com. Or you could try making one yourself!

CAMERA SUPPORTS: Using a camera support will not always be practical, but it is best to use one whenever the situation allows. When you are in a static position, working from a hide for example, use a sturdy tripod with either a pan & tilt or ball & socket head. If you are stalking wildlife, a monopod may prove a more flexible option, being instant to set up and allowing you to manoeuvre the camera and adjust composition quickly. If you are going to shoot from a car window, or from a prone position, use a beanbag instead.

DIGITAL STORAGE: When photographing nature, you will find yourself shooting a large number of frames. Therefore, a portable hard drive, or Portable Storage Device (PSD) is a useful accessory. Canon, Epson, Jobo and Vosonic all make large capacity devices with viewing screens.

Avoid shake!

To eliminate camera shake when using long, telephoto lenses, set a shutter speed equivalent or greater to the lens's focal length. For example, 1/400sec when using a 400mm lens

MICHAEL HUME

Urban wildlife

Don't think because you live in a town or city there's no wildlife for you to photograph

MICHAEL HUME

ABOVE: Foxes require a bit more effort to get anything more than grab shots, unless you are lucky enough to have them residing in your garden – often under your shed! June to October is their breeding season.

OFTEN AN URBAN ENVIRONMENT is one of the best places to get close to nature as city wildlife has become accustomed to the hustle and bustle of modern life and is regularly in close contact with people. Generally speaking, this makes urban species more approachable with your digital camera.

Nature is highly adaptable, colonising road verges, railway lines and derelict buildings. You might pass an area of wasteland every day and not realise that it is home to all sorts of nature. Rabbits will thrive in this type of environment and are often far more approachable than their rural cousins. It is best to take pictures early in the morning or late evening. Not only is the quality and temperature of light better for photography, but there will be fewer disturbances from passers-by. The equivalent of a 400mm lens should be powerful enough to record the animals sufficiently large in the frame. Disguise your outline by covering your body with camouflaged netting. Then, lie prone within approximately 20 metres of their burrows, waiting for them to emerge. A 55-200mm lens might also be useful if you want to show them within their urban environment. Wildlife photography is full of surprises and you can never predict what you might see. For instance, where there are rabbits, you will also find predators. Therefore, don't be surprised if you get the opportunity to photograph a hungry fox from time to time.

If you don't have the free time – or patience – to lie in wait for wildlife, then visit a park instead. Urban parks are excellent locations for beginners to hone their skills, as the wildlife is semi-tame.

Grey squirrels are photogenic and often grow so tolerant of humans that they can be fed by hand – although beware, they have a nasty bite. Entice them close to you with shelled hazelnuts and snap away as they feed. If you're lucky, you may get a photo of one burying or carrying a nut in its mouth. During the autumn, fallen leaves will add further colour and interest to your shots. If the squirrel will allow you to get within a metre or two, try using a wide-angle lens to create an unusual, even wacky, portrait. Turn over the page to see how we managed in our quest to capture great pictures of a squirrel!

Larger parks are often home to deer – commonly red or fallow. During autumn, they are breeding, known as the rut. This is a great time of year to take pictures, as you might see stags bellowing or even fighting. Of course, deer are large animals and you should always keep a safe, respectful distance from territorial males. However, at parks like Richmond, they can be approached with care and photographed without the need of a hide. A monopod is a quick, fuss-free form of support when stalking. Turn to page 22 to find out how contributor Helen Dixon got on tracking down deer at Richmond Park in Surrey early one morning.

Urban ideas: Birds

Starlings, pigeons and seagulls might be considered pests by some, but shouldn't be overlooked by wildlife photographers. If you know where a flock of starlings roosts, why not wait and try photographing them when they arrive for the night. Watching a large flock in the air, turning and moving as one, is a fantastic spectacle. They can create wonderful swirling shapes in the sky, but you will need to employ the long end of a telezoom to get frame-filling shots. Choose an evening when there is some colour in the sky to make a nice backdrop.

Pigeons and seagulls can also create fun, amusing images, especially when photographed perched on the head of a statue or park sign. In cities, you'll often find them close to where people eat – picnic areas, cafés etc. For a different approach, photograph groups of them feeding, using a slow shutter speed (around a second should be slow enough) to create the impression of movement. A little fill-in flash can also add a nice effect, with the benefit of creating catchlights into the eyes and softening shadows.

ALAN BASELEY

They may not be everyone's best friend, but seagulls and pigeons have a lot of character and can make fun images.

Urban park hotspots

Here are five popular parks to photograph wildlife in the UK

1) RICHMOND PARK, LONDON
The largest open space in London, covering almost 1,000 hectares. Home to an array of wildlife, including 600 free roaming deer. Over 1,000 types of beetle have been recorded in the park and rare varieties of fungi – so take a macro lens with you.

2) HOGGANFIELD PARK, GLASGOW
The park lies just a few miles northeast of Glasgow city centre. The main attraction is Hogganfield Loch, with its wooded island. An important site for migrant and wintering waterbirds, with over 100 different species recorded at the site.

3) BRADGATE, LEICESTER
Situated just four miles northwest of Leicester, Bradgate is one of the most photographically attractive deer parks in the UK. Habitat is mainly open grassland or bracken, with a scattering of mature trees. Red and fallow deer are approachable with a 300-400mm lens. Best visited in autumn.

4) FORMBY, LIVERPOOL
Not a park, but only a few miles north of Liverpool. Despite its urban surroundings, the woodland is home to a colony of friendly red squirrels. Formby is NT owned and there is a fee to park. The tree canopy can limit natural light, so flash may be required.

5) ST JAMES'S PARK, LONDON
At the very heart of London. The park only covers 23 hectares, but is home to plenty of approachable wildlife. Ducks, geese, coots and moorhens can be found on the lake and grey squirrels can be enticed within the range of a 70-300mm zoom.

Hide in your car

Your car is the perfect mobile hide for budding wildlife photographers. It breaks up a person's outline, animals in urban areas are used to seeing them and you can sit comfortably while waiting

PAUL BUNYARD

Local parks: Squirrels

We head off to a local park with a bag of walnuts, a Nikon D200 and a 18-200mm superzoom to tempt grey squirrels to strike a pose

UNLESS YOU HAVE the climbing skills of Tarzan, trying to shoot squirrels in trees is never going to be easy – they are small, a distance away and often obscured by leaves or branches. Instead, a far better option is to use walnuts to tempt them towards you. Take along a picnic rug and liey on the floor, with your lens pre-focused on the bait about half a metre away, then wait patiently.

To allow you to concentrate on framing the shot, set your camera to aperture-priority mode, using a wide aperture to help blur the background. It shouldn't be long before one of the handful of squirrels around starts moving towards the food. You'll find they are cautious at first, but once they have reached the food they should happily sit still and eat. Make sure the autofocus is set to single-shot AF (AF-S) and shoot a mixture of full body and tight head shots, always using the eye as the point of focus. The flexibility of a 18-200mm to go from wide-angle to tight portrait proves invaluable here.

This close to them, you have to try and stay quite still. Twisting the camera from portrait to landscape may result in the squirrels bolting, though zooming shouldn't frighten them. Should the squirrel finish eating before you've taken all the shots you want, throw another half a walnut just in front of the lens to keep them in situ. Having someone beside you in charge of the food servings is useful. Once you have a good mixture of portraits in the bag, experiment a little to try and capture their character, attempting to get them to climb a tree and get the classic peeping shot. To tempt them to a location, hold some food close by, just out of shot. Choose a spot with care, as you need brighter lighting conditions. They are fast so look to use shutter speeds around 1/200sec, and continuous AF, to ensure decent results without blur. Flash can frighten them away, so opting to use a faster ISO rating like ISO 400 is preferable. Once they are a little used to your presence, try some flash exposures as they may not be confident enough to stay put.

Squirrel hunt checklist

- ✔ Do your homework on locations – go to a place known for hand-feeding – wild squirrels are too nervous to come close
- ✔ **Get down low to their eye level for more engaging portraits**
- ✔ Use a faily wide aperture (eg f/5.6) and concentrate on focusing and composition
- ✔ **Always focus on the eyes**
- ✔ Try and hide your 'bait' to make the image appear more natural
- ✔ **Use slow, smooth movements**
- ✔ Take care with backgrounds and leaves in the frame, tidy the scene if required
- ✔ **Take the right bait. Squirrels enjoy walnuts and bury peanuts**
- ✔ Squirrels are terrified of dogs, they run for the hills if there is one within 50 yards
- ✔ **BEWARE! Squirrels can bite and they have very sharp teeth!**

Take an assistant
Not only can you share the fun of the experience, but your 'assistant' can be a second pair of hands, helping to tempt the squirrels with bait and also keep an eye on your gear

It is surprising how close you can get to the squirrels. The secret is to try to avoid making any sudden movements that will cause them to flee. Try and bring across the squirrel's inquisitive nature into your images, using a combination of poses and locations to do so.

Large Parks: Deer

Photographer Helen Dixon shares her techniques for photographing deer at Richmond Park in London

IN THE UK, you can generally photograph deer all year round in many of the UK's deer parks. However, if you plan your trip to coincide with the annual autumn rut – which peaks around October – you are sure to capture the stags as they compete for a mate.

Approach deer with caution: although they will be used to a human presence, they are still very much wild and dangerous. Try to wear clothing that doesn't make too much noise and use the surrounding trees and foliage to help you blend into the background.

A telezoom will give you the flexibility to shoot tight portraits or zoom out to include some of the deer's surroundings. Use aperture-priority and multi-zone metering for your exposure; an aperture of between f/5.6-9 should render your subject sharp – remember to always focus on the eyes. Also, use a tripod or monopod, the latter giving freedom to move around more quickly.

I think the best time of day is dawn, as the light is so much more attractive. Metering at dawn can be quite tricky, particularly if you are backlighting and silhouetting, so it's worth auto-bracketing your exposures by one to two stops in this situation and regularly checking the image's histogram. Look out for a cold night – this is usually followed by morning mist, creating more atmospheric shots. Mist can cause problems with your exposure too, so as a rule it is best to overexpose by 1/3 to a whole stop.

Remember to keep an eye on your shutter speed if you are trying to capture action shots. If you are struggling and still getting camera shake, and don't have a lens with image stabilisation, you can always raise the ISO rating. But don't go above ISO 400 as you will increase the amount of noise in your images.

Roaring success

If you are struggling to find a subject to photograph, listen out for a stag's loud mating roar, which it uses to try and attract a mate

ABOVE: "I heard this big male bellowing his call and followed the sound. I metered directly from the deer to retain detail."

RIGHT: "I love the majesty of the deer's antlers as it popped its head above the ferns."

LEFT: "This shot was taken when the sun went behind the clouds, giving a softer, more even light."

BOTH, FAR LEFT: "I metered off the brightest part of the background, this retained the warm glow and rendered the deer in the images as silhouettes."

Wetland wildlife

The meeting place of land and water is a wildlife haven and a photographer's paradise

REGARDLESS OF WHERE YOU LIVE, you are never far from a wetland habitat – maybe a village pond, reservoir, river or canal. Wetlands provide one of the best environments to locate wildlife. Down by the water's edge, you will find resident waders and wildfowl of all shapes and sizes, and, at this time of year, our waterways are invaded by large numbers of winter migrants too. If you're lucky, you might spot a kingfisher, water vole or even an otter. However, they are shy, rare animals and it is better to begin by trying to photograph more common species, like herons, grebes, moorhens, swans, ducks and geese.

Many wetland habitats are well visited by the public and, as a result, have viewing hides that can be used for photography. However, while they can prove useful for getting to within shooting range of your subject, they are usually in an elevated position. Shooting from above can create an unnatural-looking result in your images; it is far better to take pictures from the subject's eye-level. Thankfully, at well-visited wetland habitats, the bird life is usually well accustomed to human activity. This means that they can be photographed from the water's edge without the need of a hide. If there isn't any vegetation obstructing your view of the subject, lie prone, as this will create the most natural-looking results. Lying flat on the ground also limits body movement and thus camera shake. Use your elbows, or a beanbag, for support, as this is more practical than a tripod. The long end of a 70-300mm lens, on an APS-C sized sensor (1.5x), should be sufficient to photograph birds bobbing about on the water. But rarely do birds remain still, so employ a relatively fast shutter speed of 1/400sec – or faster if the light allows. Always focus on the subject's eyes and use a largish aperture of f/5.6 to provide sufficient depth-of-field and an attractive blur to the background.

PAUL RICHARDS

Catch a dragonfly

By mid-autumn, the days are getting shorter and colder, but some species of dragonfly can still be seen hunting around wetland habitats. They are among our most impressive and photogenic insects and are relatively big, making them easier to photograph. Dragonflies will frequently rest on rushes and vegetation by the water's edge. Being territorial creatures, if disturbed, they will usually return to the same perch. Therefore, before attempting to take pictures, first watch to see where they rest. Then simply stand nearby, camera at the ready, and move in when they next land. Approach with slow, gradual movements and be careful not to disturb the surrounding grasses. A close-up filter or extension tube will allow you to shoot frame-filling portraits. However, a dedicated macro lens will create a larger working distance and minimise the chances of you frightening it away. A mid-aperture of f/8 should provide sufficient depth-of-field to keep the insect sharp, whilst also being narrow enough to blur background vegetation.

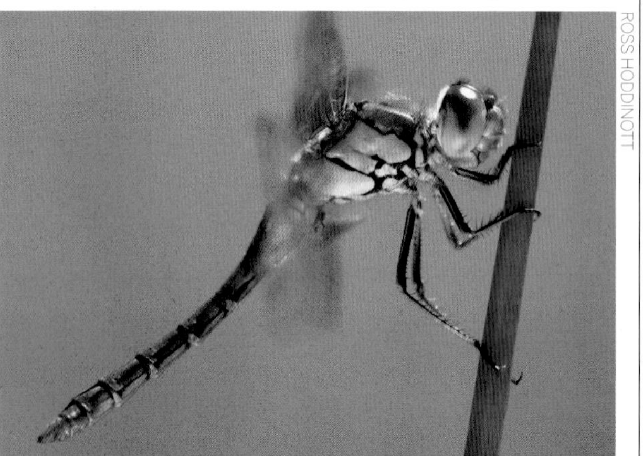

ROSS HODDINOTT

Try and get parallel to your subject so that one side of it is within the plane of focus, especially when using a wide aperture.

Shooting birds on water

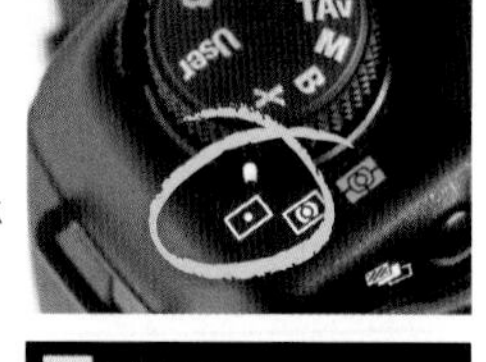

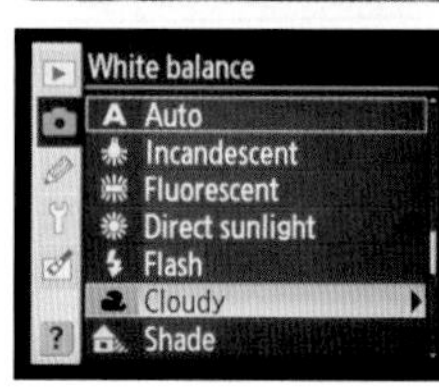

Photographs of birds on the water are usually more appealing and visually striking, especially when taking off or landing. A still day is best when there are mirror-like reflections – so check the weather forecast before travelling any distance. Reflections not only add interest to your shots, but, on sunny days, colour too. The water will adopt the colour of the sky above – or the adjacent vegetation – creating an attractive backdrop for your subject. However, bright reflections can confuse your camera's metering. Therefore, switch your camera to spot metering mode and meter from the bird's plumage – this will ensure more accurate results. On still, cloudless days, the light can adopt a slight cool, bluish cast – especially during the winter months. To restore the natural warmth to your images, switch your White Balance preset to Cloudy to simulate a warm-up filter.

PAUL BUNYARD

To make your images more interesting, try and capture some aspect of the animal's natural behaviour – bird-flight always looks dramatic.

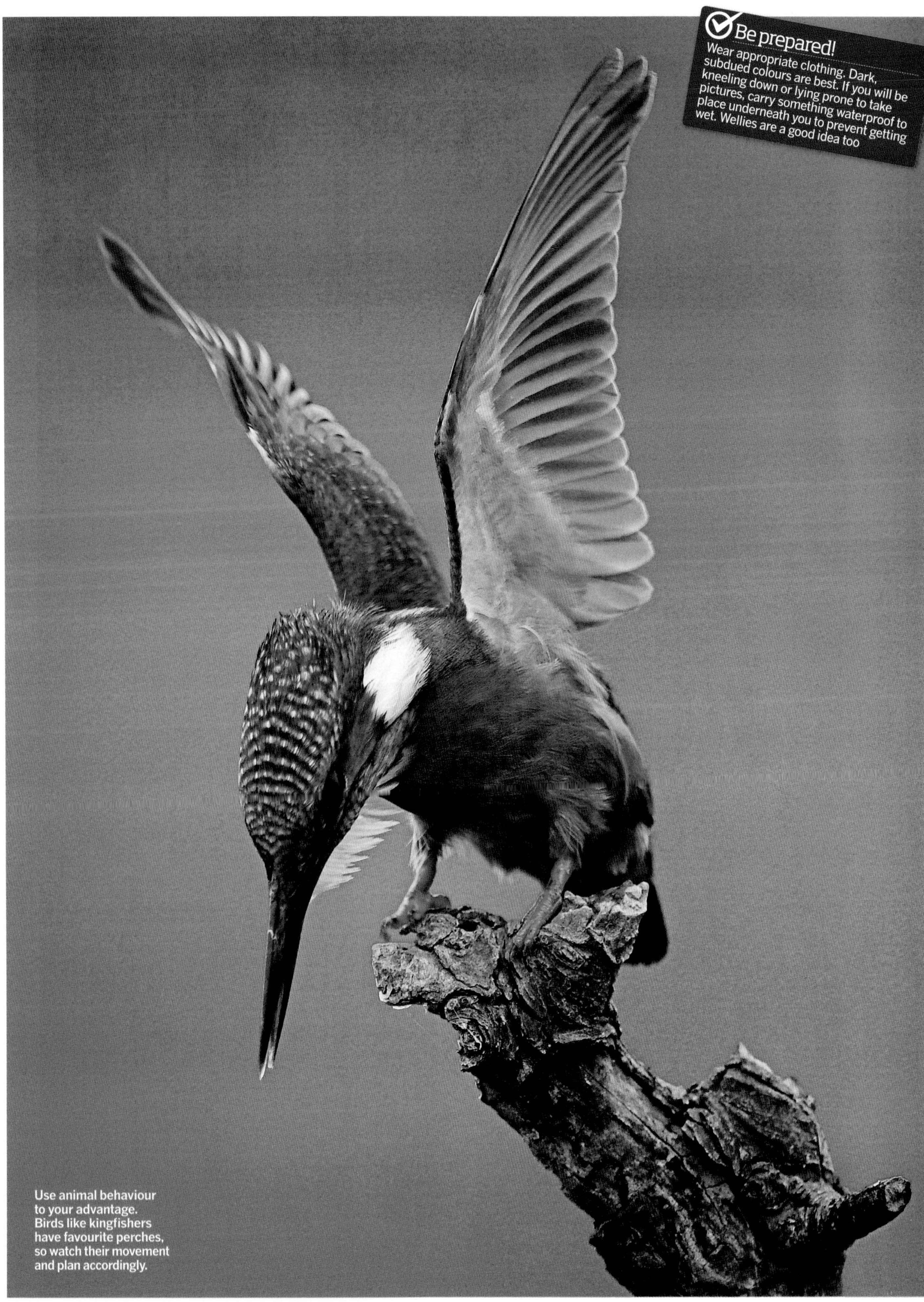

Use animal behaviour to your advantage. Birds like kingfishers have favourite perches, so watch their movement and plan accordingly.

Coastal wildlife

Not only does the coastline offer the potential for great landscapes, it's also a great place to shoot wildlife

IT IS EASY TO OVERLOOK the coast as a good location to photograph wildlife, but there is no shortage of natural subjects to find at the seaside. During the summer months, the coastal path is a good place to look for and photograph all sorts of small invertebrates. Birds of prey, like peregrines and kestrels, are a regular sight in the sky above, and sand dunes are home to a rich variety of plants and reptiles, like adders. However, it is the seashore itself where you will uncover the greatest diversity of animals to capture.

Our shorelines attract a wide variety of animals. Herring and black-headed gulls, cormorants, oystercatchers, turnstones and seals are well known and common sights along our coast. However, the molluscs, crustaceans and seaweed that cling to the rocks below the tide-line are frequently overlooked. Such subjects may have less appeal than a mammal or bird, but they still form an integral part of our natural history and warrant a closer look through the viewfinder of your digital SLR. Mussels, barnacles and limpets can create striking, abstract-looking images in close-up, either individually or in large groups. As ever, lighting is a key ingredient to success. Direct sunlight can prove too strong and contrasty, with dark shadows forming between neighbouring shells. Bright, but overcast light will provide even, flattering light – better suited to this type of subject. Alternatively, relieve distracting shadows by bouncing natural light using a reflector – or tin foil stretched over a piece of stiff cardboard.

Shells and seaweed are quite reflective, especially when wet. To reduce this sheen – and reveal their true colour and detail – attach a polariser to your close-up attachment and rotate the filter in its mount until the glare disappears. A polariser is also a fantastic accessory when photographing rookpools; you can use it to help see what is living in the pool below, like colourful snakelocks and beadlet anemones. Without one, all you will record are the reflections on the water surface.

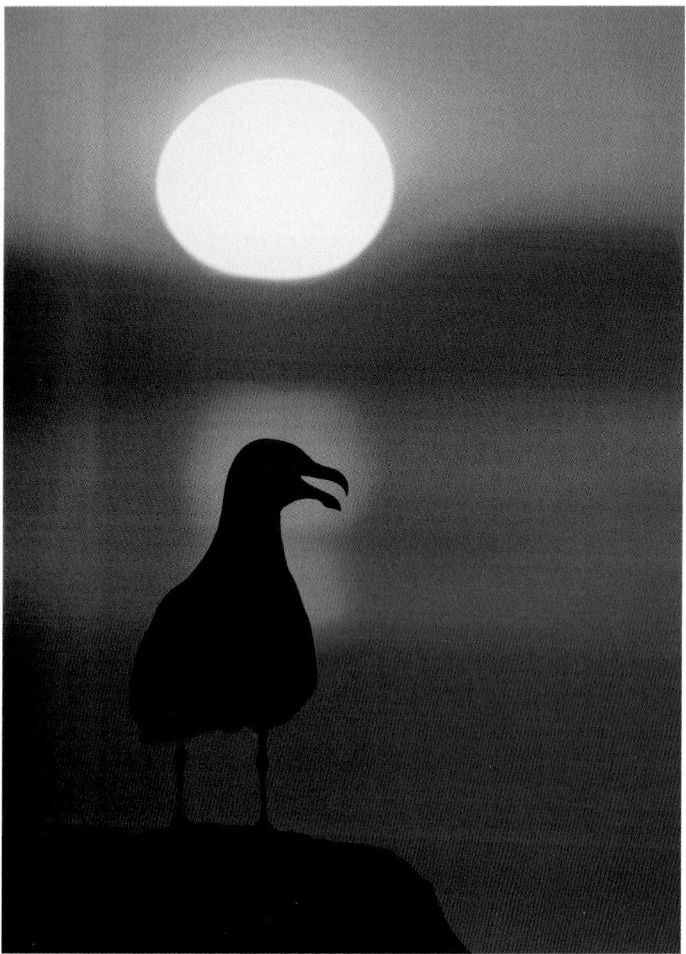

GUY EDWARDES

Seagulls are equally at home by the sea or in an urban environment. They are large birds so can make frame-filling subjects without using powerful optics.

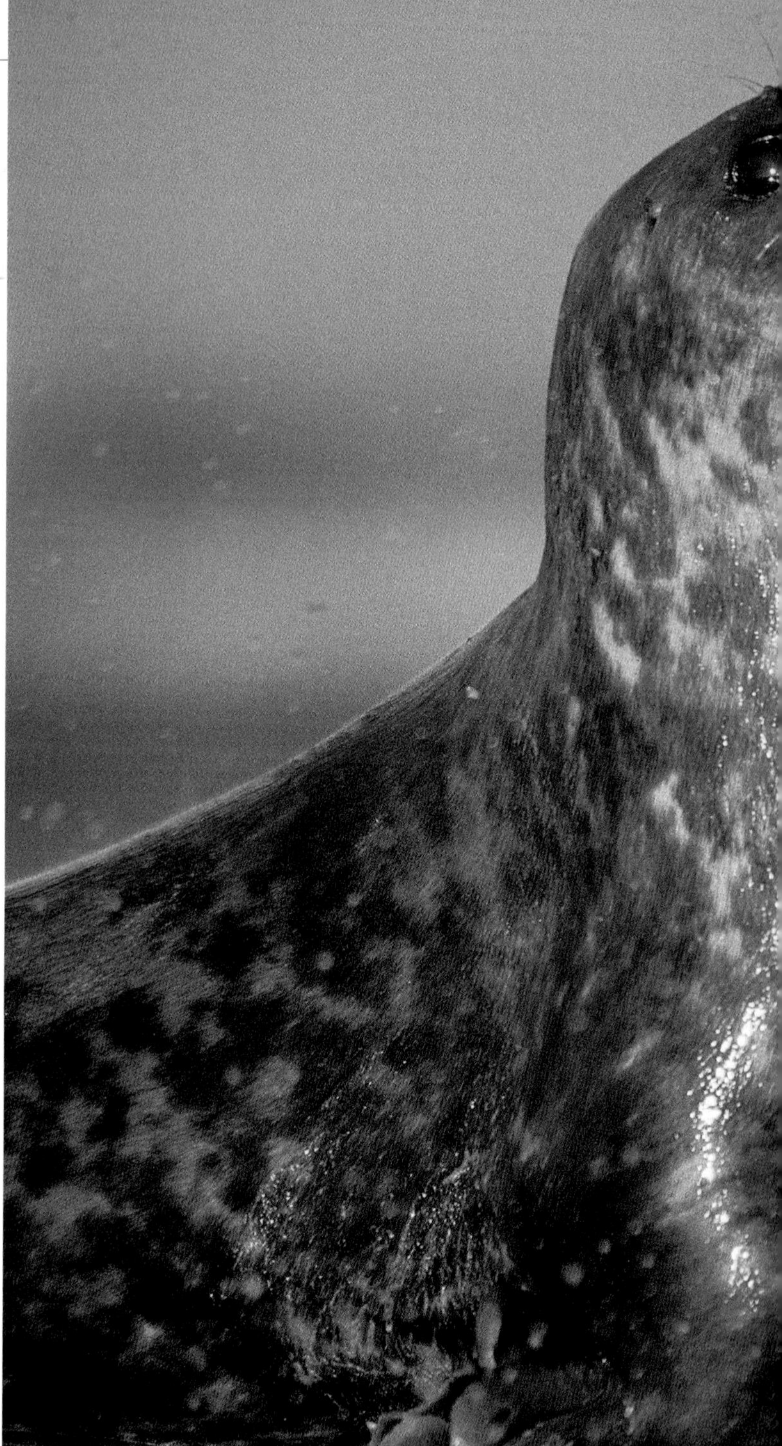

UK coastal mammals: Seals

Seals are one of our most photogenic mammals and the UK is home to large colonies of grey and common seals. The common is the smaller of the two, most frequently found on the East coast, from Norfolk to Orkney and Shetland. The West coast, the Farne Islands and West Pembrokeshire are among the best locations to spot grey seals.

As you might expect, they can be difficult animals to get close to. However, in some fishing villages where they have been fed by locals and fisherman, they can prove quite approachable. They have a tendency to 'bob' in the water, which, within a harbour environment, can be captured with a telezoom. Photographing them when they are hauled out of the water, on rocks or the shore, can be more challenging. They will often find isolated positions, which are difficult or dangerous to approach on foot. You could take a boat trip aimed at sighting seals. However, taking pictures from a boat isn't easy.

October to December is grey seal breeding season and at popular locations, like Donna Nook in East Lincolnshire, hundred of greys can be found on the beach. It's possible to get close with relative ease. It's open to the public on weekends and bank holidays, and it also has a warden to ensure eager visitors don't disturb the new mums.

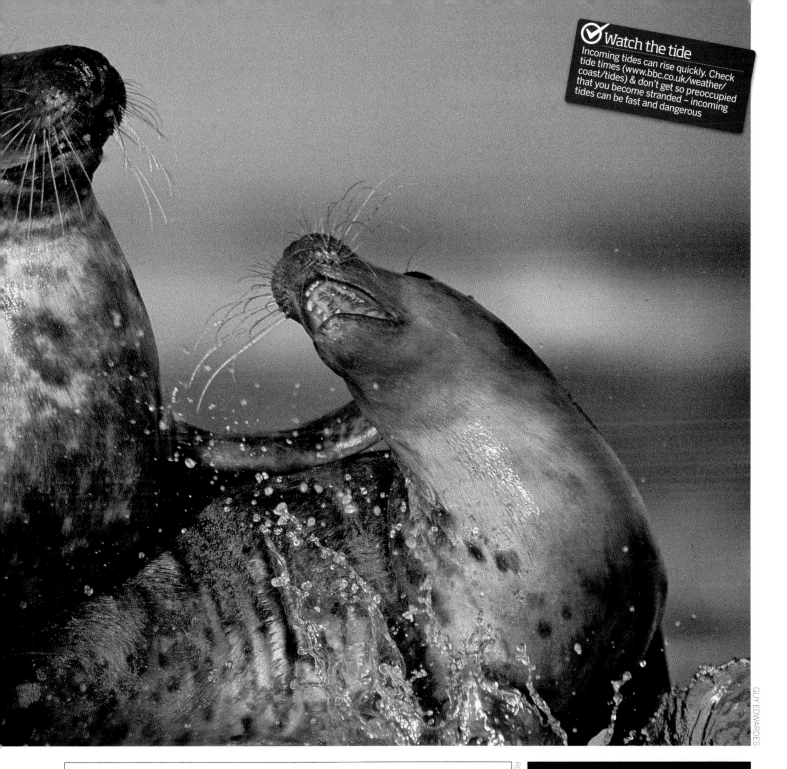

Watch the tide

Incoming tides can rise quickly. Check tide times (www.bbc.co.uk/weather/coast/tides) & don't get so preoccupied that you become stranded – incoming tides can be fast and dangerous

GUY EDWARDES

Using a tripod

Positioning a tripod isn't always easy when photographing shorelife. The rocky environment and slippery, seaweed-clad rocks can make setting up your shot a challenge. A versatile design, with legs that move independently, is ideally suited to such uneven terrain, as the legs can be locked into almost any position. Despite the potential difficulty, it is still advisable to use a tripod. Whilst you might think it isn't necessary when photographing static subjects, it is worth noting that a tripod also helps you to fine-tune composition. By slowing down the picture-taking process, it helps you to think more about viewpoints and creative possibilities.

ROSS HODDINOTT

Using a tripod means you can achieve the ultimate in image quality and not be restricted by low light, depth-of-field or a bad back!

Protect your gear

Sand and sea-spray are potentially damaging to your valuable camera equipment, so care should be taken. Sand can get everywhere. Carry a bin liner or plastic sheet to place on the beach to protect your camera bag when accessing your equipment. If it is windy, guard your set-up from spray and sand by keeping it covered – either by using a purpose-made housing or, more affordably, a plastic bag taped round the lens barrel. A lens hood will help protect the front element of your lens, and it is also worth attaching a UV or Skylight filter. They are designed to absorb ultraviolet light, but – being clear – are more often employed as an inexpensive method of protecting the front optics; they're far cheaper to replace than a costly lens.

Wildlife in the garden

You don't have to go to the Masai Mara or the Amazon rainforests to get stunning wildlife shots. Go on safari in your own back garden

Whether your garden is big, small, urban or rural, it can be used to get close to nature. In addition to resident creatures like garden birds, hedgehogs, frogs, spiders, moths and snails, your garden will be a shelter for a host of other animals visiting on a day-to-day basis, such as foxes or even deer. But before you begin taking pictures, make a list of the wildlife you regularly spot in your garden, then you can plan how best to photograph them.

Whilst garden wildlife might not be among the most glamorous, the garden is the ideal place to hone your skills. Nectar-rich flowers and plants, like buddleia and sunflowers, are well worth growing as they will attract the likes of bumblebees and butterflies. Also, with our autumns growing milder, common butterflies, like peacocks and red admirals, often remain on the wing until late October. However, by then many will look tatty, having been attacked by birds and lost some of their scaling. So only shoot those which are pristine, otherwise their condition will ruin the shot. Your camera's multi-zone metering system shouldn't have any problem with exposures, allowing you to concentrate on composition.

A small, ornamental pond is a popular feature in many gardens and these will often attract newts and frogs. Frogs are especially photogenic. Try kneeling by the pond's edge, with your telezoom, until one pops its head out of the water to breathe. When possible, shoot at 1/250sec or faster, to freeze subject and camera movement – using the eye as the point of focus. With care, you could gently move your subject to a more photogenic spot – the key is to get to their eye level.

Hedgehogs are photogenic, but being nocturnal can be difficult to photograph as a result. Enticing them with food, such as a bowl of dog food on your patio, can work. Once they're regulars, photograph them using a 50-200mm and a burst of automatic flash – again, at their level. Baiting wildlife, using suitable foods, is an ideal way to get within photographic range of nature; for example, hanging out bird feeders in your garden. Place your feeding station in a well-lit location. Also, position it close enough to a window for you to be able to take pictures while hidden indoors. The long end of a 50-200mm should be powerful enough to photograph starlings and finches feeding. For smaller birds, like blue and coal tits, attach a 1.4x teleconverter.

FRAN FRENCH

Home work

A major advantage of working so close to home is that you can quickly download and review images on your computer. This allows you to check for any technical problems and reshoot if necessary

LEFT: You may be lucky and spot a hedgehog in your garden before nightfall. Get down low and get in tight. A 50-200mm zoom should be ideal.

Take a closer look

Why not begin by finding bugs and creepy-crawlies to photograph? After a dewy night, cobwebs will be heavy with tiny water droplets, giving away the whereabouts of spiders. The web itself is photogenic, but is better photographed along with the spider that created it. Attach a +3 or +4 close-up dioptre to a standard zoom lens (at maximum zoom), or use a dedicated macro lens, to achieve an acceptable degree of magnification. Spiders are sensitive to vibration, so when using a tripod, be careful not to knock the vegetation that the web is attached to.

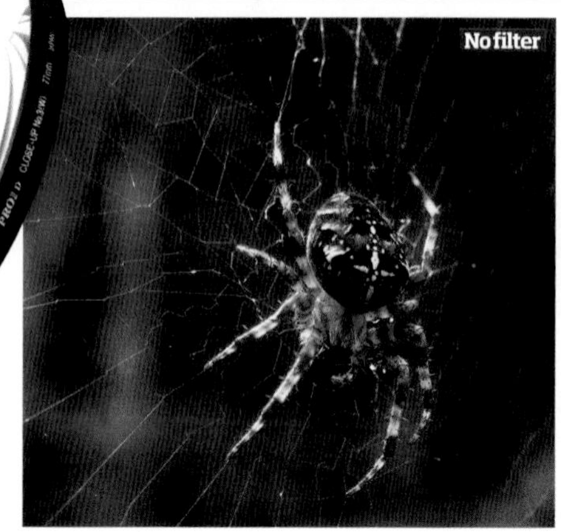

No filter

+3 dioptre

GLYNN MAY

Frogs will often sit still long enough for you to get some great shots. You can get quite near if you keep movement to a minimum.

ROSS HODDINOTT

Time to compose

Many gardeners might regard snails as pests, but they are good subjects to practice your macro techniques on – after all, they are not renowned for their speed! Experiment with depth-of-field by trying different f/stops. Do this by selecting aperture-priority mode and setting progressively smaller apertures with each frame – for example f/4, f/8, f/16 and so on. You can later examine the results, comparing the levels of acceptable sharpness and how it affects the image – knowledge you can then relate to other subjects.

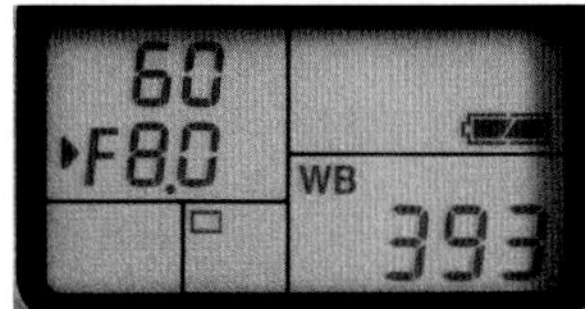

Set your exposure mode dial to A or Av, then experiment with apertures.

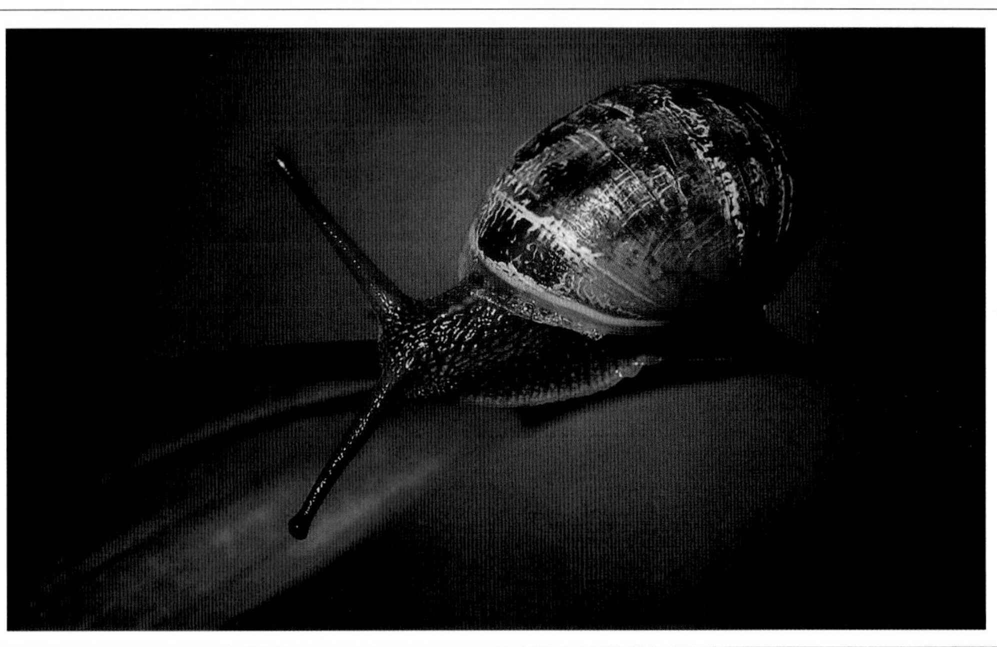

CLINT NEWSHAM

Capture clear water wildlife

Want to photograph fierce predators and their shy victims, bright colours and amazing shapes? Then look no further than your garden pond for a wide variety of wildlife inspiration

GARDEN PONDS provide a home to a range of fascinating creatures that are often ignored simply because they are largely out of sight. So long as the water is well oxygenated by plants and free from pollution, you can expect, at different times of the year, to find frogs and newts, water boatmen and water scorpions as well as voracious dragonfly nymphs and diving beetles. Spring and early summer sees the peak of activity but many of the animals are present throughout the year. So many small ponds have disappeared from the wider countryside in Britain that those in suburban gardens are assuming ever more importance as refuges for these creatures.

Even if you don't have a pond, you may still find frogs and toads in your garden, as they tend to live away from water other than when they spawn. Check among damp grass, under pots and among rocks and if you find one, as with all animals, remember to handle it with extreme care and return it if it looks like it's getting distressed. Most amphibians are pretty unprepossessing and when partly hidden amongst a tangle of weeds don't make for much of a picture. The trick is to isolate them. You can do this by placing them carefully on some grass or near some flowers and taking a low shooting position. This will put more distance between your subject and its background, throwing it out of focus and helping to isolate it from its surroundings. A telephoto lens like the 70-300mm should provide enough magnification but choose a longer focal length if you need to shoot further away so as not to disturb the creature.

Outdoor 'studio'

Creating a 'field studio' from a simple white tank will give your images a high-end studio-like finish. For the tank, all you need to do is secure acrylic panels using super glue. Acrylic has more tensile strength than glass of the equivalent thickness, so you can get away with a 1.5mm clear sheet for the front of the tank. Use 3mm white sheets for the back, sides, base and partition. Not only will the subject be seen clearly against the white set, but by backlighting it with a second flash you can see its translucent properties, giving the shot more depth. Niall Benvie explains his outdoor studio set-up.

Tools As well as the tank, have two plastic margarine tubs as holding tanks and two nets handy. You will also need two flashguns, a tripod, a plamp and a telephoto zoom set to around 150mm.

Step 1 Set up beside the pond and partly fill the tank with still mineral water (not tap water or from the pond). Put some into the two holding tanks as well so you can rinse the animal at least twice before you transfer it in to the spotless tank. Use different nets for the transfers too.

Step 2 Set up one flashgun behind the tank, far enough away to light the whole back panel. I've attached this to the leg of my Benbo tripod using a plamp. The other flashgun should be positioned above and slightly in front of the tank. Before you put the animal in the tank, do a test shot with your camera set to its lowest ISO rating and a small aperture (e.g. f/19 or f/22).

Step 3 You need to adjust the back flashgun's power and/or the camera's aperture until the background is overexposed, then switch the front flash on and adjust its output until the test subject is well exposed. This will probably be a bit less than what's needed to light the background.

Step 4 Only now should you catch and gently introduce the subject. Keep sessions down to 15 minutes per animal and do not touch it with your bare hands. Slide a clear acrylic partition into the tank to keep the subject close to the front of it. I have glued pieces of Lego to the inner sides of the tank to hold the piece of acrylic in place.

Step 5 Now, take your shots. When finished, avoid spreading disease by refraining from cleaning the nets in the pond, and pour the water into the soil at the end of a session, away from the pond.

NIALL BENVIE

Fresh-looking images

Using an outdoor studio allows you to control the lighting and means you don't have to worry about cluttered backgrounds or dirty water. You'll be jumping for joy with your results!

Stay sharp and dry

Use a telezoom or telephoto lens with at least a focal length of 100mm so you can get frame-filling images, without the risk of getting your gear wet. Try to get as close as you can to the subject too, so you can get the most out of a shallow depth-of-field

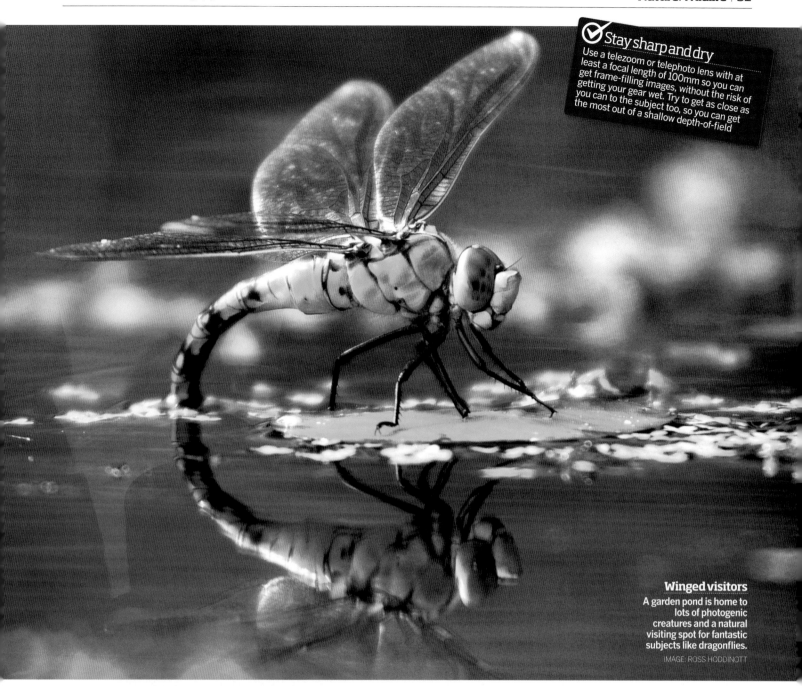

Winged visitors
A garden pond is home to lots of photogenic creatures and a natural visiting spot for fantastic subjects like dragonflies.
IMAGE: ROSS HODDINOTT

Five common water-wading creatures to try and shoot...

ISTOCK PHOTO

1) POND SKATER
Pond Skaters are common pond creatures. They 'skate' over the water's surface with their body supported on the tips of their legs. Photograph them either from overhead or as parallel as possible. Use a macro lens or a close-up attachment.

ROSS HODDINOTT

2) FROGS & TOADS
With their orange eyes, toads are very photogenic and can be found in ponds in February and March. Frogs can be also seen during this time too while spawning. Otherwise you may find one in your garden, even without having a pond nearby.

ROSS HODDINOTT

3) DRAGONFLIES
Dragonflies are beautiful insects. Broad-bodied chasers and Emperor Dragonflies are among the most likely to visit garden ponds. Due to their size, the long end of a telephoto will often be powerful enough to capture frame-filling shots.

NIALL BENVIE

4) WATER BOATMAN
This insect swims upside-down, propelled by its two long legs. The small creature has big red eyes, so it's a striking subject to photograph. Using the field studio (see left) will mean you can photograph them while they swim underwater.

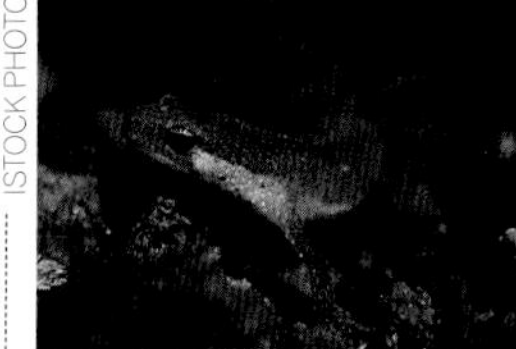
ISTOCK PHOTO

5) NEWTS
With their frog-like bodies but distinctive tails, newts are quirky animals to photograph, especially since they come in a variety of colours. You can find them in ponds, usually during June and July, when it's their breeding season.

How to get closer to insects

We show you the best ways to get close to various insects from graceful butterflies to other less beautiful but equally photogenic species

Bugs and creepy crawlies do not have a good reputation, do they? Despite their tiny size, they seem to strike terror among people. However, if you're "brave" enough to take a closer look, you'll discover that the majority of them are colourful, intricately formed and very photogenic. In the UK, few insects bite or sting, so it's an irrational fear. Therefore, rather than run away, photographers should put their phobias aside and reach for their camera instead…

Some of the techniques and principles used to photograph flowers can also be applied to photographing insects – for example the importance of lighting, originality and the need for gardening. However, the mobility, size and timid nature of mini-beasts presents photographers with a fresh set of practical and technical dilemmas. Firstly, you need to identify a suitable habitat where you'll find them. Wildlife photographers often need to research their subjects before they begin snapping, so visit your local library or check the internet for information.

1) Get up early

We won't try to pull the wool over your eyes; photographing insects is often challenging and full of frustration. For this reason, it's only logical to make life easier whenever possible. Insects are at their most lively during the warmth of mid-morning to late afternoon, so this time of day is best avoided whenever possible. It's better to shoot during the lower temperatures of morning and late evening, when their bodies are cold and they remain relatively inactive. So, if you're serious about capturing great insect shots, you need to set your alarm early…

In high summer you will need to drag yourself out of your warm, snug bed by 4.30am to be at your location by sunrise. Not fun, but the results will make it worthwhile. Look carefully amongst vegetation, tall grasses and leaves to find butterflies and bugs asleep. You will need a sharp eye, but with a little experience you will learn where to look. Tread carefully, though – a careless foot can prove fatal to these delicate, sleeping insects. One of the major advantages of photographing resting insects is that while they remain immobile, the area around them can be 'gardened'. Also, after clear, dewy nights, tiny droplets of water will form on the insect's wings and body, adding scale and further interest.

Gear up for creepy crawlies!

To photograph insects, you'll need a macro lens or close-up attachment. If your budget can stretch to it, a dedicated macro lens is a great investment, allowing a practical working distance from which to take pictures. A lens in the region of 100-180mm is traditionally best for snapping insects. However, if you are a beginner, student or have a limited budget, try using extension tubes or a close-up filter in combination with a standard focal length. Both accessories are comparatively inexpensive and provide a good introduction to the world of close-ups. A 70-300mm zoom with close focusing can sometimes be used to snap larger insects like dragonflies. If the insect is resting, a reflector may be used to bounce light onto the subject, so keep one in your camera bag. Due to the nature of insect photography, a tripod is often impractical. A monopod can prove a more practical form of support, but if you don't own one, simply keep the legs of your tripod closed together and use it as a makeshift monopod. Enthusiasts may wish to invest in a ring- or twin-flash unit. These dedicated macro accessories provide artificial illumination for close-up subjects when natural light is insufficient.

2) Camera shake

This is a common problem that occurs when the selected shutter speed isn't fast enough to eliminate your own natural movement, resulting in a blurry, ruined image. It's further exaggerated when using long focal lengths or high magnifications, so shake can prove a problem for insect photographers. The solution? Easy; just pop the camera on a tripod. Of course, it's often not that simple when shooting timid wildlife. Whilst using a support is fine for many other forms of photography, a tripod is often impractical when photographing insects. For example, a flighty butterfly won't wait and pose for you while you try to set up your tripod. Insects are highly sensitive to movement and vibration, so if a tripod leg disturbs any surrounding grasses or vegetation near to the subject, it will soon scurry or fly off. In fact, in my experience, the only time a tripod is useful is during early morning or late evening when insects, like butterflies or damselflies, are asleep or settled for the arrival of night. At other times, be prepared to shoot handheld.

It's very easy to overestimate how steady you can hold a camera, but a good general rule for macro work is to employ a shutter speed at least double the focal length of the lens in use. Therefore, when using a 90mm macro, employ a shutter of at least 1/180sec. If your camera kit offers anti-shake technology, use it; sharp images can be produced at speeds two or three stops slower than without. Alternatively, to generate a faster shutter speed, employ a larger aperture (however, this will reduce depth-of-field) or increase the ISO rating. You can also limit the effects of shake through the way you support your camera. For example, kneeling is more stable than standing. Keep your elbows to your chest and hold the camera firmly to your face. Hold it with both hands and squeeze the shutter release button smoothly. Your subject will often be low to the ground, so to achieve natural looking results, lie prone to keep the camera parallel with the subject. This will also allow you to use either a beanbag or your elbows to steady your camera. Lying flat on the ground limits body movement, greatly reducing the risk of shake.

ALL IMAGES: ROSS HODDINOTT

Bugs before bedtime

If you're not an 'early bird', look for insects before sunset instead when they are preparing for overnight. The low, warm light at this time can be great for shooting insects, especially butterflies

Turn off your beeps!
It's best to focus manually when snapping insects, but if you're using autofocus, then ensure that any noises or beeps that sound to indicate focusing are switched off before you start

3) Stalking

Suitable insect-rich habitats can be found by researching a little on the internet, or by contacting a local wildlife organisation. However, locating potential subjects to shoot is the easy bit; getting near enough to photograph them can prove far trickier. Bugs are highly sensitive to movement, as they are constantly trying to avoid predation. As a result, they will quickly scurry or fly away unless you approach them with great care. 'Stalking' is a term nature photographers use to describe approaching wild animals to within photographic range – in a stealth-like manner. Having found a suitable subject, consider your approach. Note the position of the sun and begin moving nearer, doing so slowly and avoiding sudden or jerky movements, while being mindful of where your shadow is falling. If the subject is low to the ground, get down on your knees in advance and 'wriggle' forward. Admittedly, you will look rather silly to any onlookers, but it is a small price to pay for a great shot. When you get near, slowly bring the camera up to your eye while moving yourself into a shooting position. Take a frame from slightly further away to guarantee one shot 'in the bag' and help the creature get accustomed to the sound of your shutter. Still looking through the viewfinder or using LiveView, move closer again – refocusing as you do so – compose your shot and shoot. If the insect moves; try to keep it in sight. Some insects, for example dragonflies and some butterflies, are territorial and, having flown away, may return to the same resting place a few moments later. Therefore, if you remain in position, you may well get a second chance.

4) Get your camera parallel

At the high level of magnification required to shoot insects, depth-of-field grows progressively shallow. Often it isn't practical to stop down to a small aperture of f/16 or f/22 as the shutter speed will be too slow. Also, background detail becomes more defined and can prove distracting. Even in shooting situations where you are able to use a small aperture, depth-of-field may only be a matter of millimetres, making good technique and focusing essential.

More often than not you will want to record your subject in sharp focus throughout, from its head to the tip of its abdomen. Therefore, to maximise the depth-of-field available for any given f/stop, carefully position your camera so its sensor plane is parallel with the subject. If you fail to do this, you risk the insect's body or wings drifting out of focus.

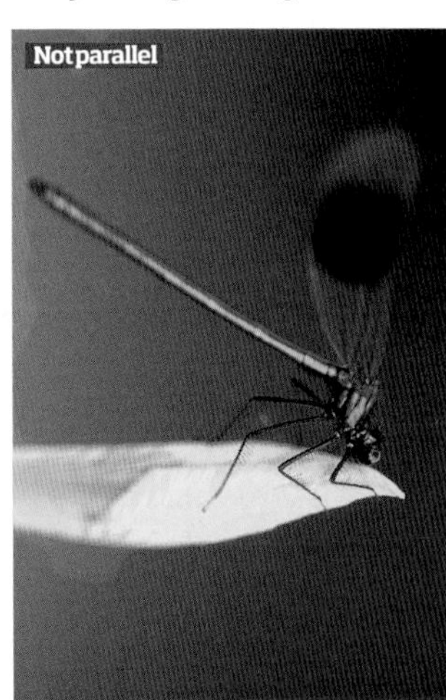

Without flash

With flash

Diffused flash

5) Using flash

There are times when ambient or reflected light is just not sufficient and a supplementary burst of flash is essential. Normal flashguns can be used for shooting some macro subjects, but a ring or twin flash unit designed specifically for macro work is better suited. A ringflash is circular in design and attaches to the front of the lens, but as they're designed to illuminate the subject evenly, lighting can look flat and dull. A twin flash unit is more flexible and works using a similar principle, but consists of two individual heads that can be moved independently and their flash output varied to offer greater creative possibilities. However, they are expensive and only close-up enthusiasts will be able to justify the added cost.

A more realistic alternative is simply to use the camera's built-in flash. What integral units lack in flexibility, they make up in convenience. Whilst their position is fixed and they can't be used off camera, they can be popped-up whenever required. This is especially handy in situations where you have to work fast – like insect photography. They are most useful for adding a touch of fill-in. Just take care not to get too close, as you risk the flash passing over the top of the subject. As a result, the built in flash is best combined at reproduction ratios below 1:2 (half life-size). With the flash being so close there is also the risk of fine detail and colour being washed out. Therefore, try softening with a flash diffuser or by taping tissue or grease-proof paper over the flash head.

Common insects

Here are five of the insects you're most likely to find and photograph in the UK

1) LARGE RED DAMSELFLY: There are many species of damselfly, but one of the most widespread is the large red. It's on the wing from May to August and favours ponds, lakes, streams and bogs

2) GARDEN SPIDER: This arachnid is found in gardens, hedgerows, woodland clearings and meadows from July until mid-autumn. Its large web comprises of radial and spiral threads

3) RED ADMIRAL BUTTERFLY: One of our most widespread butterflies. Easily enticed into gardens by planting nectar-rich plants like buddleia. Most common during July and August

4) FOUR-SPOTTED DRAGONFLY: Has distinctive spots on the leading edge of each pair of wings. It flies from May to August and hunts along hedgerows and near wetland habitats

5) ANGEL SHADE MOTH: One of the more widespread moths, on the wing from May to October. Recognised by its forewing having a ragged margin and its pinkish triangular mark

Become a lord of the wings

Bees, butterflies and dragonflies – your garden is home to all manner of winged creatures. Here's how to capture fantastic images of these beautiful airborne insects...

AMONG THE MOST colourful and attractive animals living in our gardens are flying insects, like bees, butterflies, wasps, hoverflies and moths. Butterflies and bees are particularly photogenic and can be enticed into gardens by nectar-rich plants such as Buddleia and Red Valerian. But if your back garden is brimming with flowers, it is probably also home to a variety of other photogenic insects just waiting to be captured on camera!

The most widespread garden butterflies are Red Admiral, Painted Lady, Small Tortoiseshell, Peacocks and Commas, and many of these species are at their peak during August. Quite simply, high summer is the best time of year to get out into your garden with your digital camera if you want to find several species flying about in your garden, feeding or basking in the sunshine on paving slabs, walls or fencing.

Photographing flighty insects can be frustrating as they will often fly away just as you are getting into position. However, a little patience and persistence will normally be rewarded. Before you begin taking pictures, observe the insect's behaviour. Many butterflies are quite territorial, so you may find they regularly return to the same resting place. If you notice such behaviour, wait nearby, ready to move into position the next time they land. Alternatively, you may prefer to 'stalk' them, following the insect's flight and movement before approaching them on foot once they land. The key to this technique is to keep your movement to a minimum. Most flying insects are easily disturbed, taking flight if they detect any sudden movement nearby. Bring your camera up close to your eye in advance, to limit your movement. It is also a good idea to pre-focus. This involves switching your camera to manual focus – and also the lens if it is designed with an AF/MF lever. Next, focus on an object of a similar size – a lens cap, for instance. By doing this in advance, you can then simply move the camera toward the subject until the insect is in sharp focus through the viewfinder. Pre-focusing limits any hand movement caused by adjusting the focusing ring – if focusing manually – or the potential noise and movement of using autofocus.

When photographing insects, avoid casting your shadow across the subject as it's something that will alert it to the risk of predation. Instead, consider where your shadow is in relation to the subject in advance of moving closer, adjusting the path of your approach if necessary.

For insects like butterflies, moths, bumble and honey bees, you need to get as close to them as you can. A macro lens, in the region of 100mm, is a good choice as it allows a practical working distance to minimise the risk of disturbing the creature. However, there are several excellent budget close-up attachments available, including auto extension tubes and close-up filters. Depth-of-field is restricted at high levels of magnification, so try to keep your camera parallel to the subject to maximise the back-to-front sharpness available at any given f/stop.

When photographing flighty, timid insects, you will normally find a tripod a hindrance, as opposed to a help. It will restrict your movements and positioning the legs may knock surrounding vegetation and disturb your subject. Shooting handheld will allow you to react quickly to the insect's movements and behaviour, and give you more creative freedom. Try to select a shutter speed upwards of 1/500sec in order to freeze the insect's movement and also eliminate camera shake. If your camera or lens boasts image stabilising technology, make sure it is switched on. Lastly, try to be creative with your approach and vary your angles as much as possible.

1

2

Composing insects

Butterflies are popular subjects but unless you're imaginative, you risk all your photographs looking very similar. Most photographers simply shoot butterflies, wings open, from overhead. This can work well, but to produce more original images, try experimenting with your approach and viewpoint, using different elevations. For example, a low angle from below a butterfly feeding on a flower can produce dynamic results, as can experimenting with depth-of-field. A large aperture, like f/2.8 or f/4, will generate shallow back-to-front sharpness and this can be used to draw the eye to your intended focal point.

3

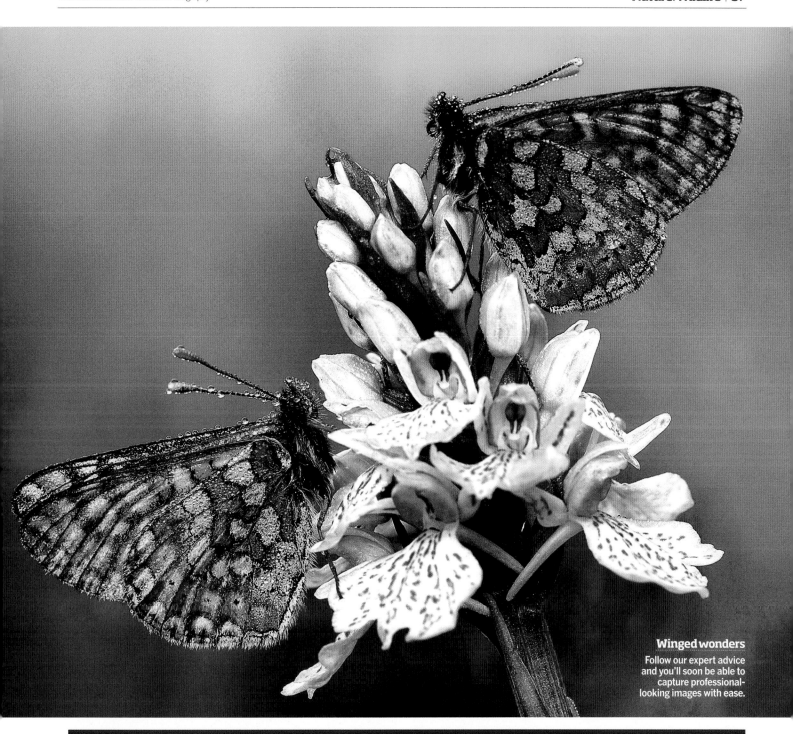

Winged wonders
Follow our expert advice and you'll soon be able to capture professional-looking images with ease.

Five common flying insects to try and shoot...

ROSS HODDINOTT

1) HOVERFLY
Hoverflies are beautifully coloured. They often land on garden flowers, which create interesting and bright backdrops. Use an aperture smaller than f/8 to generate sufficient depth-of-field.

ROSS HODDINOTT

2) MOTHS
Moths are not as colourful, but some are still attractive, such as the Elephant Hawk Moth. Search among hedges and foliage as this is where moths often rest and shelter during daytime.

ISTOCK PHOTO

3) BUTTERFLY
One of the most striking examples of garden wildlife and probably the most photographed. You will be hard pressed not to find an attractive specimen to capture an image of.

ROSS HODDINOTT

4) CRANEFLY
Don't overlook photographing Crane Flies, more commonly known as Daddy Longlegs. Their gangly appearance is best captured in close-up and in front of a clean, uncluttered backdrop.

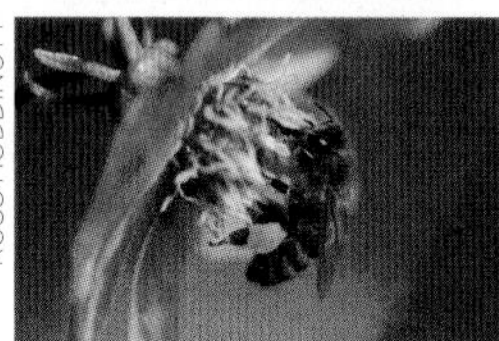

5) BEES & WASPS
Bees and wasps are regular visitors to our back gardens. Bees will be drawn to nectar-rich plants. They are always on the move, so switch from AF to manual focus if your lens struggles to lock on.

Shoot close-ups of butterflies

ROSS HODDINOTT: Summer wouldn't be complete without the graceful flight and vibrant colours of butterflies. At this time of year, they can be found in flower-rich meadowland, along the coastline, in wooded glades and in our gardens. Although wildlife photography can be tricky and frustrating, butterflies are easy to locate and get close to, particularly when feeding. Larger species are often easier to photograph, as you don't need to get so close to them to achieve frame-filling shots. Small Tortoiseshell, Peacock and Red Admiral butterflies are perfect for honing your skills. They're large and common, and will often settle on flowers or bask, open-winged, on walls long enough for you to shoot them.

Insects are highly sensitive to movement, so move slowly and don't make any sudden or jerky movements. I recommend using manual focus, as it is quieter. You also avoid the risk of 'hunting' as the lens tries to focus, which wastes valuable time. Macro lenses are best for this type of photography, providing excellent image quality and a good working distance. However, cheaper alternatives, such as extension tubes or close-up filters, will also get the job done.

Most people shoot butterflies from overhead, with their wings open flat; but to create striking, less conventional images, experiment with other angles and depth-of-field. Try shooting them from eye-level or backlit to show the transparency and markings of their wings.

To give you a few ideas, I recently visited some nearby gardens where I found a number of migrant Painted-Lady butterflies. All that's required now is a little patience and luck.

Get ready!

TIME REQUIRED
60 MINUTES

EQUIPMENT NEEDED
NIKON D300 & 105MM MACRO LENS

Essential kit

MACRO LENS: It isn't really fair to suggest that a macro lens is an 'essential' piece of kit when photographing butterflies. Budget alternatives, like close-up filters, are capable of very good results. Also, many modern zooms offer a 'macro' facility, which provides a highly useful reproduction ratio of up to 1:2 (half life-size), which is good enough to fill the frame with larger species. However, a dedicated macro is the best choice for wildlife close-ups. For flighty insects, a 'tele-macro', such as a 90mm or 100mm, is a good choice. Not only do they offer superb image quality up to 1:1 (life-size), but this type of focal length creates a more practical camera-to-subject working distance, minimising the risk of disturbance and, therefore, maximising the photographer's chances of success. A macro of this length is also relatively compact and lightweight, making sharp results possible when handheld – even without image-stabilising technology.

1 GETTING PREPARED: When 'stalking' butterflies, you have no option but to keep your set-up simple. A tripod often proves impractical – being too fiddly and time-consuming to position, and greatly increasing the risk of disturbing your subject. However, assuming it's a fine, sunny day, there should be sufficient light to enable you to select a shutter speed upwards of 1/200sec – fast enough to freeze subject and camera movement. When working handheld, keep your elbows pushed in towards your chest to limit camera shake. If you do require the added stability of a support, consider using a monopod, which is easier to position and shouldn't disturb the surrounding plants. Butterflies rarely feed or rest for long, so you will need to focus and compose your image quickly – something that gets easier with practice.

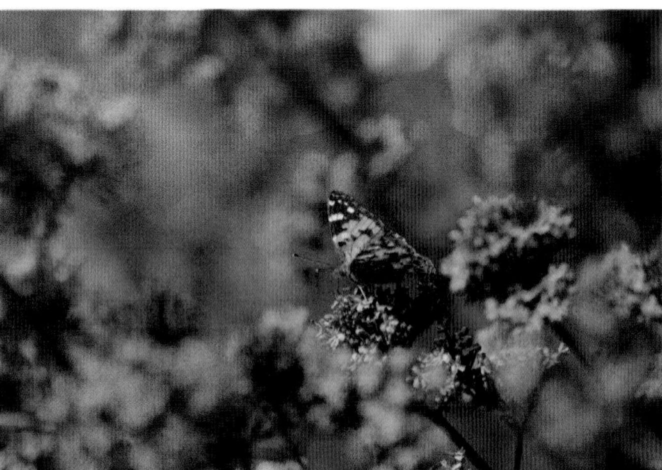

2 NOT CLOSE ENOUGH I began by simply watching the butterflies for a few minutes, observing their habits and which plants they preferred. The Red Valerian was a clear favourite, so I stood nearby, camera at the ready. As the butterfly lands, approach it slowly, gradually moving the camera to your eye. Older insects can look tatty, with faded colours, so only snap butterflies in pristine condition. My first efforts were disappointing, as I shot from too far away, so the butterfly is not large enough in the frame. I needed to get closer.

3 BE AWARE OF YOUR BACKGROUND Be aware of what is going on behind your subject, as a messy backdrop will ruin your image. With practice, it becomes easier to let your eye wander around the frame while you focus and compose your shot. A small change in shooting position can eliminate distracting foliage from the frame. Alternatively, a wider aperture will throw the background out of focus. However, sometimes, there is nothing you can do other than wait until the butterfly moves to a more photogenic position.

Final Image

Photographing butterflies is a challenge, as just as you're about to get the perfect shot, they fly away! After nearly an hour of chasing butterflies around, and a sequence of around 70 shots, I only managed a handful of images I was genuinely pleased with. Persevere and your patience will be rewarded.

Shooting mode

Aperture-priority mode allows you control over depth-of-field, whilst the camera sets the corresponding shutter speed to ensure you can work quickly and with the minimum of fuss

4 DEPTH-OF-FIELD This is crucial in close-up photography. Too much, and background detail will be too defined. Too little and the subject won't be sharp throughout. A good general rule is to set the widest aperture that will still keep your subject acceptably sharp. This also ensures that the shutter speed is fast enough to freeze subject and camera movement. In this instance, after reviewing a handful of test frames, I found that f/7.1 generated sufficient depth-of-field, whilst throwing the vegetation behind pleasantly out of focus.

5 SHOOTING ANGLE Generally, if a butterfly is resting or feeding with its wings open flat, photograph it from above. If its wings are closed, shoot from one side. Regardless of whether the wings are open or closed, try and keep your camera parallel – if not, its wings will begin drifting out of focus. However, you don't always have to opt for conventional angles. Try shooting straight on at eye-level or from a low viewpoint, for instance. With this shot, I combined the two approaches to create a more original looking result.

Wild web wonders

ROSS HODDINOTT: Rather than searching the web for ideas, why not get outside with your digital camera and search for a real web? Spiders spin beautiful cobwebs of sticky silk, and their constructions are intricate, often symmetrical and look stunning close up. Therefore, if you own a close-focusing zoom, close-up filter, extension tube or – better still – a dedicated macro lens, you will be able to capture stunning, frame-filling images.

Spiders live everywhere, so you shouldn't struggle to find a suitable web to photograph. They're easiest to find – and look their most photogenic – when smothered in tiny water droplets. Therefore, early in the morning after a clear, still night is the best time to look, when there's plenty of dew around.

Alternatively, you could spray one with water to create a similar effect by using a gardener's spray bottle to create a fine mist that won't damage the web. In autumn and winter, after a cold and frosty night, you might even find a frozen web, which is particularly photogenic and can make very arty, abstract-looking images by using a shallow depth-of-field, together with careful focusing.

Get ready!

TIME REQUIRED
30 MINUTES

EQUIPMENT NEEDED
NIKON D300, SIGMA 150MM, TRIPOD & REMOTE RELEASE

EQUIPMENT NEEDED
REFLECTOR

Essential kit

REFLECTOR
A compact, fold-away reflector is an essential close-up accessory. They are designed to bounce natural light onto miniature subjects in order to relieve ugly shadows. A reflector will normally create a more natural-looking form of illumination than flash. However, I have often employed a reflector as a makeshift background for small subjects. Its black cover can be held behind the subject to create a clean, simple backdrop. In some situations, you can even use a reflector's silver or white side in order to create high-key results.

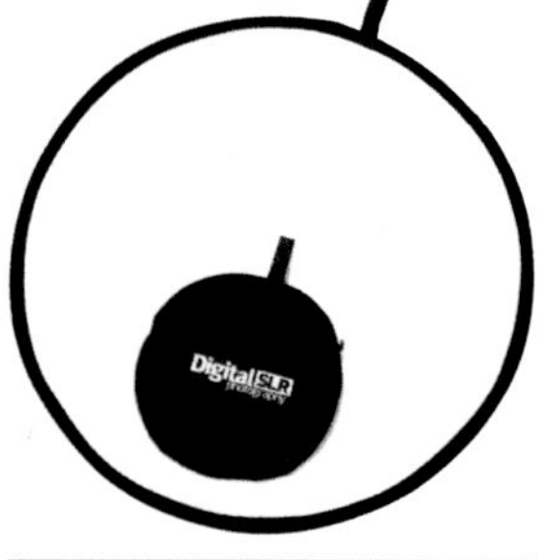

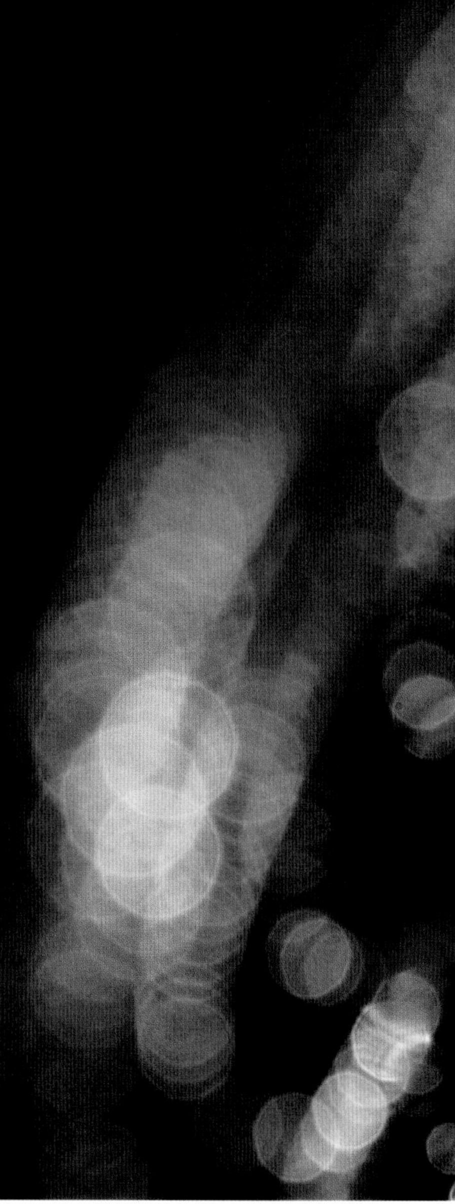

1 I didn't have to search my local area long before finding a dew-laden web. I composed the image quickly, and decided to include the entire web in the frame. I opted for an aperture of f/8, hoping that this would create sufficient depth-of-field to keep the web sharp, while not recording too much background detail. However, I didn't pay enough attention to the background and the web doesn't stand out very well against the light backdrop.

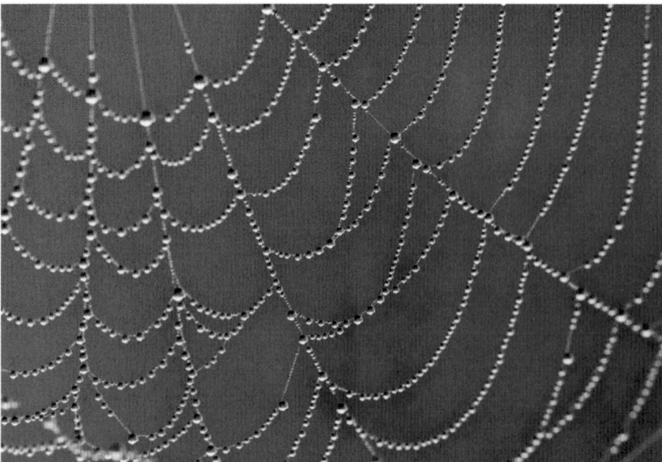

2 The subject's backdrop is often a major contributing factor to a photo's success or failure. By simply changing viewpoint, shooting angle, focal length or aperture, you can alter the background's colour and appearance. To eliminate the white sky from the image-space, I selected a higher angle by extending the legs of my tripod. A grassy bank now created a more attractive green background. I also opted for a tighter composition.

3 I wanted to create a more arty looking result, so I selected a wider aperture of f/4, and placed my set-up at an angle to the web. This would allow me to record just part of the web in focus. Focusing needs to be accurate when working with such a shallow depth-of-field. I checked the image on the LCD monitor, zooming in to check the subject's sharpness. Unfortunately, my focusing wasn't precise enough and the image is soft.

4 I tried again. Using a shallow depth-of-field at this level of magnification allows the photographer to direct the viewer's eye precisely to a specific point of focus. If your camera has a preview button, use it to review the distribution of depth-of-field. This time I took an extra few moments to ensure my focusing was accurate and released the shutter remotely to prevent any camera movement spoiling the image.

5 Although happy with the previous shot, I felt a black backdrop would suit the subject better – thinking it would contrast starkly with the glistening water droplets. The cover of my foldaway reflector is black, so I held it around 40cm behind the web and used the self-timer to trigger the shutter. Finally, I had the result I wanted. If you'd prefer a more colourful look, you could try using brightly coloured card to alter the appearance of the background.

How to shoot garden birds

Ross Hoddinott reveals how you can set up your garden to help you capture great images of the small birds that visit throughout the year

Regardless of where you live in the UK – rural or urban – common and widespread song birds are rarely far away. Due to their familiarity, it's easy to overlook just how attractive our popular garden residents are. For example, blue tits, great tits and greenfinches are all hugely photogenic. They also tend to be fairly tolerant of human activity and can be enticed near to a camera using suitable food. However, getting close enough to birds to take pictures is just the beginning. A good photograph is the result of a combination of background, surroundings, light and exposure. All these things can be controlled and influenced by the photographer; they shouldn't be left to chance. Once your set-up is complete, you then need to wait. Nature is unpredictable, so patience is required. However, photographing birds can prove addictive. You just never know what might happen next... that 'once in a lifetime' shot might be just around the corner.

Gear up for birds!

To photograph birds of this size, you will need a minimum focal length of 300mm, otherwise they will appear too small in the frame. A 70-300mm zoom is good, or you could even combine a shorter focal length like a 55-200mm with a 1.4x or 2x tele-converter. A sturdy tripod is essential to support your set up. Select your digital SLR's continuous shooting mode, so when your subject is in position, you can capture a quick burst of images. As you will be shooting a large number of frames, keep spare memory cards nearby ready to replace full ones. Whether you focus using autofocus or manual focus is personal preference. Finally, don't worry if your success ratio is small at first. Digital doesn't cost and it really doesn't matter how many images you take to achieve a good one.

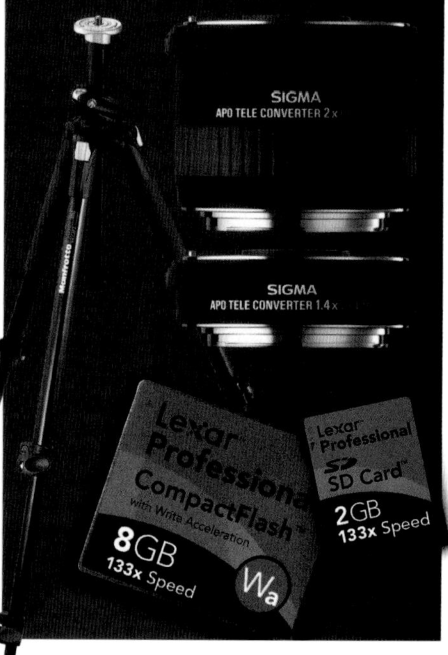

1) Camouflage

Baiting garden birds with nuts and seed will only entice them close to you if your set-up is carefully concealed. Otherwise, your every movement will frighten them away. In this instance I simply hung scrim netting across my studio window. This allowed me to change memory cards and camera settings without risk of disturbing the birds feeding just a few metres away. If you don't have a suitable window or shed that you can use is this way, consider buying a hide. The foldaway Dome hide, available from Wildlife Watching Supplies (WWS), is quick to erect using aluminum flexipoles. The hide is free-standing, but in strong winds the guy ropes and pegs provided can be used. To further disguise your whereabouts, buy a camouflaged lens hood sleeve. The scrim netting from WWS is a soft, quiet lightweight material, ideally suited to wildlife photography.

For more options, visit: www.wildlifewatchingsupplies.co.uk and www.stealth-gear.com

2) Bait the subject

Enticing birds within range of your camera is only possible using bait. They will soon learn to visit a feeding station to supplement their natural diet. It's important to provide suitable food; safe for wild species to digest. Common garden birds like tits and finches enjoy wild bird seed and peanuts – available at a local garden centre. Keep food replenished regularly – while this can prove quite costly, it will be money well spent. Once birds are regularly visiting your feeding station, introduce a hide or move the food source within range of a window. I took all the images for this feature from my studio in Cornwall. My simple set-up used two feeding poles placed 2m from my window. I hung a seed feeder from one and a nut feeder from the other in an attempt to attract a greater range of species. I placed the poles parallel to each other, with a 0.5m gap between, where I fixed a perch for birds to use when not feeding.

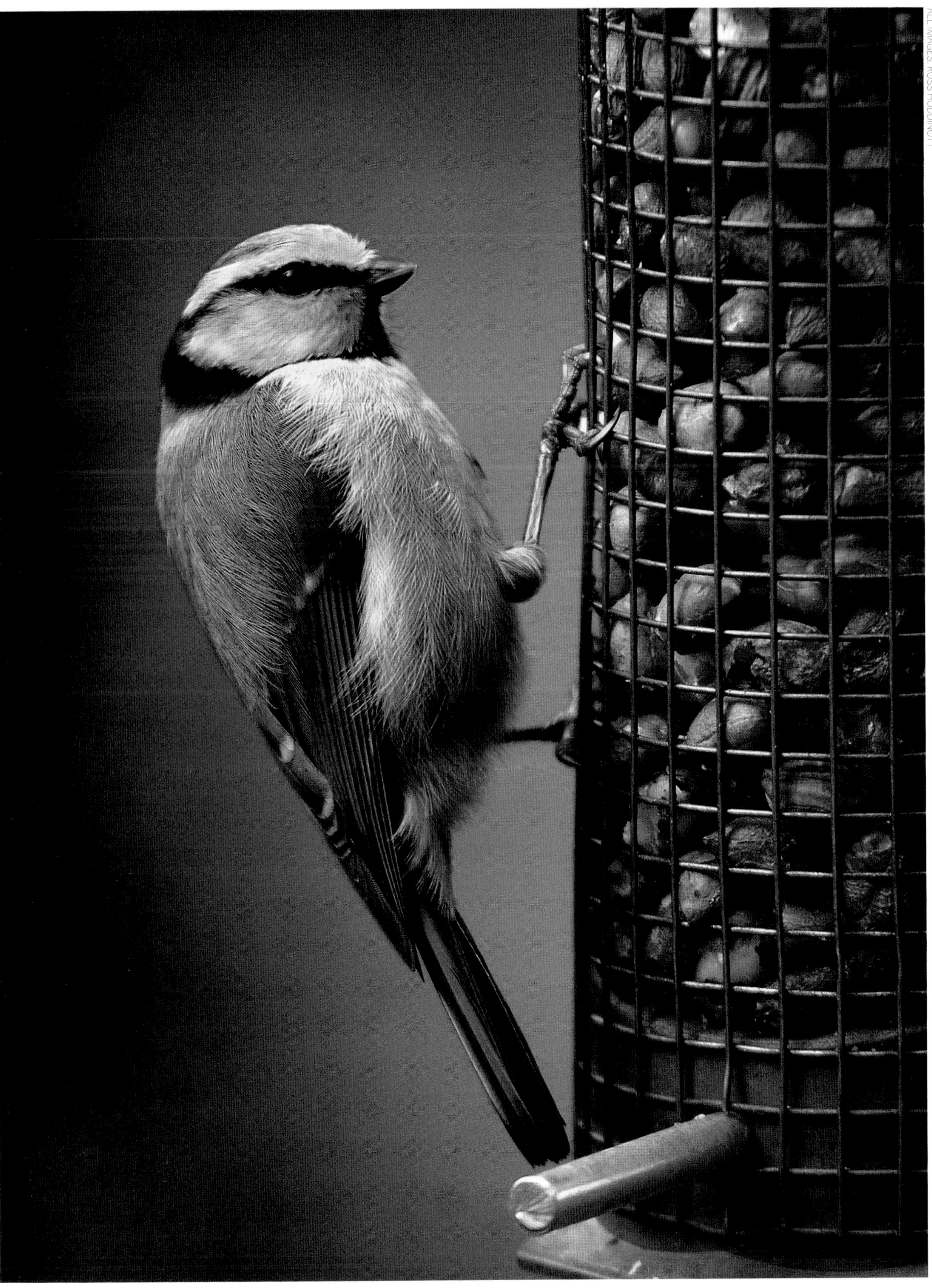

ALL IMAGES: ROSS HODDINOTT

3) Create your own background

Many wildlife images fail as a result of insufficient attention being paid to the subject's background. A dull or messy backdrop will ruin an otherwise technically good image, so this is a key area. When photographing small garden birds, you will normally be using a focal length upward of 300mm. A useful characteristic of telephoto lenses is that they condense perspective, creating an attractive, diffused background at wider apertures. However, to ensure you create a clean, simple backdrop, your perch should have a minimum of 2m of empty space behind it. Any twigs or background elements nearer than this will remain defined and draw the eye away from the subject.

The background colour is also important. A vibrant backdrop will help give your image added punch. Therefore, try to align your setup so that a colourful shrub or painted garden fence creates your background. If this isn't possible – or you are taking pictures in winter when colours are more subdued – introduce an artificial backdrop. In this instance, I constructed a simple wooden frame (1m square) which I erected roughly 2m behind my feeding station. I then attached coloured cloth to the frame using finger tacks, being careful to keep the material taut to prevent distracting creases from forming. Alternatively, you could use card, but this is more likely to tear if windy.

Positioned at this distance behind the subject, the material is rendered in soft focus, creating a clean, flattering backdrop. Any colour will do, so experiment. However, greens, blues and browns will create the most natural-looking results.

4) Choosing the shutter speed

Small garden birds are extremely flighty and active. They rarely remain still long to allow you to comfortably compose and focus on them, and even when they are resting, they are constantly looking about and altering position. Therefore, you need to prioritise a relatively fast shutter speed to freeze their rapid movement. Ideally, a speed of 1/400sec or faster is required. Otherwise you will take a high percentage of images that suffer from subject blur. If necessary, select a higher ISO sensitivity to generate a fast enough shutter speed. Even at ISO 800, levels of noise remain acceptable. However, to maximise image quality I recommend you do not exceed a sensitivity of ISO 400. Being able to increase the ISO rating at the flick of a switch is hugely beneficial to wildlife photographers who need to set a faster shutter speed to freeze movement or flight. It can make the difference between a blurred image or one that's pin-sharp.

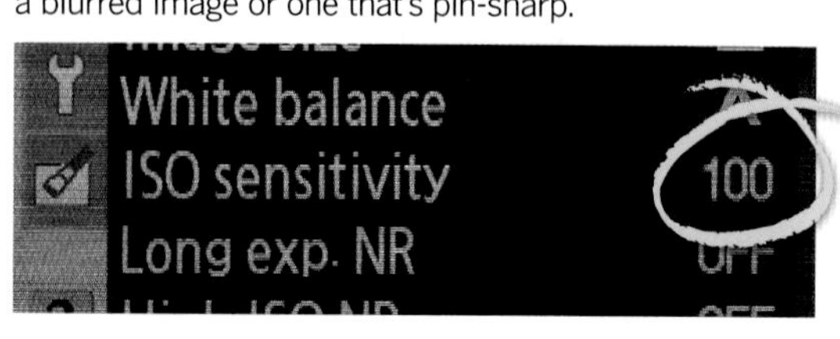

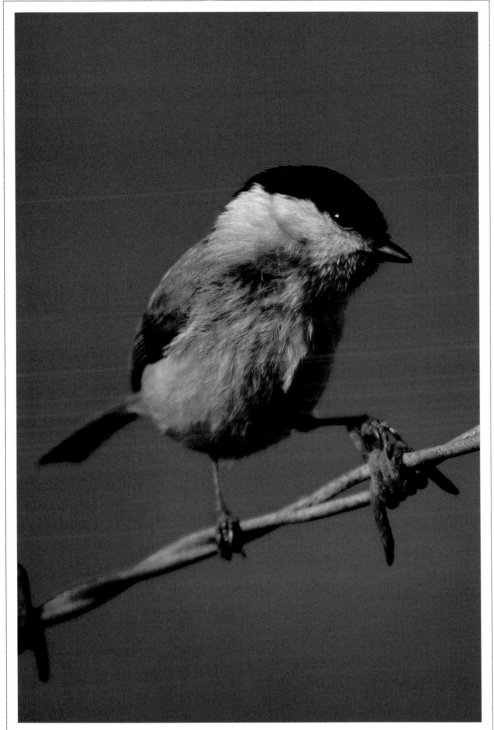

5) Consider using props

Using feeders is the perfect way to bring birds within range of your longest lenses. However, images of birds clinging to a feeder don't look very natural and you will soon get tired of taking this type of shot. To make your images look more wild and natural, introduce a prop near to your feeding station that the birds can use as a perch. This can be anything, as long as it is photogenic and in keeping with the species. An attractive, colourful branch works well. You can even make your images look seasonal by utilising a sprig of spring blossom or branch of autumn berries. If you want to be more adventurous, try using a rusty piece of barbed wire, washing line or maybe a milk bottle. Just use your imagination. The drawback of using a prop is that typically birds will only rest on the perch very briefly before hopping onto the feeder. Therefore, you will need to react quickly and remain patient. Experimentation is key. You will find that some props look and work better than others. If you're using an artificial background, you might also want to alter its colour to complement the type of perch you are using. Introducing a prop allows you more control and creativity over the look and feel of the final image. You're also able to create a more interesting overall result. Another advantage of using an attractive perch is that it will allow you to place less emphasis on the bird and, as a result, employ a shorter focal length. Shooting at a lower magnification is technically advantageous, as depth-of-field is extended.

Common garden birds

Here are five of the most likely visitors to your garden if you live in the UK...

1) BLUE TIT: Arguably the UK's most popular and common garden resident. Has elements of blue, green and yellow in its plumage with striking dark markings on its head.

2) ROBIN: One of our favourite song birds. They are highly territorial and are not adapted to cling on to feeders, but will use perches and often be found eating fallen seed beneath feeders.

3) COAL TIT: Widespread and common in UK, the coal tit is one of our smallest birds. Has black and white markings on head with conspicuous white patch on nape. Underparts are pale, pinkish buff.

4) CHAFFINCH: Male has reddish-pink face and underparts, bluish crown and chestnut back, female is more uniformly buffish brown. Both have white shoulder patch & white wingbar.

5) GREENFINCH: Widespread in the UK. Male is bright yellow-green, female is less colourful. Both have yellow wing patches, rumps and sides to tail. Bill pink and conical for feeding on seed.

ALL IMAGES: ROSS HODDINOTT

FLOWERS & FLORA

Nature is one of the most popular subjects to photograph, but it is also one of the most technically challenging. However, the beauty of flowers and flora means it is incredibly rewarding when you have captured images that encapsulate the delicate, stunning beauty of our natural world. And we often don't have far to look. Travelling by car, train and plane is so convenient today that it is easy to ignore the photogenic potential waiting for us much closer to home. Our own gardens are often brimming with picture potential. During summer, our gardens are at their best, brimming with colourful flowers, tree blossom and interesting plants. Whether your garden is big or small, rural or urban, there will be no shortage of things to shoot. Flower close-ups are always popular, but there are also many other less obvious subjects for instance, beautifully backlit foliage or abstracts focused on shape, form and texture. If you don't own a garden, don't be deterred. You could always head out to a public garden or well kept part to try your hand at nature photography. Or you could head out into more rural areas and use the techniques and advice covered here to capture great images of the wild flowers and plants you'll find along hedgerows, countryside and woodlands.

HELEN DIXON

Get geared up for the garden

Get prepared to venture outside to shoot stunning garden images once you've read our top advice on techniques and gear

ONE OF THE BIG APPEALS of garden photography is that it is possible to capture great images within the confines of your backyard, without the need for pricey or specialist equipment. Your camera with standard zoom is enough to get you started. For many garden images, you will want to get close to your subject in order to isolate it from its surroundings and to exclude anything distracting from the background such as a shed, greenhouse or garden fence. Thankfully, most standard zooms are designed with a useful close focusing distance. While the 'macro' facility on such lenses does not offer the same high level of magnification as a true, dedicated macro lens, they allow photographers to get close enough to capture frame-filling close-ups of larger plants such as dahlias, aliums, lilies and irises.

If you already own a macro lens, then you will find it well suited to garden photography. A dedicated macro will allow you to shoot at high levels of magnification, up to 1:1 (life-size). This is perfect for shooting miniature detail such as petals, sharp thorns or tiny water droplets suspended on a branch. Not all photographers can justify the cost of buying one but there are several cut-price alternatives, including close-up filters and extension tubes.. Close-up filters are available in a variety of diameters and simply screw onto the front of your lens. They act like a magnifying glass, allowing you to focus nearer to the subject than you could otherwise. You can buy a set of three dioptres, of varying strength, for as little as £10 – what great value for money!

Telephotos can also be very useful for garden photography. Longer focal lengths, like the telephoto end of a 70-300mm zoom, appear to condense perspective. They naturally exhibit a shallower depth-of-field, throwing background detail quickly out of focus. This is perfect in situations where you wish to isolate a single flower against an attractive wash of colour, for example, a single tulip among dozens.

Finally, don't overlook the creative possibilities of using a wide-angle for garden photography. A short focal length is useful for taking shots of plants in context with their surroundings. While, instinctively, you might want to capture garden subjects close up, a wider approach can also be effective. For example, use a lens in the region of 17-35mm and you can capture dynamic-looking images due to the distorted perspective.

Quite simply, great garden images are within your grasp whatever equipment you own. Of more importance is a good, creative eye. Follow our advice and you will quickly learn new skills and capture brilliant garden images.

Essential garden gear

Lenses: A standard 18-55mm kit lens will get you started, but you may also want to look at getting a macro lens for close-ups or a telephoto lens so you can capture detail in objects that are far away. Wide-angle lenses can introduce some quirky distortion to your shots.

Tripod: A tripod is the perfect companion for garden photography. Not only does it provide the stability you need to capture shake-free images, but it also helps slow down the picture-taking process so you take longer fine-tuning the composition. You can buy a decent support for around £100.

Plamp: The Wimberley Plamp acts like an extra arm, with a clamp fixed at each end. You can attach one end to a tripod leg and the other to hold a flower. Thanks to its ball and socket segmented arm, it can be positioned quickly and costs under £30. Bargain!

Reflector: A perfect windbreaker and lighting supplement, a reflector is ideal for bouncing natural light or flash onto your plants for extra illumination and to protect your shots from movement caused by wind.

Spray bottle: Water droplets add scale, sparkle and interest to plant close-ups. A spray bottle or atomiser only costs a few pounds, but by spraying your subject, you can transform an ordinary subject.

Use your polariser

Although better known for their ability to saturate blue skies in scenic images, polarising filters are very useful accessories for garden photography. A polariser will remove the reflective sheen from foliage and petals, restoring a subject's natural vibrancy and help to make sure your shots are colourful and stand out. These filters reduce the light entering the lens so shutter speeds will be lengthened as a result. This isn't a problem when using a tripod in still weather, but on windy days or when shooting handheld, a faster shutter speed may be a priority to reduce the risk of camera shake.

LEE FROST

Garden viewpoints to try...

1) OVERHEAD: Some subjects suit being shot directly from overhead. You can capture symmetrical-looking compositions of flowers such as roses, gerberas or dahlias by placing them centrally in your camera's viewfinder.

2) PARALLEL: A parallel viewpoint is best for natural-looking shots of plants. This viewpoint is also a good way to create distance between your subject and its background to achieve a clean, diffused backdrop.

3) LOW: An upward shooting angle is a good approach for creating unusual, dynamic-looking compositions, particularly in combination with a wide-angle lens. Use a right-angle finder or your digital SLR's LiveView to aid composition.

ALL IMAGES ROSS HODDINOTT

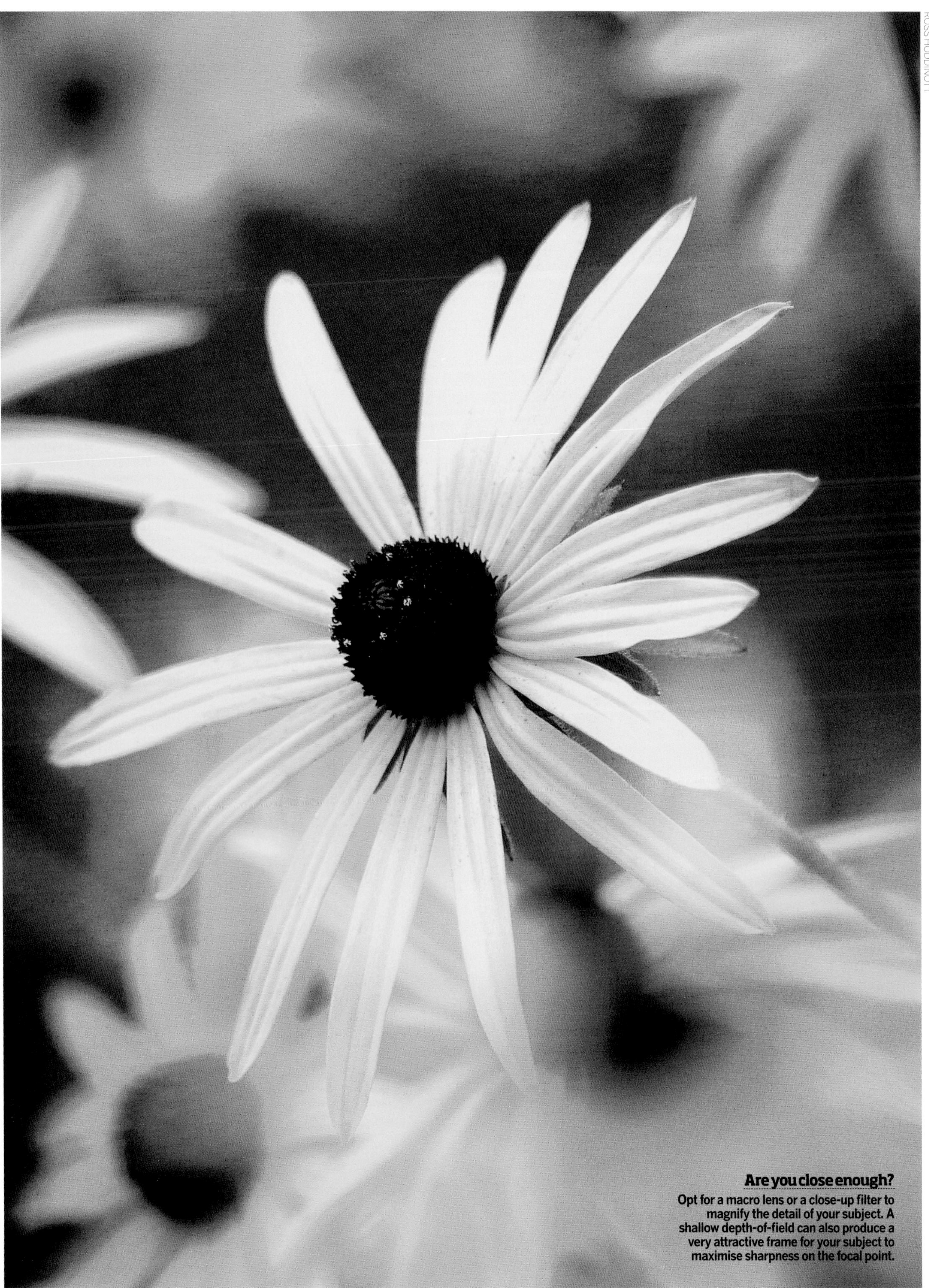

ROSS HODDINOTT

Are you close enough?

Opt for a macro lens or a close-up filter to magnify the detail of your subject. A shallow depth-of-field can also produce a very attractive frame for your subject to maximise sharpness on the focal point.

Fundamentals of lighting

Turn your average garden flora photography into beautiful still-lifes by learning how to master and manipulate the basics of daylight

JUST LIKE ANY OTHER SUBJECT, lighting is the key ingredient to success when photographing the plants growing and flowering in your garden. Good lighting will make your images stand out from the crowd, while poor lighting will undermine your efforts. Early morning and late evening light are traditionally the best times for photography, with the sun's low position providing warmth and softness to the quality of light. However, neighbouring buildings, hedges and fencing mean that many gardens fall into deep shade prematurely. As a consequence, photographers may be forced to take pictures during the day instead. Daytime light can prove harsh and contrasty. However, when shooting close-ups, photographers possess far more control over lighting. It is possible to manipulate light, using shade, altering shooting position or through the use of flash or a reflector.

Bright, overcast lighting is an underrated form of illumination, but one that is well suited to plant photography. Subtle, overcast light reduces the glare from foliage, restoring natural colour saturation. It also reduces contrast, allowing photographers to record fine detail that might otherwise appear washed-out in direct light. In fact, if the light is particularly harsh, casting your subject into shade – using your own shadow, or even an umbrella – is a useful trick for reducing contrast and producing a better result. Shooting in overcast light isn't without drawbacks, though. It is important to note that shutter speeds are longer as a result, so if it is windy there is an increased risk of unintentional subject blur. It is also trickier to focus and compose your shot with any accuracy in windy weather. Thankfully, when shooting in a garden environment, it is usually possible to find a sheltered corner where you will be unaffected by blustery conditions.

On-camera flash and frontal lighting can create very flat, shadowless light, which – in truth – is often best avoided. Overhead light, from the mid-day sun, can cast dark ugly shadows beneath the subject, which can be a problem if shooting from a low or parallel viewpoint. In this type of light, a small handheld silver/white reflector is an essential aid. By holding the reflector adjacent and angling it so that light is bounced back onto the subject to relieve dark shadows, it is possible to balance the light and create a more attractively lit close-up. You can alter the intensity of the light by moving the reflector closer or further away.

Side lighting is well suited to garden subjects, enhancing texture and creating a greater impression of depth in a photo. For more dramatic results, opt for backlighting. Backlighting will highlight fine detail, like hairy foliage, stamens and veining. This type of light works well with translucent subjects like leaves.

Shooting backlit plants

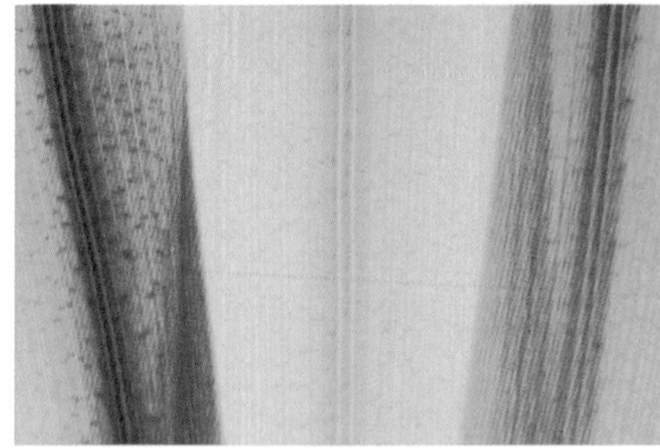

When shooting garden plants, backlighting is a very creative form of illumination. It highlights shape, form and miniature detail that might otherwise get overlooked. It is particularly well suited to translucent subjects, for example backlighting will emphasise every tiny vein found running through a leaf. However, this form of lighting is also one of the most technically challenging. When shooting toward the light source, the risk of flare is enhanced. Therefore, attach a lens hood or carefully shield the front of the lens using your hand or a piece of card. Also, backlit subjects are more likely to fool a digital camera's multi-zone meter. Metering can be erratic at times, so it is important to regularly assess exposure when shooting backlit subjects. Review your histogram screen and be prepared to adjust your exposure compensation settings.

Garden lighting tutorial

To explain the basics of using light in a garden photography situation, nature photographer Ross Hoddinott ventured into his back garden armed with his DSLR. His task was to shoot a flower while contending with bright sunshine, using just a tripod and a reflector. A collapsible silver/white reflector can be picked up for as little as £15 to £20, while a decent tripod (essential for garden photography) will set you back around £80 to £100.

Set-up

1 In deciding to shoot a handful of close-ups, I opted for a parallel viewpoint and selected a large aperture of f/2.8 to create a shallow depth-of-field. However, the bright, overhead sun was creating dark, ugly shadow beneath the flower and along its stem.

2 When working in close proximity to the subject, a burst of camera flash can look artificial unless carefully regulated, so a reflector is often a better option. I simply held it in place nearby and angled the reflected light onto the flower to relieve the shadow areas.

3 You can reduce contrast by taking photographs in shade. If there are no passing clouds that will oblige, simply use your own shadow to cast over smaller garden subjects. Shooting in shade can lead to longer exposure times, so be wary of blur in your shots.

4 I increased the ISO sensitivity of my DSLR from 100 to 200 to get a faster shutter speed. I then waited for a lull in the gentle breeze before releasing the shutter. This time the shot is pin-sharp. By controlling the light, this image looks much better than the original.

ALL IMAGES: ROSS HODDINOTT

Backlit subjects

Adding backlight to subjects like leaves can highlight detail that would otherwise have been invisible.

Water droplets

Daniel Lezano explains how adding water droplets to a subject can give extra visual interest to flower images

ROSS HODDINOTT

WITH SO MUCH RAIN FALLING in the UK, it's easy to understand why producing a guide on mimicking raindrops in your garden photos could be deemed as a little odd. Unfortunately, most of our rain falls during the colder months when our gardens are bare of flowers, so with fewer showers during the summer, the only way to be sure we'll have raindrops on our flowers when we want them is to make them ourselves.

This is easily done using a water spray bottle, watering can or garden hose. If you're using one of the latter two options, be sure that the nozzle has an attachment that sprays water over your flowers, rather than providing a strong solid stream, otherwise you may cause damage to delicate flowers and plants.

There are a number of different ways that droplets can settle on your garden flowers and plants and they can give very different types of results. One of the most popular is capturing droplets hanging off stems, usually in groups of two or three. This is an effective technique that takes on an added dimension if there are flowers nearby that are captured within the droplets, such as in the image above. If you want to try this technique, choose a viewpoint that takes the backdrop into account. The other common image is a far simpler one and that is to spray droplets on leaves, so they cover the surface with dozens of small droplets.

For this step-by-step, I wanted to try a technique that I'd not seen before and that was to create a single droplet that rested on a flower, rather than hanging from it. My chosen flower was a purple alium, one of my favourites to photograph due to the intricate nature of its multi-flowered bloom. As I'll be moving around trying different angles, I'm shooting handheld and using a 100mm macro lens to help me get close. The bright sunlight means avoiding camera shake won't be a problem, but the odd breeze means I need to keep shutter speeds relatively high to avoid blur caused by the subject's movement during the exposure. I use aperture-priority mode as I want to retain close control of depth-of-field.

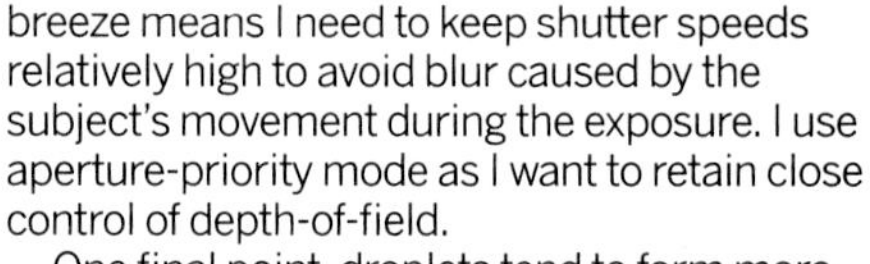

One final point, droplets tend to form more easily and hold their cohesion better on humid days when there is more moisture in the air. Therefore, if a summer storm is brewing, head into the garden and you'll find this technique easier to achieve than on hot, dry days.

1 **I start off by spraying the alium with a water spray to spread a light dusting of water over the flower. Unfortunately, while the spread of water is good, the droplets are too small, meaning that they're not large enough in the frame. I need to find an alternative!**

2 **I try using a hose but the result is the same. I decide I need to apply a larger drop with more control and attempt to do this using a straw dipped into a jar of water. By using my finger on the top end of the straw, I do my best to control the release of water onto the alium.**

3 **It takes a few attempts but I eventually manage to settle a large droplet of water on a flower. It's proof that with a little patience and luck, the straw method can work. This particular droplet is way too large, so I shake the alium and keep trying until I manage to do better.**

4 **It takes a few more attempts but I have a droplet that is a more suitable size. Now it's a case of trying to find a suitable viewpoint and the best aperture setting. I start by shooting from above, but the result is too two-dimensional, so I shift my position and look for alternatives.**

5 **Adopting a lower viewpoint provides a more three-dimensional feel to the image and the flower with the droplet is clearly visible due to the shallow depth-of-field from a wide aperture (f/5.6). However, the out-of-focus foreground is distracting and the dark backdrop is unattractive.**

Final image

By shifting my position slightly higher, I've made a dramatic improvement to the composition. Not only does the subject now dominate the frame, the foreground is less cluttered and the green vegetation in the background is far more appealing. The aperture of f/8 provides the perfect amount of depth-of-field too.

Weeds, glorious weeds!

Daniel Lezano shows that unwanted weedy visitors to your garden can make for great still-life images

UNLESS YOU'VE SOMEONE in your home who's totally dedicated to their garden, chances are there are areas where weeds make an unwelcome appearance. Normally, that calls for a small trowel to dig them up or a dose of weedkiller. However, the dandelion is one weed that photographers should look forward to seeing as it makes for very photogenic images. Rather than the actual flower, it's the dandelion clock, also known as a parachute ball, that deserves your attention. This delicate head is made up of small, lightweight seeds that break apart from the clock and float off with the breeze. This makes them beautiful but difficult to handle, so while it's possible to pluck one and move it into a suitable location, you'll often find it's best to shoot it where it has grown.

There are various ways you can photograph a dandelion clock, so it's worth trying out as many as you can before it breaks up. One of the most popular is to adopt a low angle and shoot it against a dark backdrop or a blue sky, polarised to boost the contrast. Another is to fire a sequence of images while some seeds are blown off the head, so that they are caught in mid-air, then shooting the clock, with its remainder of seeds.

All these ideas are worth trying, but for this step-by-step, I've decided to shoot something a little different from the other garden images in this guide. Instead of going for a colourful image of the clock, I'll be looking to produce a more detailed, monotone and abstract result. I've set up my camera with a 100mm macro lens on a Manfrotto 190XPROB, which has a useful collar that allows the centre column to be quickly adjusted for low-level shooting. It's a bright day, so I set a low ISO of 100, and with aperture-priority mode selected, I shoot each frame at f/5.6, f/8 and f/11 to vary the depth-of-field – I'll decide later which I prefer. As focusing is critical, I set single-point AF to ensure I focus on the centre of the clock.

In situ

Reflector cover

Diffuser

Set-up 1

Set-up 2

Set-up 3

1 Dandelions are one of the most common garden weeds, so you shouldn't have much trouble finding a suitable crop. I discovered one growing through some gravel beside my shed, where it has been sheltered from the wind. Here's a 'straight' shot taken of the dandelion clock to show it in its natural setting. The green and brown backdrop is not particularly inspiring so some measures need to be taken to improve the result.

2 I place the black cover of my reflector behind the dandelion clock and it makes an instant improvement, with the white head standing out from the backdrop. I need to dial in -1EV exposure compensation to prevent the clock losing detail – check exposures via your LCD monitor. While better, the result is still too bland. To reveal the intricacies of the clock, I need to work out a way to shoot the subject backlit.

3 The solution is easy – I place the diffuser of my 5-in-1 reflector behind the dandelion clock (a sheet of white paper or net curtains can also be used if you don't have a diffuser panel). Due to the low angle, I shoot handheld, using the tripod to support the diffuser. The image is instantly much better than previous attempts. The bright sunlight gives a near-white backdrop and the dandelion clock is recorded as a near-silhouette.

Wonderful weed

A quick tweak in Levels (*Image>Adjustment>Levels*) to improve the contrast of the silhouette effect, followed by the addition of a slight tint using *Image>Adjustments>Hue/Saturation*... and I'm done.

The wonder of wild flowers

As Ross Hoddinott reveals, woodland, forests and rural areas are not just perfect for scenics, but also for capturing its beautiful flora

In spring and early summer, you'll find hedgerows and woodland brimming with colour. Wild flowers are just reaching their annual peak, presenting outdoor photographers with countless opportunities to capture stunning floral images. They can literally spring up anywhere, growing along roadside verges and even appearing between cracks in pavements, so regardless of where you live, you shouldn't need to venture far to find flowering plants to snap. Wild flowers can be shot using practically any focal length; a wide-angle lens can be used to photograph them in context with their surroundings, a zoom or telephoto to shoot small groups and a macro or close-up attachment to isolate individual flowers. As a result, regardless of your kit and budget, great shots are within your grasp.

The size, shape, colour and form of our native wild plants varies tremendously, making it tricky to give specific advice on how best to photograph them. To a great extent, the subject, its particular environment and the light conditions on the day will dictate your approach. However, I guarantee your wild flower images will benefit from these tried and tested tips and guidelines.

Without reflector

With reflector

1) Using a reflector

When photographing wild flowers, I only employ a burst of flash when the fastest available shutter speed remains too slow to freeze movement. Personally, I feel flash ruins an image's natural feel – destroying subtle colouring and fine detail. Instead, when the lighting is poor, I prefer to manipulate the natural light available. This is possible with the use of a reflector, such as the collapsible, lightweight types made by Lastolite. Alternatively, it is possible to make one by stretching kitchen foil over a piece of cardboard. A reflector couldn't be easier to use. Simply position it near to your subject and angle to direct natural light onto the area required. The intensity of the 'bounced' light can be increased or lessened by moving the reflector closer or further away from the subject. Whilst an essential aid when it's overcast or while taking pictures in woodland under a thick canopy of leaves, a reflector is also useful in bright, sunny conditions. For example, overhead sunlight will create ugly, harsh shadows that can be lifted by bouncing light onto the shaded regions. A reflector can prove fiddly and awkward to accurately position whilst taking pictures. Personally, I use a Wimberley Plamp to position my reflector. This is a ball-and-socket segmented arm with a clamp at either end. One end can be attached to a tripod leg, whilst the other holds the reflector.

Gear up for wild flowers!

To photograph wild flowers, you ideally need a macro lens or close-up attachment. If you can't justify the cost of a dedicated macro, consider using either extension tubes or a close-up filter combined with a standard focal length. A telephoto – in the region of 200mm to 300mm – is useful for shooting larger flowers, like orchids. Also, a wide-angle lens can prove handy if you wish to photograph carpets of flowers or images including the subject's surroundings. Always carry a sturdy tripod to avoid camera shake and aid composition, although if you're shooting from ground level, a beanbag will prove more practical – along with a groundsheet to lie on. A reflector is another 'must-have' accessory. An atomiser (water spray bottle) can be employed to add fine, dew-like water droplets. A polarising filter is useful to reduce reflective glare from foliage and a soft focus filter can work well in combination with backlit subjects. An angle-finder is ideally suited to shooting wild flowers at ground level. Always focus manually for precision, unless your eyesight won't permit. Also, if your camera has a depth-of-field preview button, use it to check your selected aperture has generated sufficient depth-of-field. Release the shutter using the self-timer to minimise the risk of camera movement.

2) Gardening

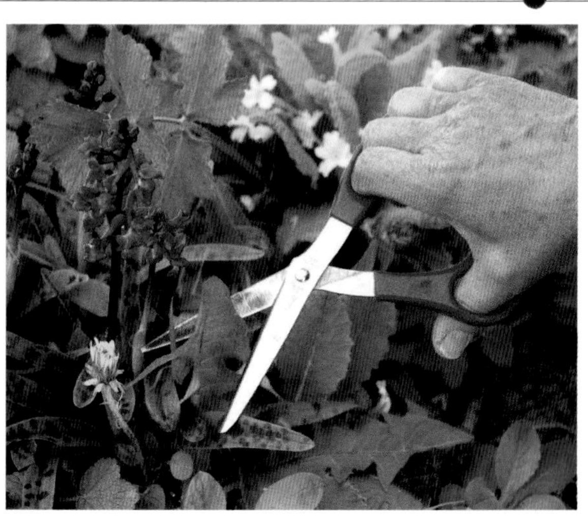

Gardening is an essential part of wild flower photography. Don't worry, though; you don't need green fingers. Gardening is a term given to the selective removal of grasses and other distracting elements from the foreground and background of the frame. Rarely, in my experience, will you photograph a plant in the wild without having to do some degree of tidying first – unless the subject is filling the viewfinder. The extent you have to garden depends on the environment and f/stop employed. At wide apertures, depth-of-field is shallow, so less tidying is required as the subject's background quickly drifts out of focus. In contrast, when using small apertures, the extended depth-of-field created retains more detail and definition in the subject's surroundings – making gardening a more fiddly, time-consuming process.

While minor background distractions can be removed later using the clone tool in Photoshop, others cannot, without it being obvious in the final image. It is far better to get the image right in-camera. My approach is to first compose the image and set the exposure. I then preview the depth-of-field, carefully studying the frame to identify anything that might prove distracting. If your camera lacks a preview facility, take a shot and scrutinise it on the LCD monitor. I then carefully flatten them with my hand or use scissors to remove them. This should be done with care and consideration. Only remove grasses and stray leaves; never cut or destroy other wild flowers. Ultimately, you are striving for a clean and diffused background.

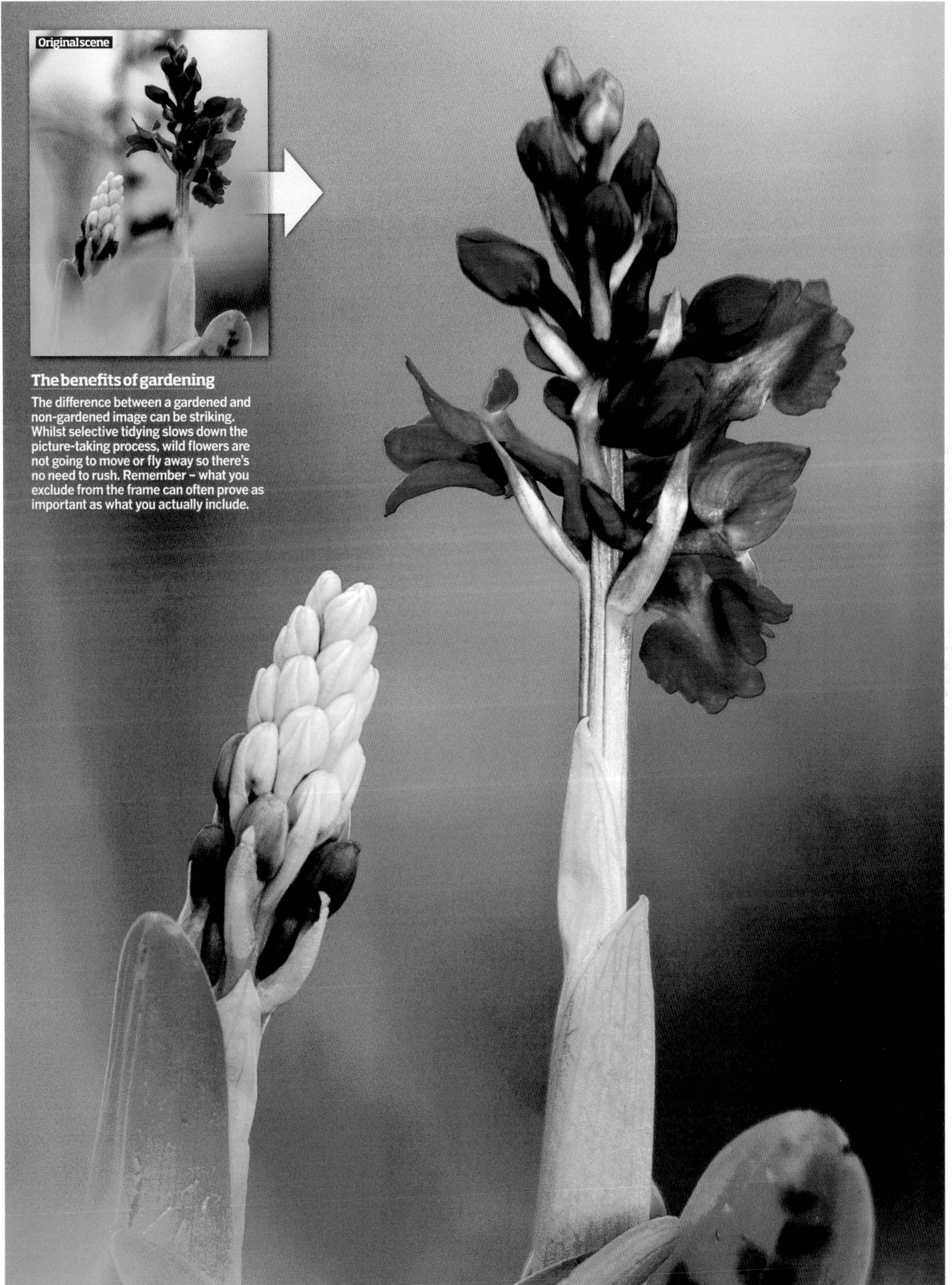

The benefits of gardening

The difference between a gardened and non-gardened image can be striking. Whilst selective tidying slows down the picture-taking process, wild flowers are not going to move or fly away so there's no need to rush. Remember – what you exclude from the frame can often prove as important as what you actually include.

3) Lighting

As with any subject, lighting is a key area and the way in which you use ambient light greatly dictates the look of the final image. I often prefer to work on bright, but overcast days. Foliage glare is reduced, colours are more saturated and lower contrast allows me to capture fine detail that might otherwise be washed out. However, shutter speeds are lengthened in overcast conditions, so a still day is required and a camera support essential. Side or frontal light is fine, but avoid shooting around mid-day when the overhead sun is harsh. If unavoidable, cast your shadow across the subject to lower contrast and use the self-timer to trigger the shutter.

To capture wild flower images with more drama and impact, backlight them. Evening or morning light is best, when the sun is low in the sky and is perfect for highlighting shape and form. It can create wonderful results – illuminating tiny hairs and detail on stems, and giving petals a translucent appearance. To backlight a subject, you need to shoot in the direction of the light, so there is the risk of lens flare. To avoid this problem, use a lens hood or shield it with your hand or a piece of card. The tricky lighting conditions can easily deceive metering systems, so check images via the LCD and bracket settings.

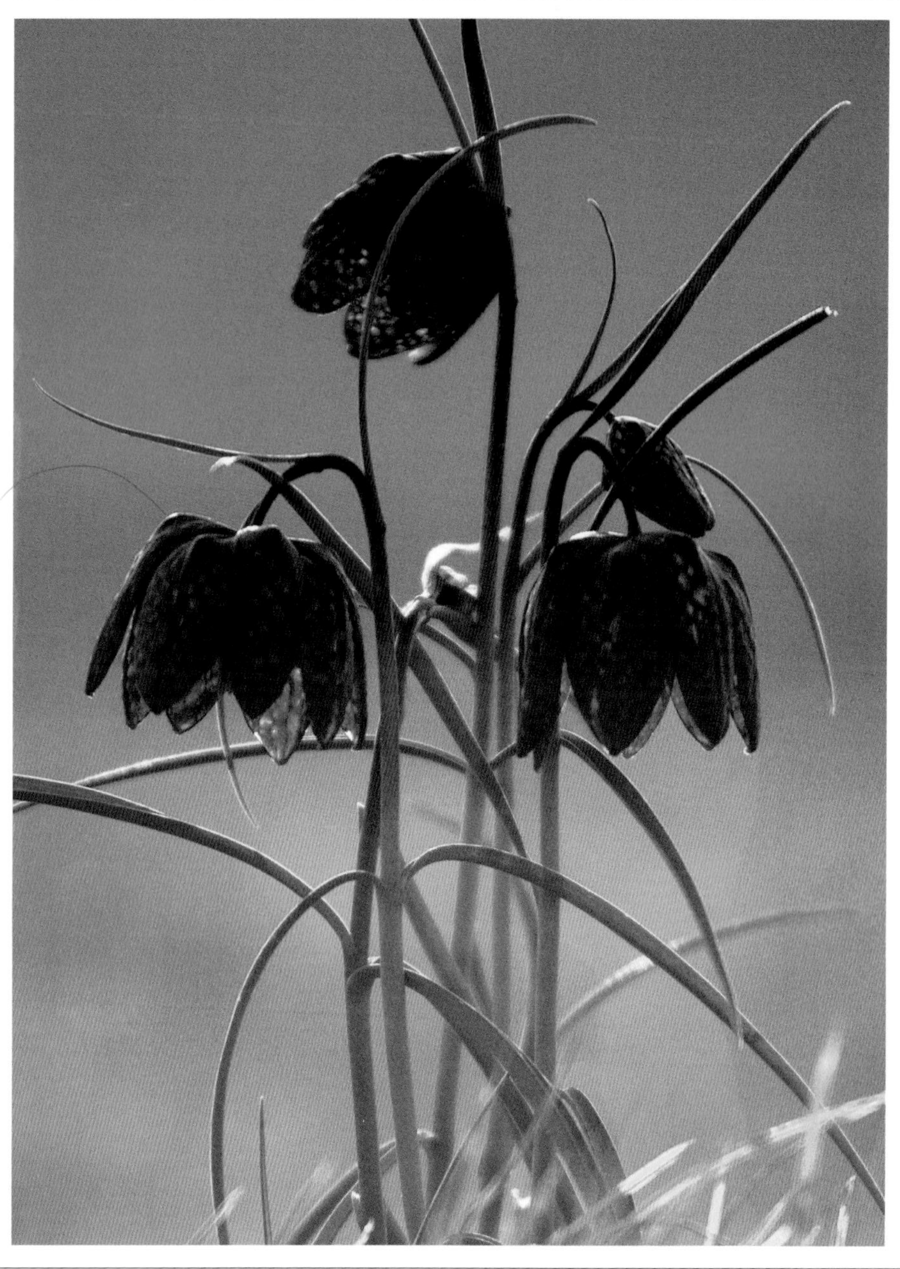

4) Depth-of-field

The aperture you select, and the resulting depth-of-field, will greatly dictate the look and feel of the final image. There is no definitive rule regarding how much, or how little, depth-of-field is required; this is a decision you need to make at the time of taking the picture based on the effect you wish to achieve. If you want to draw the eye of the viewer to a specific point of focus, use a large aperture, like f/2.8 or f/4. If you want to maximise back to front sharpness, opt for a small f/stop, like f/16 or f/22. Your camera cannot predict the effect you desire, so it is important to set apertures manually, rather than rely on one of your camera's automated exposure modes. If you are unsure which aperture will create the best effect, why not simply take a sequence of images with different f/stops and decide later which you prefer. I did this when I photographed this close-up of a celandine flower. In this instance, I much prefer the images taken with a shallow depth-of-field.

f/22

f/5.6

f/2.8

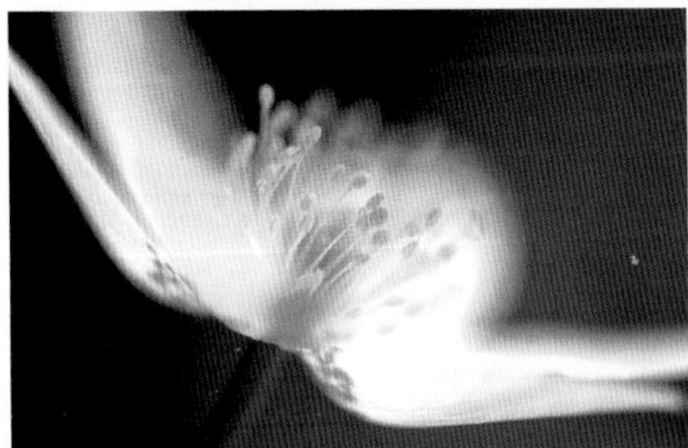

5) Originality

Producing fresh images of common, well-photographed flora is far from easy and too often we record a subject in a certain style or way, simply through habit. In other words, preconceived ideas can stifle our creativity. Digital capture has made it easier than ever to experiment, so be imaginative. Each species has the potential to be shot in an infinite number of ways. It is possible to produce a varied set of images from the same subject by simply altering the viewpoint, focal length, lighting, exposure, background or camera-to-subject distance. Each parameter can have a dramatic effect over the look and feel of the final image. In my experience, it is best to begin by taking the image that is immediately most obvious, then move around the subject and consider different approaches. Try shooting from low and high viewpoints, then vary focal lengths and depth-of-field. Fill the frame with the flower, but also take a shot showing it small within its environment. If it is breezy, use a long shutter speed to blur the flower. The possibilities are only limited by your imagination. To illustrate this point, I visited a local woodland where wood anemone grow in large numbers and captured these very different results within minutes.

Original scene

Common wild flowers

Here are five of the most popular wild flowers to photograph in the UK.

1) EARLY PURPLE ORCHID: One of the most widespread wild orchids, thriving in woodland, scrub and grassland. Glossy, dark green leaves are spotted and flower spike is pinkish-purple.

2) PRIMROSE: Familiar perennial of woodland, hedgerows and shady meadows. Also a garden favourite. Flowers are 20-30mm across and borne on long, hairy stalks.

3) BLUEBELL: Although common in the UK, bluebells are scarce abroad, with Britain home to more than 50% of the world population. Often found as impressive, dense, photogenic carpets.

4) WOOD ANEMONE: Widespread and locally common woodland perennial. Long stalked stem leaves are divided into three lobes. Shoot them individually or as large carpets of flowers.

5) FOXGLOVE: Tall, recognisable flower – common along coast paths, woodland glades and scrub. Its spike bears a succession of pink-purple, tubular flowers, which are also poisonous.

ALL IMAGES: ROSS HODDINOTT

Visiting public gardens

Don't have a garden? Or is yours better described as a jungle? No problem. Head to a public garden to capture stunning images

GARDENS ARE UNDENIABLY full of picture potential, but not everyone has one. If you live in a flat or apartment, you may not have access to a garden. Alternatively, you may simply not enjoy gardening and, as a result, don't have anything of great interest growing in your backyard. If this is the case, don't worry – you can still take great garden photos. Family, friends and neighbours are sure to say 'yes' if you ask them if you can photograph the plants growing in their gardens. Failing that, why not visit one of the many beautiful formal gardens open to the public throughout the UK.

A quick look on the web will inform you of the gardens you have near you. For example, the RHS (Royal Horticultural Society) owns several gardens (and is affiliated to many more) that are home to beautifully manicured flower beds brimming with colour. The cost to enter such places is normally quite reasonable, and you can spend all day taking pictures.

Formal gardens are great places to visit. They are full of unusual and exotic plant species and trees, providing far more variety and choice than most family gardens. In addition to being home to an array of plants, shrubs and grasses, formal gardens often have flowers growing together in large numbers, creating impressive displays of colour. They are carefully designed and lovingly maintained to ensure they always look pristine. Month after month, different flowers come into bloom in natural cycles, so it's worth visiting the same garden again and again throughout spring and summer. The majority of shots will be obvious – close-ups of beautiful blooms and backlit leaves, for example. However, with so many exotic, non-native plants growing, you will find plenty of other opportunities. Look for unusual flowers – large or small – with either long stamens or long colourful spikes comprising dozens of individual flowers. Such intricate and interesting detail lends itself to photography. By experimenting with depth-of-field and the point of focus, you can radically alter the end result.

Public gardens are often home to features like waterfalls, small fountains, attractive archways and gazebos. Frequently, these are surrounded by vibrant flowers or smothered in climbing plants and make great shots. A short telephoto (around 50-100mm), is well suited to this type of garden image, flattening perspective and allowing you to isolate key areas of interest and detail. Keep an eye on the background too as you'll want to avoid other visitors appearing in your images, so wait until the frame is clear of people before shooting.

Many gardens close around 6pm, meaning photographers are unable to enjoy the best hours of light. Therefore, take a small foldaway reflector when you visit in order to manipulate the natural light in your close-up shots.

Find a public garden near you

Visit www.parksandgardens.ac.uk to get information on over 5,000 parks and gardens in the UK. You can browse the directory alphabetically or by area, so finding a garden close to you should be a walk in the park!

HELEN DIXON

Things to look out for...

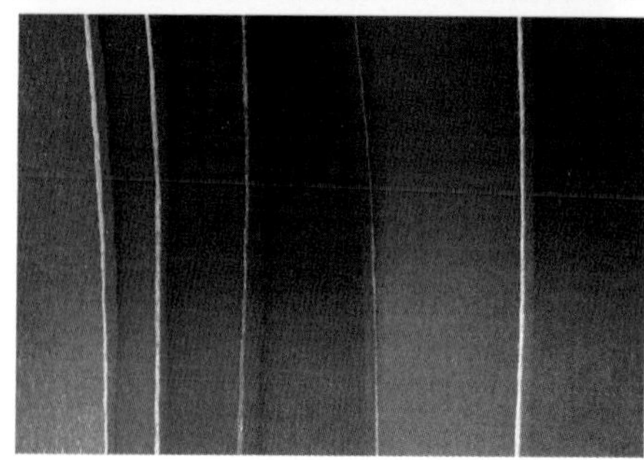

ROSS HODDINOTT

1) BARK: You will often find exotic, non-native species of tree – like Himalayan Birch and Eucalyptus – growing in public gardens. Many have wonderfully textured, colourful bark. Get in close for eye-catching natural patterns.

HELEN DIXON

2) BLOCKS OF COLOUR: In formal gardens, flowers are often grown in huge numbers that far exceed what you have growing at home. Look for large beds of tulips or daffodils. Try different lenses, from wide-angle to telephoto.

ROSS HODDINOTT

3) BUILDINGS: Many large public gardens have attractive buildings set within the grounds, often partly covered in ivy, wisteria or other climbers. Using a telezoom, you can isolate areas of interest for perfect compositions.

ISTOCK PHOTO

4) AUTUMN GLORY: Several of the larger public gardens are home to species of trees and plants that produce a spectacular golden display in autumn. Make sure to research gardens in your local area and contact them to help you plan the best time to visit for stunning results.

Public garden step-by-step

Public gardens are great places to visit with your camera, as there's so much more variety and space than the average back garden – you can easily spend a day wandering around taking pictures. Summer is a great time to visit formal gardens as flowers are in full bloom and foliage is fresh and vibrant. The entry fee to this Cornwall property was under £10 – fairly reasonable considering the choice of plants to photograph.

ALL IMAGES ROSS HODDINOTT

1 **The formal gardens at this local property were full of picture potential when I visited recently. A flower bed brimming with colourful tulips caught my eye and I could tell there were so many different ways to photograph garden subjects. By simply altering focal length, depth-of-field or viewpoint, I could radically alter the look of the end image.**

2 **I attached an 18-270mm superzoom for versatility and began by using the wide end together with a high, overhead viewpoint. I filled the frame with the tulips for maximum impact. The stretched perspective, created by the wide-angle effect, adds interest. The result is abstract looking, but I felt I could be somewhat more creative.**

3 **I was drawn to the tulip's long shadows cast on the ground. I decided to make them a feature by including them as part of the composition. Again, I adopted a high viewpoint, but this time I used a longer focal length and shot from further away. A vertical composition worked the best, creating the impression of height.**

4 **I changed viewpoint, sitting on the floor to shoot from a parallel angle. I used the telephoto end of my zoom and opted for the zoom's widest aperture. This, combined with the long focal length, created a shallow depth-of-field and a nicely condensed perspective. However, the frontal lighting looks a bit flat.**

5 **I moved to the opposite side of the flower bed and shot towards the light's direction instead. The backlighting helped give the tulip's translucent stems and leaves an attractive glow. I continued to shoot using a shallow depth-of-field, using it to help draw the viewer's eye to my intended point of focus.**

Magic mushrooms!

ROSS HODDINOTT: Autumn is a wonderful time of year for outdoor photography. Photogenic mists hang in valleys and trees and woodlands turn golden brown. This is also the season for photographing fungi. While they may not be considered the most exciting or glamorous subjects, toadstools and mushrooms are highly photogenic. There are thousands of types, ranging greatly in colour, size, shape and design. Fungi can grow practically anywhere, from parks to garden lawns. However, many species enjoy damp, mature woodland, where there are fallen trunks, mossy stumps and deep leaf litter. October and November are the best times to visit your local woodlands in search of fungi. This is a subject accessible to all photographers, with only a basic set up required. Naturally, you will need a digital camera – preferably with LiveView – and also a macro lens or close-up attachment, such as extension tubes or close-up filters. Fungi enjoy growing in dark environments, so the stability of a tripod is essential and also a reflector or flashgun to help to illuminate your subject. Whether you capture a solitary mushroom or toadstool or a group clumped together, spend a few minutes assessing the best viewpoint and choice of lens to use and whether using a reflector or not is beneficial. Your subject isn't going anywhere, so take some time and have fun capturing great images!

Get ready!

TIME REQUIRED
45 MINUTES

EQUIPMENT NEEDED
NIKON D300, SIGMA 150MM LENS TRIPOD, REMOTE RELEASE

ALSO USED
SCISSORS & REFLECTOR

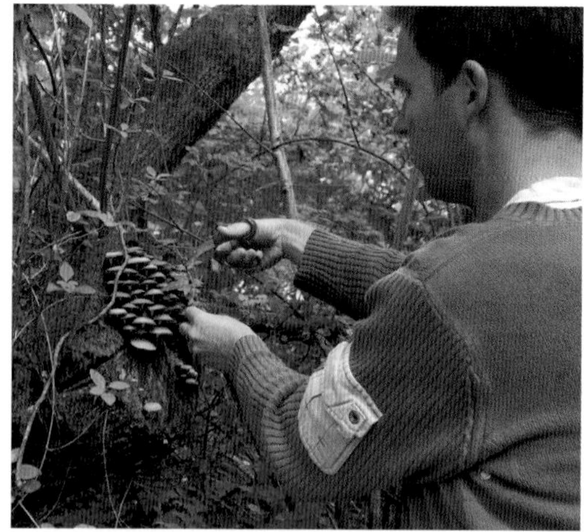

1 **You have to pay particular attention to your subject's surroundings when shooting close-ups. I always keep scissors in my backpack to tidy up the frame – a technique known as 'gardening'. I removed some ivy from the tree stump the mushrooms were growing on, but was careful not to damage the fungi themselves.**

Tripod and remote release

When photographing fungi in dark woodland the light is often limited. This, combined with the fact that you will often want to select a small aperture in the region of f/16 or f/22 (to generate sufficient depth-of-field), means shutter speeds are typically slow. To ensure pin-sharp images, a tripod and remote release are essential. A tripod will give the stability you need. If the woodland floor is damp and soft, push the feet into the ground for extra security. Even when using a tripod, physically pressing the shutter release button can cause small vibrations that soften images, so fire the shutter remotely, using a cabled or wireless remote release. If you don't have one, use the camera's self-timer function instead. If your camera has a 'mirror-lock' function, use it. This works by locking up the reflex mirror before releasing the shutter, eliminating internal vibrations.

2 **To eliminate the problem of the distracting background, I opted to move my tripod slightly closer and go for a tighter composition. The result is an improvement, but the parallel viewpoint is rather uninteresting and overall, the shot lacks impact. The parallel viewpoint may work with some subjects, but in this case it clearly doesn't do the job.**

3 **The intricacy and pattern of a mushroom's gills is usually their most photogenic and interesting feature. Therefore, low viewpoints, looking upwards, often work well and produce the best images. Next, I repositioned my tripod, but due to the low, awkward angle, I was struggling to compose the image accurately and comfortably through my DSLR's viewfinder.**

4 **When shooting at low, awkward angles, LiveView is a really helpful feature. I switched on LiveView and using the screen, I composed the shot without having to contort my body. The low angle really emphasised the fungi's gills, creating a more interesting shot. Cameras with a vari-angle LCD monitor are even better adapted for this type of photography.**

Be prepared!
To avoid getting damp, muddy clothing, wear waterproof trousers or carry a ground sheet or bin liner to kneel on

Final image
A mushroom image that's truly magic. Why don't you head out to the woods and give this technique a try?

5 The disadvantage of using a low viewpoint is that the underneath of the fungi is in dark shadow, obscuring detail and proving quite ugly – especially as light levels in a dense woodland can be quite low to start with. A burst of fill-flash can be used to relieve this, but it can be too harsh and unnatural in such close proximity to the subject.

6 I prefer using a reflector. You can instantly see its effect on the subject and alter the light's intensity by moving it closer or further away. I think it's the most natural-looking way to illuminate miniature subjects and it is also the simplest. Holding the reflector close, I bounced light back up onto the fungi and released the shutter again until I was happy with the result.

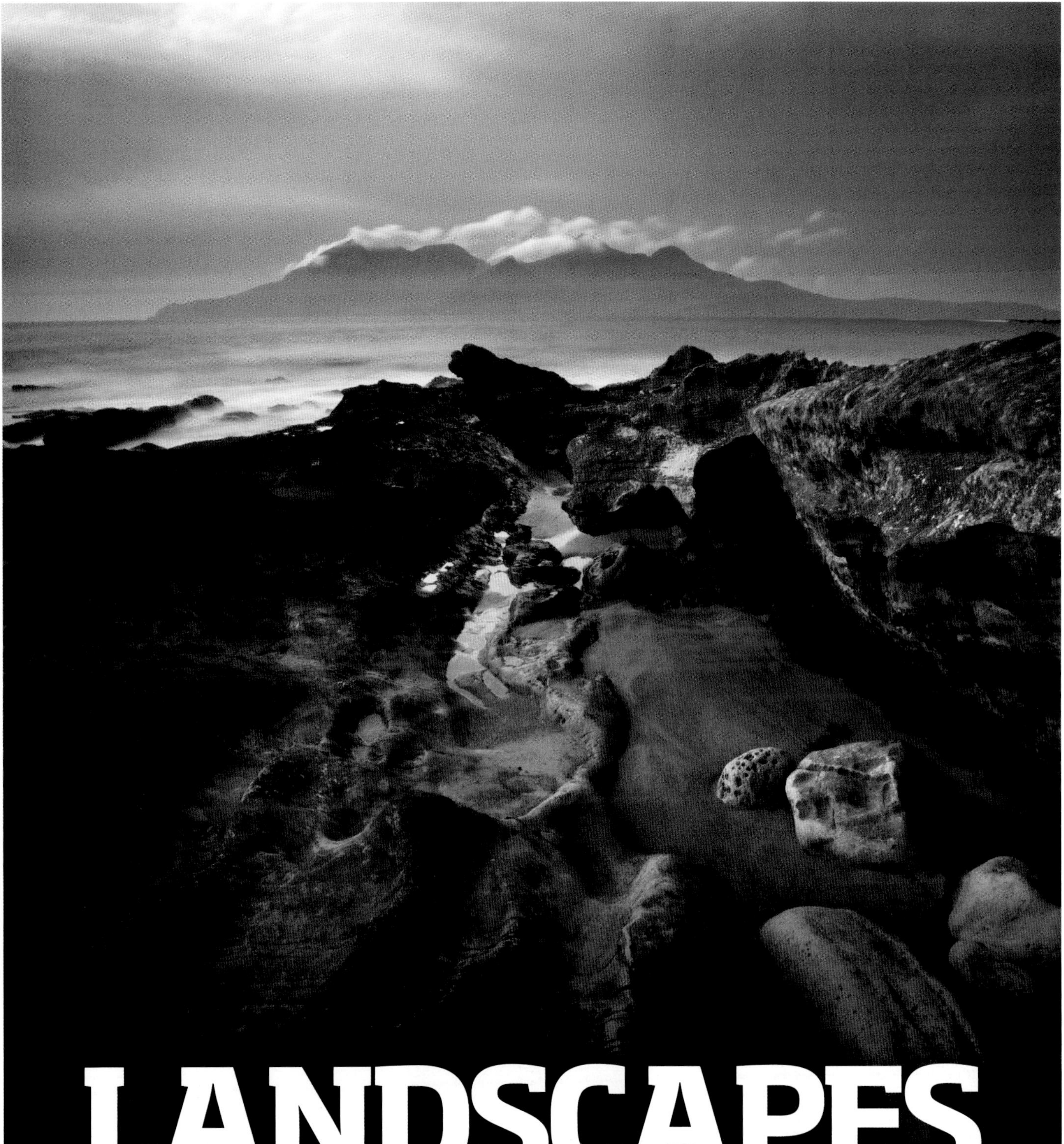

LEE FROST

LANDSCAPES

The wonders of the great outdoors offer endless potential for stunning photography. This major section provides all the essentials you'll need to take your best ever landscape shots

Capturing beautiful landscapes is a pursuit shared by millions of photographers around the world. Whether shooting in the UK or abroad, the diversity of the scenery and how it appears at different times of day, in each of the four seasons and under different weather conditions, means that the great outdoors can offer an ever-changing range of scenery for you to photograph. We cover all the core principles and techniques that will help you to take your best ever landscape photos, as well as provide a huge selection of stunning images to inspire you.

Creating balance: The 'rule-of-thirds'

Before you shoot a single image, you need to practice this simple framing technique

The word balance implies an equal weighting. In a picture, this would mean symmetry, but visual balance – or rather harmony – is not usually achieved this way. Placing a subject centrally in the picture frame usually results in a static rather than a dynamic composition. Placing the subject off-centre, on the other hand, encourages the eye to move around the frame more, resulting in a more dynamic picture.

One way of dividing the frame up to achieve harmony is to use the 'rule-of-thirds'. This is a simplified version of the 'Golden Section', a proportion which has been used in art and architecture for centuries. This proportion also occurs with great frequency in nature, and there is research to suggest that our brains are 'hard-wired' to respond positively to images and objects that follow this proportion – for example, people whose faces are proportioned according to the golden section tend to be thought of as more attractive.

The practical application of this in landscape photography is to divide the frame up into thirds, horizontally and vertically, and organise the elements in the scene to fit into the grid, for example by placing the horizon line on one of the dividing lines. The points where horizontal and vertical lines intersect can be particularly powerful places for putting strong focal points in scene.

RIGHT: This image follows the rule-of-thirds quite closely. There is approximately two-thirds land and one-third sky, the main part of the hay bale is in the left third of the frame and the sun is placed on an intersection of thirds.

Breaking the rules: Horizons

Like all rules, however, the rule-of-thirds needs to be applied with judgement rather than as a matter of course, and there will always be situations where it needs to be ignored. For example, when shooting a scene where the sky is reflected in water, you might well want to place the horizon across the middle of the frame, giving the two elements of the shot – sky and reflection – equal weighting. If there is no interest in the sky, the horizon can be placed higher in the frame or cropped out altogether, or to increase a sense of emptiness and isolation, the horizon can be placed very low in the frame. The beauty of shooting digitally is reviewing your efforts and shooting to ensure the perfect composition.

ALL IMAGES: MARK BAUER

Order & balance

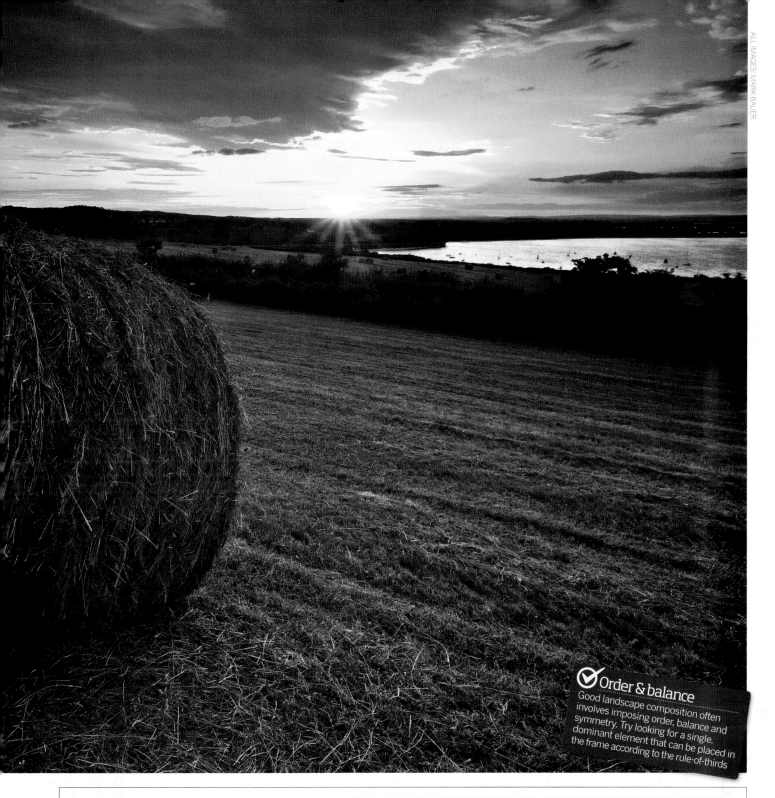

Good landscape composition often involves imposing order, balance and symmetry. Try looking for a single, dominant element that can be placed in the frame according to the rule-of-thirds

Experiment with viewpoints

Finding the right viewpoint is key to successful landscape composition. Rather than shooting everything from head height, experiment with high and low viewpoints. Higher viewpoints have the effect of opening up the planes in the image and are useful with standard and telephoto lenses. When photographing well-known landmarks, it's tempting to use the established viewpoints, but spend time looking for a fresh view, as it's much more satisfying to capture something original.

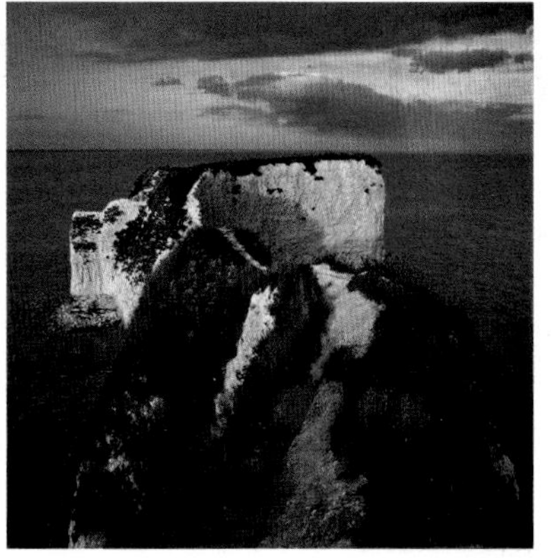

While there's nothing wrong with the first picture, it's the 'standard' view of Old Harry Rocks in Dorset, taken by countless photographers before. Without having to move very far, however, I found a less photographed and more dramatic viewpoint.

Creating the illusion of depth: Foreground interest

This simple compositional tool works by including a strong visual element in the bottom section of the frame to give extra interest

ONE OF THE BIGGEST problems facing landscape photographers can be summed up quite simply: the world is three-dimensional and a photograph is two-dimensional. One of the main reasons that landscape photographs fail is that they don't convey the sense of depth that our eyes perceive when we view a scene with our own eyes. Fortunately, there are a few compositional tricks we can employ to get round this problem.

A very effective way to create depth in a photograph is to include a strong foreground, often in conjunction with a wide-angle lens. Emphasising the foreground in this way will add depth to the picture by creating an 'entry-point' for the eye, pulling the viewer into the scene and giving the picture a sense of distance and scale. Wide-angle lenses work best for this technique because of the way they stretch perspective, exaggerating the elements close to the lens and opening up the view beyond the foreground. This can cause problems, however, because it can result in the middle distance looking empty and lacking in interest. The trick is to shoot from a lower viewpoint, which has the effect of compressing the middle distance, so that there isn't too much empty space in the composition. Avoiding the use of ultra wide-angle zooms can also reduce this problem. You'll also need to use a small aperture and focus carefully to maximise depth-of-field.

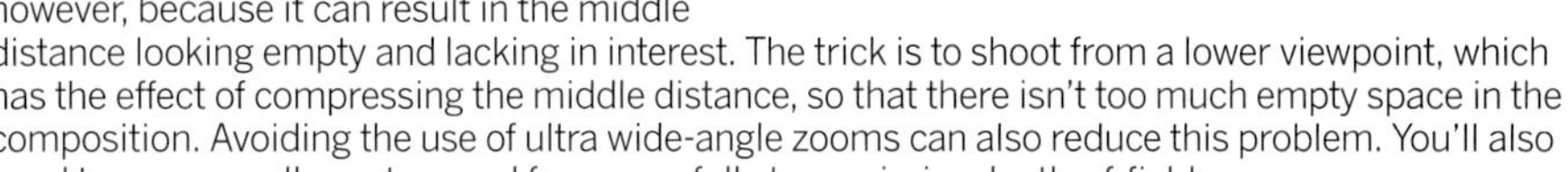

Natural frames

There are a couple of other points that are worth bearing in mind too. When people first start experimenting with this technique, there is a tendency to stick anything and everything in the foreground – regardless of whether or not it actually suits the shot. It's worth spending time looking around a scene and trying to find foreground elements that complement the background. Also, try not to ignore the middle distance – after the viewer has been pulled into the scene by the foreground interest, the eye needs to be guided through the middle distance to the background.

The 'big' foreground is a technique that has been well exploited by landscape photographers in recent years and is in danger of becoming a bit of a cliché. It's worth remembering that foreground interest doesn't have to be 'big' to be effective. Subtle elements often work just as well – for example, reflections in wet sand, the pattern of waves breaking on the shore, or the shadows cast by trees.

Essential kit

To make the most of foreground interest, you will need a wide-angle lens. A 'standard' wide-angle zoom rather than an ultra wide-angle often works best. I'd recommend a 17-40mm zoom rather than a 10-22mm as this enables you to give it impact, but without leaving the scene beyond looking too empty.

A sturdy tripod is a must – when exploiting foreground interest in a landscape we usually need to use a small aperture to maximise depth-of-field. Exposure times can be quite long so hand-holding becomes impractical. A tripod that allows you to set the camera low to the ground is also useful, as low viewpoints can be used to hide or minimise empty spaces in the middle distance when using wide-angle lenses.

A set of Neutral Density Graduate filters should always be with you when shooting landscapes as they help control the difference in contrast between the land and the sky.

Finally, two small but very useful pieces of kit are a remote release, to avoid camera shake, and a hot-shoe-mounted spirit-level to keep your horizons straight. It's possible to correct a wonky horizon in post-processing, but it's much better to get it right in-camera.

INSET: MIDDLE DISTANCE
The cow parsley makes an attractive foreground to lead the eye into the scene and provides a suitable frame for the view beyond. A wide-angle lens and a small aperture of f/22 provides plenty of depth-of-field.

LEFT: CORFE CASTLE
It's important to choose a foreground that suits your subject. In the first picture, the thistles complement the castle rising out of the mist. In the second, the yellow gorse is too colourful to frame this view successfully.

RIGHT: SMALL DETAILS
It's not always necessary to have a 'big' foreground; a small object such as this shell can be effective in a more minimalist composition.

Keep it simple!

Composition is all about what you choose to include in the frame – and also what you choose to leave out. Often, less is more and compositions that are uncluttered can be the most successful

Solitary shell

You don't need imposing boulders to create strong foreground interest. A wide-angle lens and low viewpoint emphasises this single shell, which forms a natural starting point for the eye to settle on before following the sand trails into the distance.

Step-by-step guide: Finding a suitable foreground

We have introduced you to the practice of placing something in the foreground to create depth, and to use a small aperture to give front-to-back sharpness, now we need to show you how to lead the eye into the frame

1 The beach at Osmington Mills is filled with large, round rocks – an ideal choice as foreground interest. With this first shot, however, although the eye is led into the shot by the line of rocks, there's not much to see in the middle distance.

2 Using the rocks along the water's edge to lead into the picture and then on to the headland in the background works much better. However, this particular group of rocks is a little dull and the picture needs more atmospheric lighting.

3 With the sun obligingly appearing from behind the clouds, I tried a different foreground. The sky and the light on the headland are dramatic, but the foreground is a bit messy and needs a greater sense of order and neatness.

4 The three foreground rocks in this composition stand out from the others and lead the eye successfully along the shoreline to the headland. The light and sky are still good and, overall, this shot works much better than the previous three.

5 A slight change of position and a switch to a landscape format gives a much more successful and balanced composition. Your eye is drawn first to the solitary rock (bottom right) and then follows the shoreline to the headland beyond. Nice!

Format choice

There is no straight answer as to whether an upright or landscape format works best. That said, an upright format often places emphasis on foreground subjects better than landscape format images

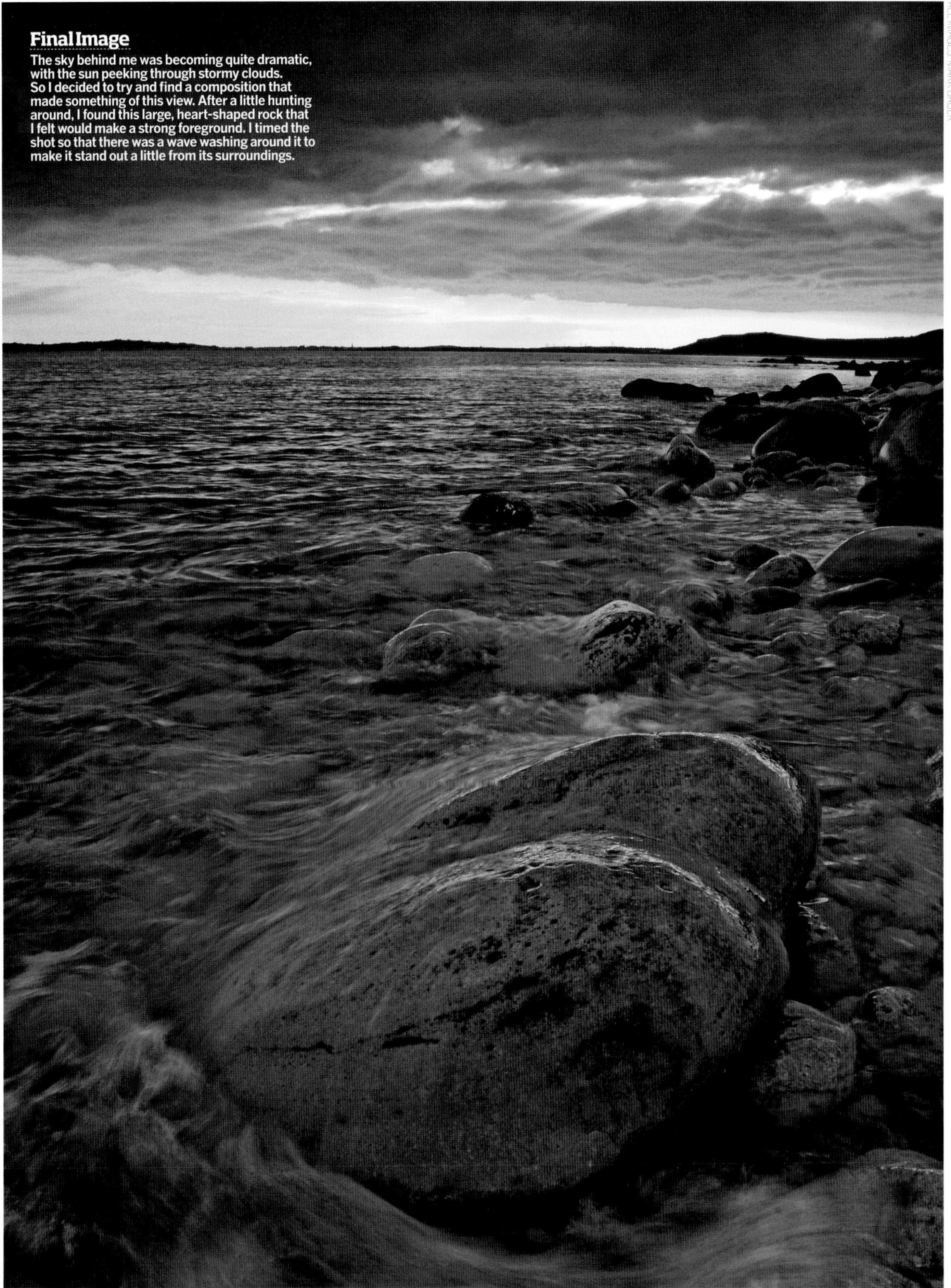

Final Image

The sky behind me was becoming quite dramatic, with the sun peeking through stormy clouds. So I decided to try and find a composition that made something of this view. After a little hunting around, I found this large, heart-shaped rock that I felt would make a strong foreground. I timed the shot so that there was a wave washing around it to make it stand out a little from its surroundings.

ALL IMAGES: MARK BAUER

Light direction

The position of the sun in context of how you frame a scene plays a major role in the mood of the image

THE DIRECTION OF LIGHT has a dramatic influence on how the landscape will appear behind the lens. Front lighting, with shadows falling behind the subject away from the camera, can make a scene look flat and uninteresting, although with the sun low over the horizon, it can provide good colour saturation. With low front lighting and wide-angle lenses, an added problem is that you have to be careful to avoid getting your own shadow in the picture.

Side-lighting is a favourite with many landscape photographers, because it reveals texture and shadows falling across the scene that highlight shape and form, therefore adding more depth to a scene.

Backlighting can be very dramatic, with shadows racing towards the camera, and the emphasis is very much on shape and form, with objects being recorded as silhouettes. Depending on the conditions, these objects might be placed in front of a boldly coloured background. Trees, backlit by the rising or setting sun, can look very effective, with shadows spreading out in front of them and the sun's rays bursting through the branches. Do be careful, though, not to look directly at the sun, especially if viewing the scene through a telephoto lens, as this can cause permanent damage to your eyes – not worth it, even for that Pulitzer prize-winning shot. The technical danger here is that your camera will probably tend to underexpose backlit scenes, so you will probably need to add a little more exposure than suggested by your camera's meter. Remember to check the histogram and be prepared to reshoot if necessary.

Essential kit to deal with light

STURDY TRIPOD: This is a must, especially when shooting in the low light of dawn and dusk

NEUTRAL DENSITY GRAD FILTER: Well worth having – again these are particularly handy at dawn and dusk, when the sky can be quite bright in relation to the ground. They help equalize contrast between the two

POLARISING FILTER: Useful for saturating colours and removing glare from bodies of water

Low front lighting

Capture the right mood for the scene

Perhaps the most important thing to remember is to shoot in lighting conditions that will enhance the natural mood of your subject. For example, some scenes are naturally more tranquil and will look best in the corresponding soft light of dawn and with pastel colours. Others have a naturally brooding atmosphere and demand more dramatic, theatrical and directional lighting.

NORMAN CHAPEL, ST ALDHELM'S HEAD: Make sure you shoot in conditions that suit your subject. The Norman Chapel at St Aldhelm's Head in Dorset has a brooding presence, which, as can be seen from these pictures, is best suited to low light and heavy skies.

Enhance low light with reflections

Pre-dawn and twilight are very moody times for landscape photography, but the land itself can be almost completely in shadow, with very little detail. If you shoot near water, you can include reflections as a foreground, which will help to balance the shot and throw more drama and impact into your image. The stiller the conditions the better for a more mirror-like surface.

MUDEFORD: With the sun yet to appear above the horizon, the wonderful colours in the sky can be used to add colour and impact into the foreground. In this shot there was a slight breeze across the water surface so I had to wait for it to drop for a clearer reflection.

ALL IMAGES: MARK BAUER

Back lighting

BOLDERWOOD, NEW FOREST
Backlit trees can make for dynamic images, especially with the sun's rays bursting through the branches.

Seasonal light

How light bathes a scene changes throughout the year, so be sure to revisit your favourite locations

ALTHOUGH NOT OBVIOUS on a day-to-day basis, the different seasons have an impact on the way the light falls on the landscape. In winter, with the trees having dropped their leaves, the landscape is more exposed and the low sun casts long modelling shadows throughout the day. The air is more humid and has less dust than at other times of year, giving the light a clarity not often found in the other seasons. Clear, cold nights often lead to a frost in the morning, complemented by pastel colours in the sky.

The light in summer is often less favourable for landscape photography, with the high sun creating harsh light for a large part of the day, with more dust and heat haze meaning the light is generally less clear.

In early spring and late autumn, the light and clarity are better than in summer and it's possible to shoot for most of the day. The weather is also quite changeable at these times of the year, which can create moody and dramatic photo opportunities. In late spring and early autumn, after a cool night, mist can often form at dawn as the land begins to warm up. This is the time to head for rivers, lakes or hills overlooking valleys. Certain locations will look more photogenic at different times of day and year than others. Researching locations and deciding what time of day or year will suit them best is time well spent.

DAVID ENTRICAN

MARK BAUER

Effect of weather on light

In theory, there's no such thing as good or bad weather in landscape photography – good images can be produced in any conditions. The reality is, however, that certain conditions will produce more dramatic shots. The trick is learning to recognise and anticipate them. For example, if planning a sunset or sunrise shoot, don't cancel it if there's cloud cover. If there's a break on the horizon, there's a good chance that the clouds will be lit from below when the sun is at or just below the horizon, with the result being a very dramatic sky.

One of my favourite conditions is sunshine and showers – the light can be stunning in the moments when the rain stops and the sun breaks through, with foreground objects spot-lit against a dark, brooding sky. These moments are fleeting, however, and don't last for long, so you need to have your camera prepared beforehand.

If the weather is bad – grey, overcast and raining – there are still shots to be made. In these conditions head for woodland: the diffused, less contrasty lighting suits this type of location and, surprisingly, using a polariser can really enhance a picture, by cutting out the reflections and glare from wet foliage and saturating the colours.

Ironically, probably the least inspiring weather for landscape photography is provided by what most people would describe as a 'perfect' day – blazing sunshine and clear blue skies.

ROSS HODDINOTT

Above: These two pictures illustrate that moment when a storm gives way to a brief burst of beautiful sunlight through a break in the clouds. Right: The overcast conditions give a diffused effect to the light. A polariser has taken the sheen off foliage and enhanced saturation.

MARK BAUER

Know your weather

The weather forecast is the butt of many jokes, but I've found there are one or two websites which are more reliable than others. My two favourites are: **www.metoffice.gov.uk/weather/uk** and **www.accuweather.com/ukie**

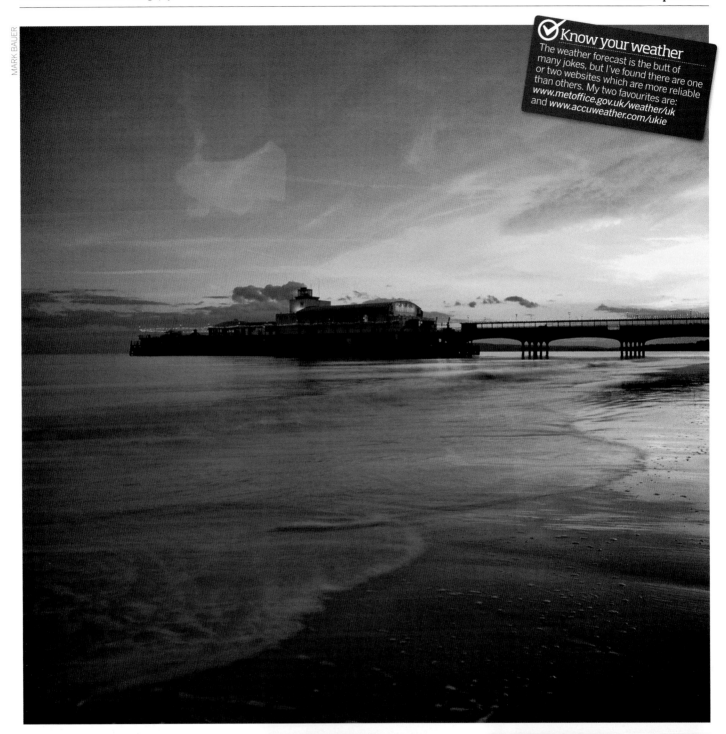

Light 'on the edge'

A lot of the action in landscape photography happens 'on the edge' – the transition between one state and another. In terms of light, this means the transition from day to night or vice versa, the change from one season to another, the transition from calm to stormy weather and so on. Capturing these moments can result in powerful pictures, especially when combined with other edge themes such as the edge between land and water, wilderness and civilisation etc.

TOP: Lots of 'edge' themes come together in this shot – it was taken in the time between one storm passing and another arriving, at the edge of land and water and at the transition between night and day.

RIGHT: The shots before and after show how rapidly light changes. In the first, the storm is still clearing as the sun sets, and in the second there was a fantastic afterglow before the next storm rolled in.

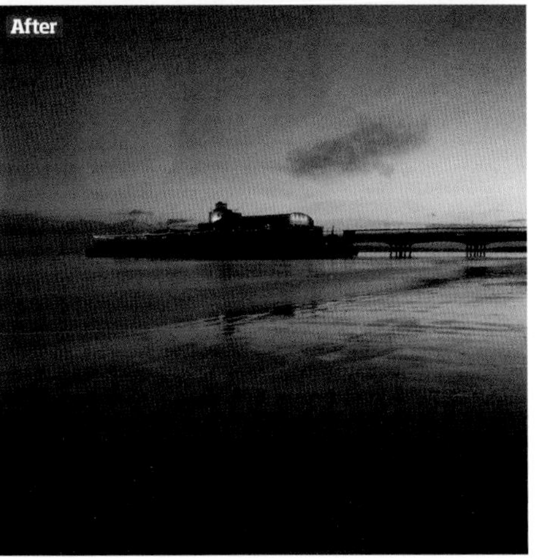

Time of day

Over the course of a day, from sunrise to sunset, the constantly changing path of the sun results in scenes taking on a new light

THE CHANGING LIGHT at different times of day makes a huge contribution to the mood of a shot. Pre-dawn light is cool and blue, but as the sun gets close to the horizon, pink tones start to appear in the sky. If there are clouds, these will be lit from below. But if the sky is clear, there may be an 'Alpenglow' with the blue shadow of the earth at the horizon and pink tones above. The mood of this lighting is one of calm, stillness and tranquillity. When the sun breaks over the horizon, the light is warm and the low sun highlights texture and form, creating a warmer mood (though still with cool shadows) or, depending on what's happening in the sky and composition, added drama. This is the lighting for the big vista.

With the sun high in the sky, creating a moody shot is more challenging. The high contrast and harsh shadows provide little textural relief or modelling of objects, for a large part of the day. There is little warmth in this light and scenes can look 'flat'. However, it is still possible to take good shots at this time of day. Strong colours can be intensified, especially if using a polariser, and scenes with structures in them can also work well, including in black & white.

The light towards the end of the day, and at sunset and post-sunset, is similar to the light at the beginning, but it tends to be warmer – more orange/yellow. This is because the air is drier and more filled with dust and other particles, such as pollution, stirred up by activity during the day. The warm light of the sun is therefore more diffused. I've also read that these particles block blue light to some extent, which makes sunset redder. The mood here is often high drama, rather than the more subtle, peaceful mood at the beginning of the day.

1

2

3

4

CHANGING LIGHT THROUGHOUT THE DAY: 1) The pre-sunrise light is cool, with pink tones in the sky. The amount of colour will depend on how much cloud cover there is to pick it up. 2) With the sun over the horizon, the light is generally warmer, but the shadows are still a little cool. 3) With the sun almost directly overhead, there is little shadow to add depth or texture to the scene and the colour temperature is fairly neutral. Despite some interest in the sky, not a moody result at all. 4) There is more drama and more yellow and orange tones in the sky at sunset.

Pre-dawn

'Alpenglow'

Crossover light

Urban landscapes can benefit from the low light treatment. With city night shots, the trick is not to wait until it's completely dark, but shoot while there is still some colour in the sky and the city lights are on. This period when the natural light and artificial light are balanced is sometimes referred to as 'crossover' light.

Nightshots of urban landscapes look their best when you get clear, unpolluted air and balance the natural and artificial light levels together. The contrast range is lower and the light can give bags of atmosphere.

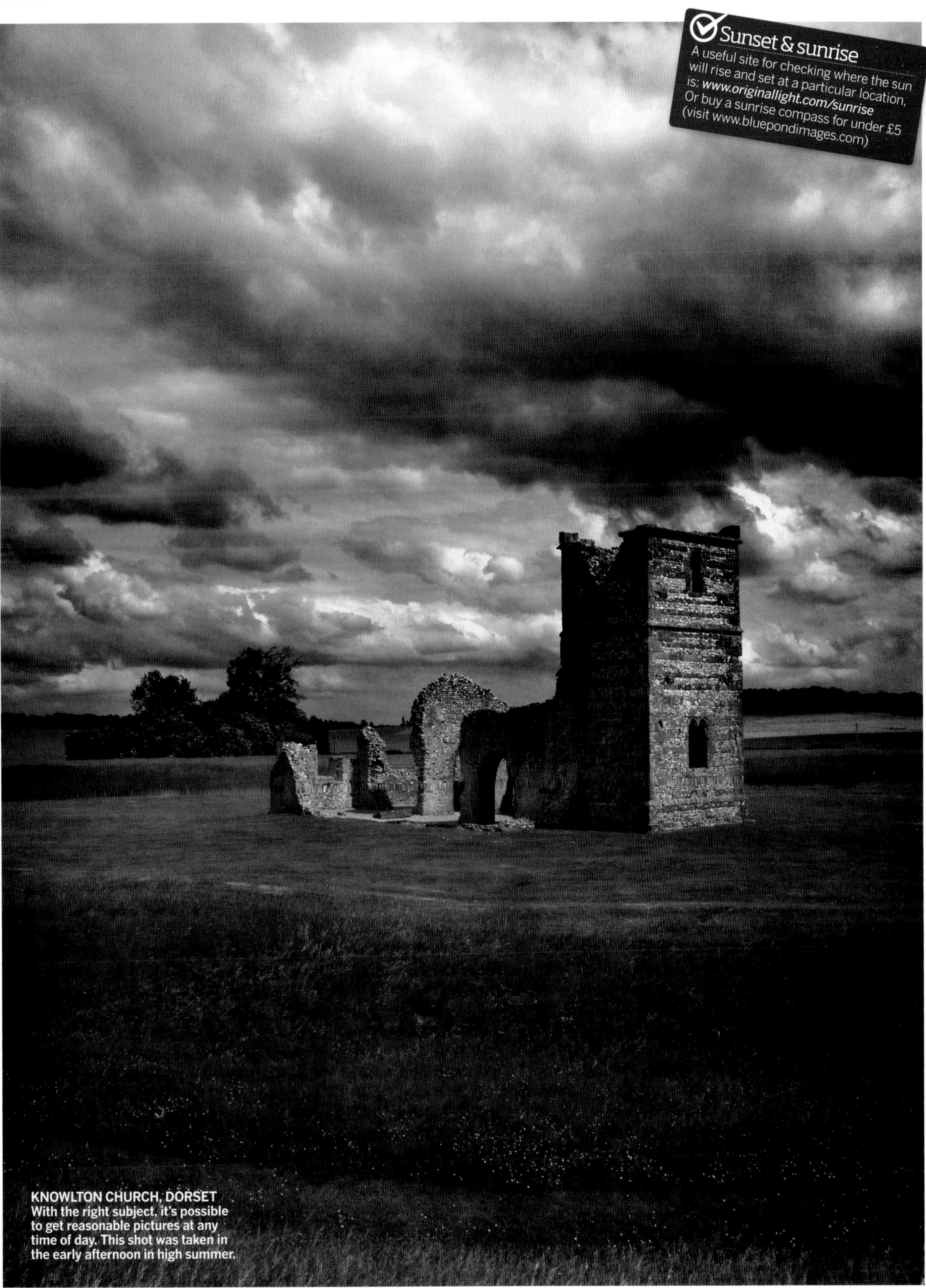

Sunset & sunrise

A useful site for checking where the sun will rise and set at a particular location, is: ***www.originallight.com/sunrise*** Or buy a sunrise compass for under £5 (visit www.bluepondimages.com)

KNOWLTON CHURCH, DORSET
With the right subject, it's possible to get reasonable pictures at any time of day. This shot was taken in the early afternoon in high summer.

Sharpness

When shooting landscapes, it's important to work at capturing the most detail possible within the scene. This is achieved through using the appropriate equipment and employing the proper techniques

Essential kit

TRIPOD: Always use a tripod, together with a remote release. Use the sturdiest tripod you can comfortably carry and don't forget to use a good quality head. If your camera has the facility, use mirror lock-up and wait a few seconds before releasing the shutter to avoid camera shake caused by mirror 'slap'.

LENSES: Good quality lenses are essential, so buy the best that you can afford. In general, fixed focal length lenses are sharper than zooms, although modern zoom lenses are actually very good and the slight loss in quality is usually more than made up for by the convenience they provide.

Depth-of-field

Usually, though not always, the aim in landscape photography is to keep everything from foreground to background sharp. Several factors play a role here: wide-angle lenses have inherently more depth-of-field than longer lenses, smaller apertures give more depth-of-field than wider apertures and accurate focusing is obviously also important.

There is greater depth-of-field behind the focal point in an image than in front, so a rough method of maximising depth-of-field is to focus about a third of the way into the scene. The more accurate way is to use the hyperfocal distance technique. If you set the hyperfocal distance on the lens, depth-of-field extends from half that hyperfocal distance to infinity. So for example, with a 28mm lens stopped down to f/16 on my Canon EOS 5D (full-frame sensor), the hyperfocal distance is about 5½ feet. Setting 5½ feet on the lens gives a depth-of-field from about 2¾ feet to infinity.

Finding the hyperfocal distance using prime lenses is relatively easy. Using the lens's depth-of-field scales you simply line up the infinity symbol with the correct aperture mark on the lens barrel. On zoom lenses, it's more complicated as there are no depth-of-field markings to help, so you need a chart to make an educated guess at the distance. It's also important to remember that depth-of-field scales are different for full-frame and APS-C-sized sensors, so the hyperfocal distances will be different. The tables below give some distances at common focal lengths for both types.

Right: Setting the hyperfocal distance is a useful technique with longer lenses, as well as wide-angles. In this example, a 100mm lens was used – notice the foliage in the foreground is in focus. A 0.6ND grad helped tone down the sky. Inset right: On fixed focal length lenses, you are given a distance scale and a depth-of-field scale to help gauge the hyperfocal distance.

HYPERFOCAL DISTANCE: APS-C SENSORS

Focal length	12mm	15mm	17mm	20mm	24mm	28mm	35mm	50mm	70mm	100mm	135mm
Aperture f/8	3.2ft	5ft	6.4ft	8.9ft	12.6ft	17ft	27ft	55ft	105ft	218ft	395ft
f/11	2.3ft	3.5ft	4.5ft	6.2ft	9ft	12ft	19ft	39ft	75ft	155ft	280ft
f/16	1.7ft	2.5ft	3.3ft	4.4ft	6.4ft	8.6ft	14.5ft	27ft	54ft	110ft	198ft
f/22	1.2ft	0.9ft	2.3ft	3.2ft	4.5ft	6ft	9.5ft	19.2ft	38ft	77ft	140ft

HYPERFOCAL DISTANCE: FULL-FRAME SENSORS

Focal length	16mm	20mm	24mm	28mm	35mm	50mm	70mm	100mm	135mm
Aperture f/8	3.8ft	5.6ft	8.0ft	11ft	17ft	35ft	68ft	138ft	250ft
f/11	2.6ft	3.9ft	5.8ft	7.8ft	12ft	25ft	48ft	98ft	178ft
f/16	1.9ft	2.9ft	4.0ft	5.5ft	8.5ft	17.5ft	34ft	70ft	125ft
f/22	0.4ft	2.0ft	2.9ft	3.9ft	6ft	12.5ft	24ft	49ft	89ft

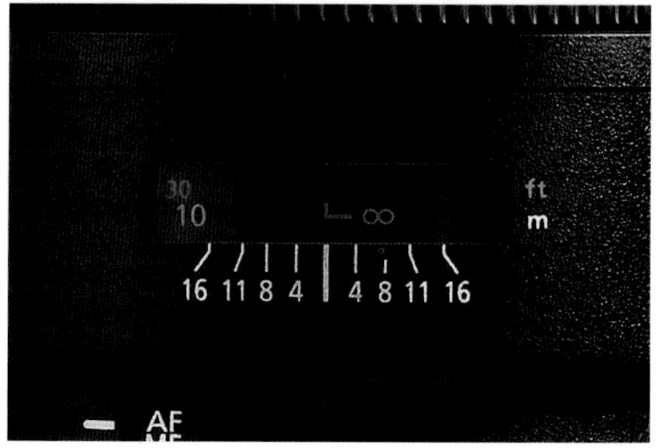

The effects of diffraction

The more you close the aperture down, the greater the depth-of-field, so the usual advice given is to use very small apertures, such as f/16 and f/22. However, stopping down too far can actually be detrimental due to an optical effect called diffraction. The simple explanation of diffraction is that when light passes through the aperture of a lens, the edges of the hole disperse the light waves. As the aperture is stopped down, the amount of diffracted light becomes a larger percentage of the total amount of light being recorded and the image becomes noticeably less sharp, meaning less detail is resolved. APS-C and full-frame sensors are affected slightly differently, and certain lenses will be more prone to diffraction than others. But in general, with an APS-C-sized sensor, you'll start to notice the effects of diffraction if you stop down beyond f/11, and with a full-frame camera, once you go beyond f/16.

Of course, that's not to say that you should never use apertures smaller than that. You will need to make a decision on the compromise between overall sharpness and depth-of-field relevant to the amount of fine detail you think it's necessary to record in any one particular image. That said, it's worth remembering that a 17mm lens on an APS-C-sized sensor will give you a depth-of-field from 2¼ feet to infinity when set to the hyperfocal distance at f/11 – enough for most situations.

To show the effects of diffraction at different apertures, I took a series of pictures at f/8, f/11, f/16 and f/22 – focusing and overall exposure remained constant – the only change was the lens aperture. The pictures were all processed using the same software and settings when post-processing. I used more sharpening than usual to make the effects more obvious.

Post-processing

All digital images benefit from sharpening; it's best done in post-processing for more control. If using Photoshop's USM filter, a smallish radius such as 0.6 will give the best results.

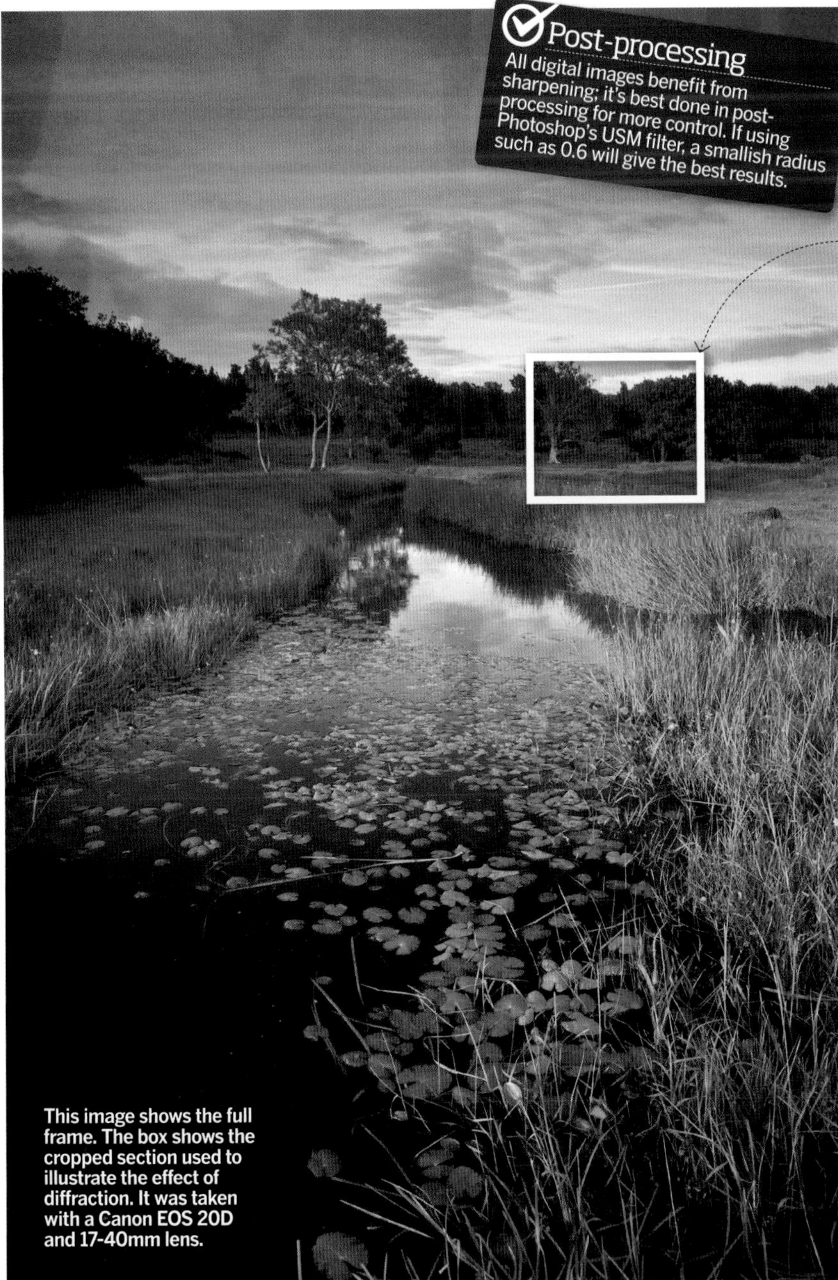

This image shows the full frame. The box shows the cropped section used to illustrate the effect of diffraction. It was taken with a Canon EOS 20D and 17-40mm lens.

The results may not be so obvious in magazine reproduction, but are very clear in large prints. At f/8, everything looks pretty sharp, with good detail in the background foliage. Things still look good at f/11, but once stopped down further, instead of becoming sharper as depth-of-field increases, the image becomes noticeably less sharp and detailed. This is crucial in landscape photography, especially large prints, and it was this 'mushy' looking foliage that put me off shooting digital landscapes for a long time – until I realised what was going on.

Exposure

Digital SLRs have extremely accurate, multi-zone metering systems with a histogram function to help us check accurate exposure, so getting it right has never been easier. However, to take more creative control, you need to take things into your own hands. Here are a few techniques for perfect exposures

Getting the right exposure

I was after a 'different' view of Corfe Castle in Dorset, so sauntered along to the graveyard in the village. Having found a composition based around one of the crosses, the next problem was sorting out the exposure.

1) This is what the camera's meter came up with, without the aid of any filtration. The scene is very contrasty, and the camera has struggled to capture all the tonal information.

2) A spot meter reading from the base of the cross and one from the sky revealed a difference in brightness of about 4½ stops. Setting an exposure for the land, I then fitted a 0.9ND grad (three stops) and pulled it down below the level of the horizon, to the edge of the darkest shadow area at the bottom of the frame. I used a soft grad, so that it wouldn't cut into the cross. But there is some loss of detail in the brighter parts of the sky. It might be possible to recover this in the Raw converter, but I reduced exposure by two-thirds of a stop and reshot.

3) The result is 'exposed to the right' as far as possible without clipping the highlights – the histogram shows there are still quite a lot of dark tones, but also plenty of information in the top section of the histogram, and crucially, no 'clipped' shadows.

4) A straight conversion of the Raw file looks a little dull, as the picture lacks contrast. For the final version, I've brought the exposure down slightly and added more contrast, especially in the shadows, to recreate the drama of the original scene. I've also tweaked the white balance to add a bit of warmth and increased saturation too.

5) For comparison purposes, I also took a shot underexposed by one stop. This leaves the shadows muddy and lacking in detail, which is very apparent in the crop.

Mid-tone metering

DSLR meters are calibrated to an 18% grey mid-tone. Basing exposure readings on a mid-tone, such as grass, is a good starting point for accurate exposures

Shadows

These two examples on the right show why it's not a good idea to underexpose and then try to pull up the shadows in the processing. The nearest image is around one stop underexposed (to maintain highlight detail) and the shadow curve has been pulled up to match the exposure in the correctly exposed version on the right. As you can see, not only is there 'posterisation' in the shadows, rather than smooth tonal transitions, and tons of noise, but also the sensor has recorded significantly less detail.

Colour histograms

Some DSLRs allow you the option to view separate histograms for the red, green and blue channels. You're better off ignoring this option and using the standard greyscale histogram option

Expose to the right

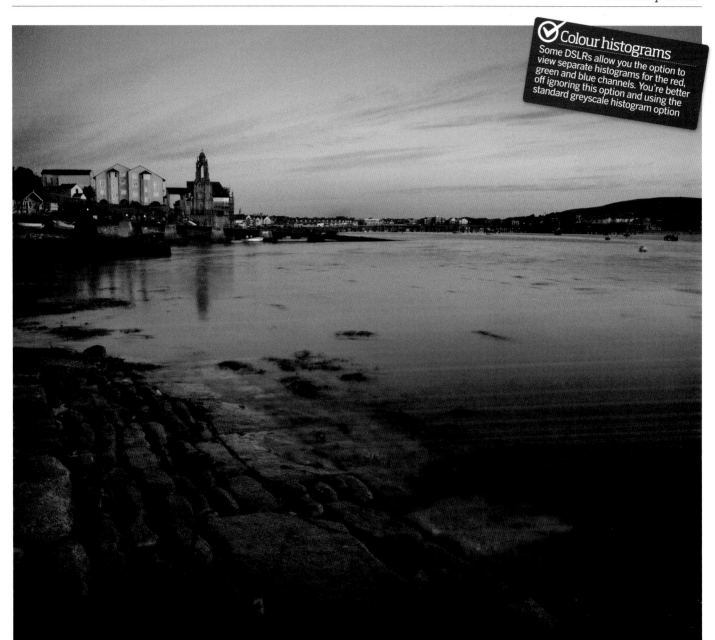

'Exposing to the right' is fast becoming a widely-accepted approach to help maximise image quality – although it only applies if you shoot in Raw. With this technique you effectively push exposure settings as close to overexposure as possible without actually clipping the highlights. The result is a histogram with the majority of pixels grouped to the right of mid point – hence the name 'expose to the right'. So, when you're confident you understand exposures well enough, give this technique a try and try pushing the exposure as far to the right of the histogram as you can, without clipping the highlights. The image will probably look a little light once in the Raw converter, but this is easily corrected with the brightness and contrast controls and will give much better results than trying to lighten a darker image.

CCD and CMOS sensors count light in a linear fashion. Most digital SLRs record a 12-bit image capable of recording 4,096 tonal values over six stops. But the tonal values are not spread evenly across the six stops, each stop records half the light of the previous one. So, half of the levels are devoted to the brightest stop (2,048), half of the remainder (1,024 levels) are devoted to the next stop and so on. As a result, the last and darkest of the six stops, only boasts 64 levels. This might seem confusing but, simply, if you do not properly use the right side of the histogram, which represents the majority of tonal values, you are wasting up to half the available encoding levels. So if you deliberately underexpose to ensure detail is retained in the highlights – a common practise among many digital photographers – you are potentially losing a large percentage of the data that can be captured.

MAIN IMAGE & INSET: Exposure to the right of the histogram will capture maximum detail and minimum noise. Once in the Raw converter the image will look too light and washed out so use the brightness and contrast controls to adjust the image's appearance.

MARK BAUER

Filters for exposure

There are a few filters that can help the landscape photographer gain more control over the light entering the camera and fine tune and enhance these lighting effects for more pleasing results

Neutral density (ND) graduated filters

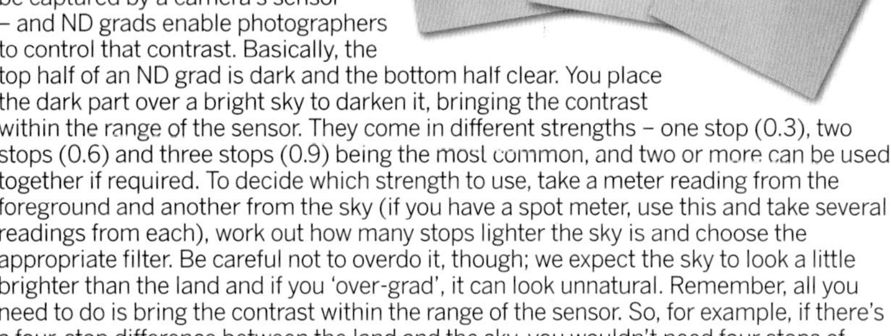

These are an essential part of any landscape photographer's kit. Depending on the lighting conditions, there can be a big difference in brightness between the land and the sky – often a greater range than can be captured by a camera's sensor – and ND grads enable photographers to control that contrast. Basically, the top half of an ND grad is dark and the bottom half clear. You place the dark part over a bright sky to darken it, bringing the contrast within the range of the sensor. They come in different strengths – one stop (0.3), two stops (0.6) and three stops (0.9) being the most common, and two or more can be used together if required. To decide which strength to use, take a meter reading from the foreground and another from the sky (if you have a spot meter, use this and take several readings from each), work out how many stops lighter the sky is and choose the appropriate filter. Be careful not to overdo it, though; we expect the sky to look a little brighter than the land and if you 'over-grad', it can look unnatural. Remember, all you need to do is bring the contrast within the range of the sensor. So, for example, if there's a four-stop difference between the land and the sky, you wouldn't need four stops of filtration – two or possibly three would be sufficient.

Polarisers

The other filter that is useful for digital landscape photography is the polariser, which cuts down reflections and increases saturation, especially of blue skies. The effect is strongest when the camera is at a 90° angle to the sun. To use a polariser, simply put it on the lens, look through the viewfinder and rotate the filter until you see the effect you want. The only thing to bear in mind is that the filter will cut out about two stops of light.

Without polariser

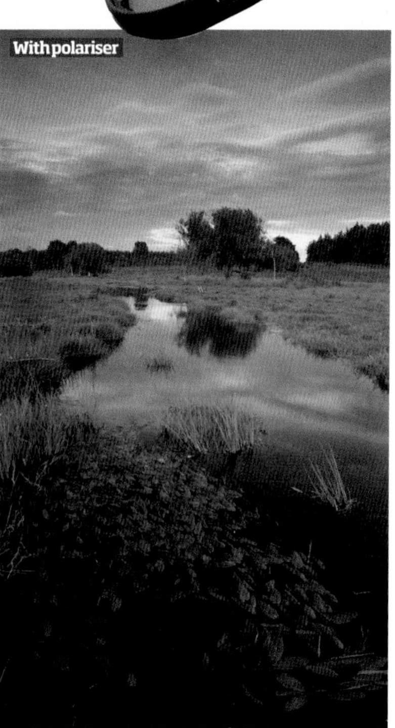

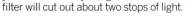

With polariser

WITH & WITHOUT POLARISER: As well as being useful for saturating blue skies, a polariser cuts down glare and can be useful for making reflections in water richer and more saturated.

Hard or soft grads?

ND grads come in two varieties – hard and soft-edged, which are pretty much as they sound – hard-edged grads have a 'harder', more abrupt transition from the dark to clear sections. Debate rages among landscape photographers about which is 'best' and to be honest, there is no definitive answer here – they each have their own advantages and disadvantages. Hard-edged grads are much easier to line up in the viewfinder and are very useful when there is a very bright area near the horizon (e.g at sunset) but can more obviously 'cut into' features on the horizon such as trees, hills or buildings. Because of the gentle transition from light to dark, soft-edged grads look a lot more natural when there are features breaking the horizon (which is most of the time) but are harder to line up in the viewfinder and are not so effective if the horizon is very bright. Personally, as a general rule, I prefer to use soft-edged grads and over time have got used to lining them up; I find using the depth-of-field preview makes it a little easier. If the horizon is very bright, I like to pull the dark area down just a little bit below the horizon.

Hard grad

Soft grad

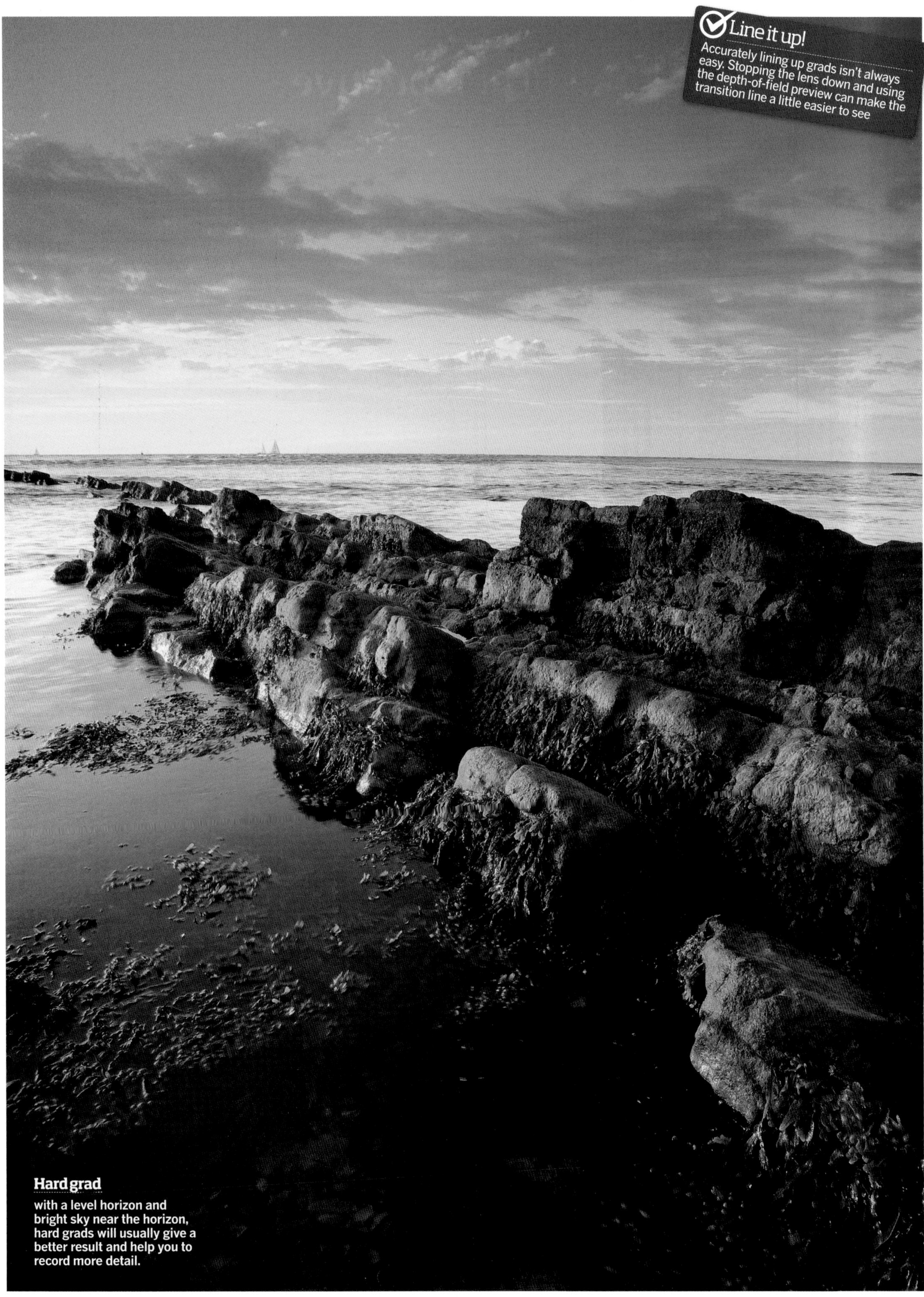

Line it up!

Accurately lining up grads isn't always easy. Stopping the lens down and using the depth-of-field preview can make the transition line a little easier to see

Hard grad

with a level horizon and bright sky near the horizon, hard grads will usually give a better result and help you to record more detail.

The fundamentals of perspective

Trying to imagine how the real-life three-dimensional scene in front of you can be successfully translated into a two-dimensional image is all a matter of perspective

Use different lenses

A good method for learning about perspective is to shoot the same scene using different focal lengths, learning how they affect the relationship between foreground and background

THE MOST COMMON SUGGESTION OF DEPTH in an image is created by including overlapping planes or features – if one thing is partly obscured by another, such as a small hill in front of a big hill, or a tree in front of a building, there must obviously be distance between them, so our brain tells us that we're looking at something with three dimensions.

Another common method of identifying depth or perspective is size recognition. When we're born, we're very naïve as to how the world around us works – we don't know what things are or how they're supposed to look because we've never seen them before. So as a baby, if we saw a photograph of an elephant standing in the middle of a dusty plain, we would have no idea if it were big or small – we wouldn't even know that it was an elephant! As we grow and our brains record experiences, we build a database of information that is constantly updated and subconsciously referred to every second of the day. That's why you know how to find your way home, how to tie your shoelaces, how to use a knife and fork and how to speak. Size recognition works in the same way. Once you've seen something, you not only remember what it is and what it looks like, but with a reasonable degree of accuracy, you know its size.

One thing you'll need to learn to identify and use is 'diminishing perspective'. This type of perspective relies on the fact that the further away an object is from the camera, the smaller it appears in the photograph. For example, if you stand next to a building, it will dwarf you, but walk 100m down the street and it will appear much smaller – more diminutive than a car that is right next to you will appear, even though you know that in real life, the building is far bigger.

This is why the inclusion of foreground interest in a landscape photograph gives a strong feeling of distance and depth – an old wooden gate that you use to fill the foreground appears far bigger than the barn behind it, but you know the barn is bigger than the gate, so your brain deduces that the barn must be far away and depth is implied.

Diminishing perspective can also be exploited by photographing a series of similar-sized objects, such as an avenue of trees. The nearest tree to you will appear to be tallest and the one furthest away, the smallest, with each tree appearing smaller than the one before. This diminishing scale again adds a powerful feeling of depth because we know that the trees are of a similar size, so the fact that they're getting smaller suggests they are getting further away.

Wide-angle lenses are ideal for exaggerating diminishing perspective because they appear to stretch the distance between the elements in a scene. The wider the lens you use for this (the shorter the focal length) the better. If you crawl up to a snail in your garden with a 15mm lens, in the shot, it will look bigger than your house!

Conversely, telephoto lenses appear to compress or flatten perspective, so elements in a scene will appear closer together than they really are; and the longer the focal length of your lens, the more pronounced this 'foreshortening' is.

Telephoto lenses also allow you to emphasise aerial perspective, which is based on the fact that colour and tone diminish with distance, due to atmospheric haze, mist and fog. If you gaze across a mountainous scene at sunrise, for example, the mountains closest to the camera will appear darker in colour or tone than those further away. The same applies with trees in mist, or the undulations of a rolling landscape. As Mark Bauer reveals later in this section, use a telezoom and home in on the more distant parts of the scene, where the haze or mist is stronger. Alternatively, shoot into the sun (not at it!), so the distant parts of the scene are much brighter than those closest to the camera.

Aerial perspective can also be implied through colour. Cool colours such as blue and green appear to recede, so they make ideal background colours for foreground objects with warmer hues such as red, orange and yellow, which are said to 'advance'. You can make use of this by composing photographs with warmer colours in the foreground, such as a bed of spring flowers, against more distant green foliage and blue sky.

What you need to remember is that although lenses appear to change perspective, in reality, they don't. The easiest way to demonstrate this is to photograph a scene with both wide-angle and telephoto lenses from exactly the same position. The two photographs will obviously look different, but if you crop an area from the wide-angle shot that covers the same area covered by the telephoto shot, you'll see that the perspective is identical in both. To change perspective, you not only have to change lenses, but also change camera position, so a key element appears the same size in both pictures.

Let's say you're photographing a person standing in front of a building. First take a picture with a wide-angle lens so the person is just about the full height of the frame. You'll see that perspective appears to have been stretched, with the building seeming to be much further away than it really is. Next, use a telephoto and back off until the person is the same size in the frame as they were in the previous shot. Now you'll see that perspective has been compressed and the building appears much closer to the person than it really is. It's worth shooting comparisons like this to help you get a better understanding of how perspective works and how you can use it effectively in your photography. A photograph only ever has two dimensions, but by harnessing and exploiting perspective, you can at least give the impression of a third.

Making the most of scale

LEE FROST

As well as perspective, scale is also a powerful compositional tool, because if you include something of recognisable size in a photograph, the viewer can compare it to all the other elements and form conclusions about how big, or small, those elements are. For example, 'average' humans are of a similar size, give or take a few inches, so if you photograph a person standing in front of a statue and they seem dwarfed by it, because you know roughly how tall a person is, you can then deduce that the statue is enormous. However, if that person is excluded from the composition, you would have no idea of the scale of the statue because it's an unfamiliar object and you have nothing to compare it to. That said, don't always feel that you must include scale 'markers' in your photos. Intentionally avoiding them produces images that are intriguing because the viewer isn't entirely sure what they're looking at, so they're forced to keep looking in an attempt to satisfy their curiosity. Details in the landscape are ideal for this type of image because you'll find many subjects on a very small scale that could equally be very big. Ripples on a sandy beach, captured in close-up, look remarkably similar to towering desert dunes, for example. Similarly, the nooks and crannies in a slab of rock can be made to look surprisingly like the Grand Canyon when all traces of scale are excluded from the composition.

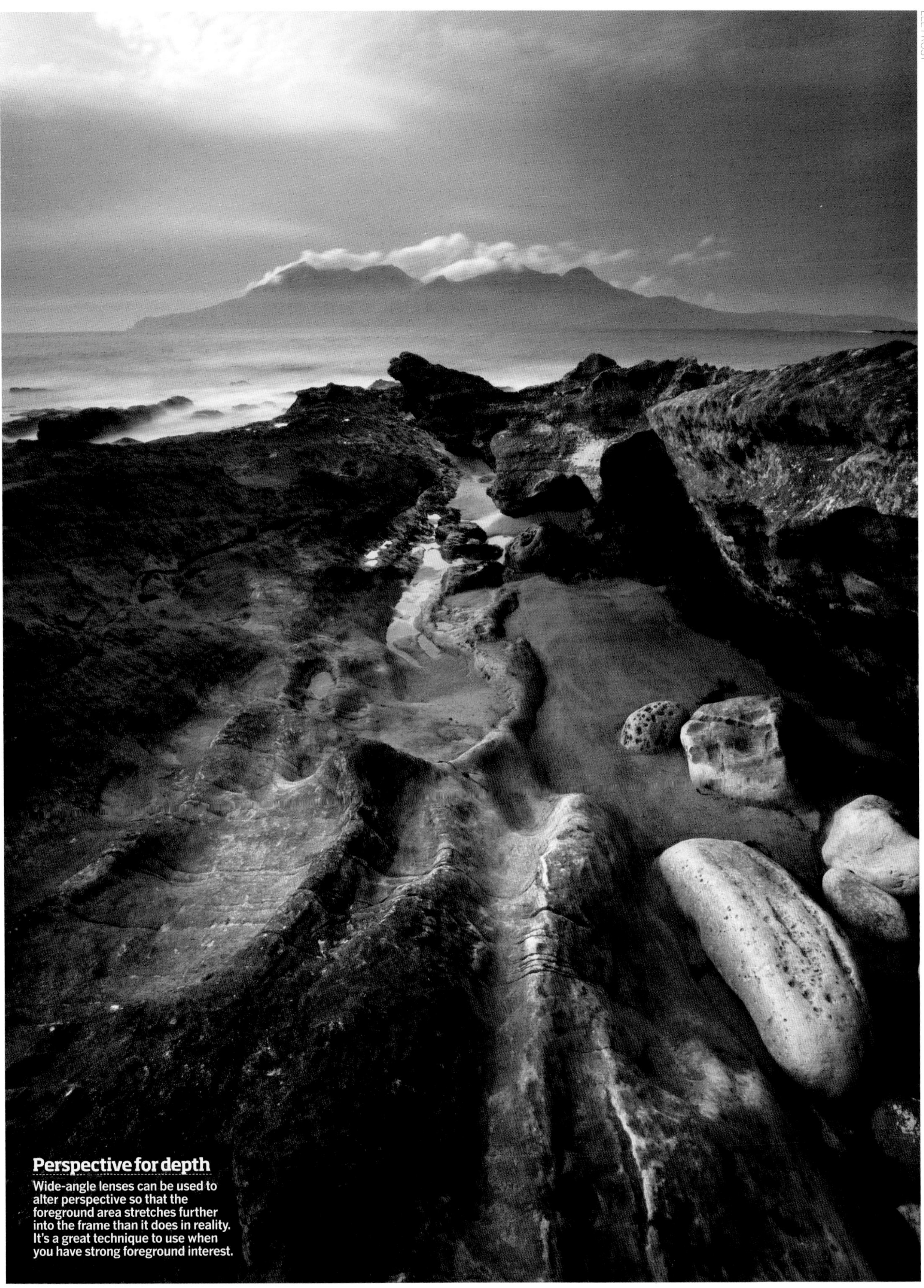

LEE FROST

Perspective for depth

Wide-angle lenses can be used to alter perspective so that the foreground area stretches further into the frame than it does in reality. It's a great technique to use when you have strong foreground interest.

Perspective compression

Photographers often talk about using a telephoto to compress perspective, but what does it mean?

TECHNICALLY SPEAKING, telephoto lenses don't 'compress perspective', but practically speaking, you do get a different feeling of perspective from a telephoto shot than from a scene captured with a wide-angle lens.

Wide-angle lenses seem to open up perspective and create a sense of depth, because nearby objects appear big, and further objects appear to be very small, suggesting distance. Added to this is the fact that wide-angle lenses create strong diagonals, which enhance the sense of depth (if arranged carefully within the frame). On the other hand, telephotos make distant objects appear larger, apparently compressing the planes of the image and therefore reducing the impression of depth. Lines tend not to stretch into diagonals, and parallels remain parallel, which increases the two-dimensional feel. Compared to a wide-angle view, this all adds up to an image that has a more static feel. And of course, the longer the lens, the greater the effect. So what kind of images benefit from the compression effects of longer lenses? The static character of telephoto images suits tranquil scenes, so hilly landscapes are ideal, especially where there are several planes or 'layers' that can be visually pulled together, so that they appear to be almost stacked on top of each other. The feeling of tranquillity can be enhanced by early morning mist, with the tops of the hills rising above a sea of mist. More dramatic images can be created in the right lighting conditions – look for alternating bands of light and dark, creating a 'layering of light'. Urban landscapes also work well, as you can use compression to juxtapose elements or to suggest a crowded environment.

Mark Bauer shoots Corfe Castle

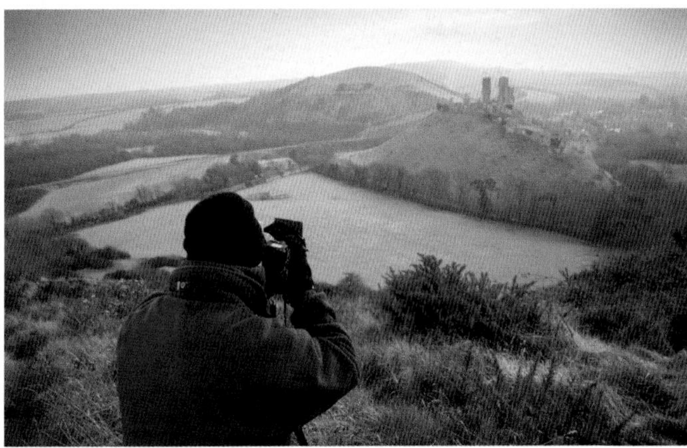

Telephotos have inherently less depth-of-field than wide-angles, but you're also more likely to be at a distance from your subject, without anything close to the camera in the foreground. However, it's still a good idea to use a small aperture to make sure everything appears sharp. This can make it difficult to get a fast enough shutter speed to shoot handheld, so a tripod is essential. Ideally, you should also use a remote release and mirror lock-up.

50mm

75mm

It's just an illusion!

While telephotos appear to compress perspective, the truth is that they don't. Magnify an area of a shot taken with a wide-angle lens and you'll see that it gives a virtually identical effect!

28-35mm

The apparent distance between the foreground and castle creates a sense of depth, with the hills and village behind the castle stretching away into the distance.

60-85mm

Even at moderate telephoto settings, the perspective seems much flatter, and the castle seems to loom over the distant hills and the village.

105-200mm

As the focal length increases, perspective seems to flatten out, so that the castle and the hills behind seem to be almost in the same plane.

Add impact with vanishing points

One of the most powerful forms of perspective involves the use of converging lines to create an illusion of distance and space. Lee Frost shows you how

LINES, IN ALL THEIR VARIOUS FORMS, are useful compositional aids. Horizontal lines echo the horizon, so they help to create balanced, calm compositions, whereas vertical lines are more active and add tension to an image. Neither suggests distance or depth though. To achieve that, you'll need lines that appear to carry the eye through the scene. Diagonal lines work well, especially when they're running from the bottom left of the frame towards the top right corner, because that's the natural way we tend to view a photograph. However, the effect is at its strongest when you have a series of diagonal lines travelling from different corners of the composition and converging towards the centre of the frame.

Use your LCD not only to check exposure, but also to ensure that the horizon is level.

The picture area then becomes like an open window, framing the scene beyond, while the converging lines act like visual rays, carrying your eye to a point in the distance. The photograph no longer seems flat – you feel as though you could walk right into it. To use linear perspective in this way, you need to find a scene that contains or creates parallel lines. Roads, railway tracks, paths, fences, rivers and streams, jetties and piers are all ideal. All you do then is position yourself between the parallel lines, so that you're looking down them. What you'll see is that, as the lines move further away from the camera, they appear to move closer together – or converge – and eventually appear to meet at a point in the distance, known as the 'vanishing point'.

To maximise the effect, use a wide-angle lens to stretch the perspective, so the lines appear really wide apart in the immediate foreground and converge dramatically. Anything from 28mm will do the trick, but once you get down to 20mm or wider, the effect becomes extreme. You should also include the vanishing point in your composition because that brings everything to a satisfying conclusion and heightens the sense of depth. If you exclude the vanishing point, the viewer's eye will want to keep going beyond the picture to see where the lines meet, and this creates an odd effect. To show how linear perspective works, I photographed a local pier in a variety of different ways.

Maximise depth-of-field

Make sure the whole scene is recorded in sharp focus by stopping your lens down to a small aperture such as f/16 and focusing on the hyperfocal distance. The table below shows the hyperfocal distance for popular wide-angle focal lengths and apertures from f/11 to f/22. Focus the lens on the hyperfocal distance and everything will appear sharp from half the hyperfocal distance to infinity.

Aperture (f/stop)	Lens focal length (mm)				
	16mm	20mm	24mm	28mm	35mm
f/11	0.75m	1.0m	1.5m	2.0m	3.0m
f/16	0.5m	0.7m	1.0m	1.4m	2.1m
f/22	0.35m	0.5m	0.7m	1.0m	1.5m

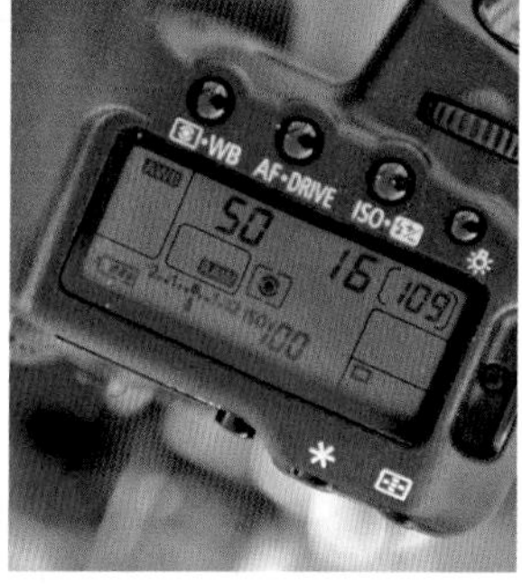

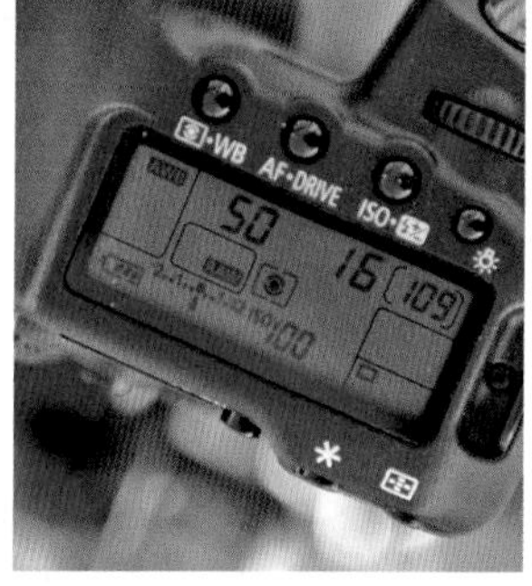

1 This was my first glimpse of the pier, and you can see that when viewed side-on, and at a distance, it appears flat because the lines formed by the pier structure are running horizontally across the frame. No sense of depth is implied, and the overall effect is two-dimensional and dull.

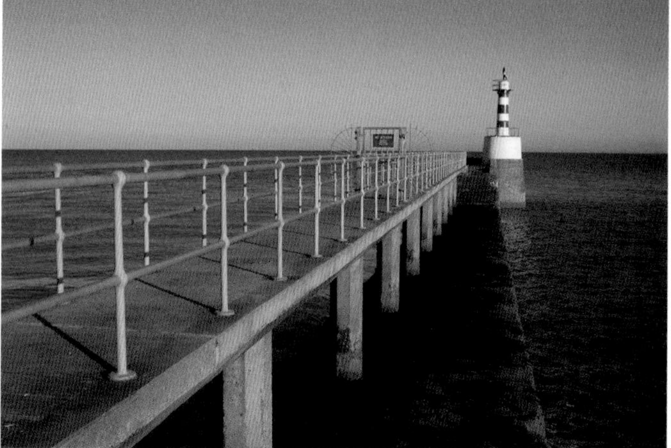

2 Moving closer to the pier is more effective and creates more depth. Now you can see that the lines created by the walkway, the foundation slab and the handrails are all converging from bottom left to top right and carrying the eye to the lighthouse, which is the main focal point in the composition.

Keep horizons level

Use a spirit level, or if your camera has one, an electronic level, to avoid wonky horizons. The frame markings in the camera's viewfinder also help achieve a balanced, symmetrical composition

Final image

In the end, I decided the most effective composition was created by lowering the camera position a little more than for step 3, so the top handrail was pushed above the horizon. I also set the zoom to a slightly wider focal length to really emphasise those lines.

3 By looking straight down the pier, the parallel lines formed by the walkway and rails are converging from both sides to a central vanishing point. This shows linear perspective much more effectively, and while more three-dimensional than before, the image can still be improved.

4 For a more extreme effect, I set my zoom lens to 16mm and placed the camera almost at ground level, so that there are lines converging from all four corners of the frame and the vanishing point is emphasised further. It produces an effective result, but the wide expanse of concrete is off-putting.

More tools for perspective

Still short of ideas for ways to use perspective? Then try out these three simple, yet highly effective techniques

1) Adding depth

Although images are only two-dimensional, our brain will use the elements within the image to determine scale, distance and depth. As a result, photographers have the ability to 'stretch' or 'flatten' perspective, depending on their viewpoint and the focal length of the lens that they decide to use. Longer focal lengths compress perspective, creating quite flat-looking results, while, in contrast, short focal lengths appear to stretch perspective, making nearby objects look larger and more dominant, whilst distant objects will look smaller, further away, and less significant. In other words, wider focal lengths will help you to create the appearance of depth.

Adding depth to your shots is a powerful visual tool that can suit any type of subject. However, it's most commonly used by landscape photographers, who will often place a nearby object – like a rock, some flowers or a pathway – in the foreground of their photo, to contrast with a distant view. As a result, this serves to heighten our perception of depth. It works particularly well in combination with a focal range in the region of 10-28mm. Due to the extensive depth-of-field this type of lens gives, it is possible to get close to your foreground interest and exaggerate its size, making it appear bigger in comparison to its background. The nearer the foreground object is to the camera, the greater the perception of depth. Remember that while you'll often want to manipulate perspective by exaggerating foreground interest, you should be careful, as it's easy to overdo it by including a very prominent foreground at the expense of the middle distance and backdrop of your scene. Although wide-angles naturally have a large depth-of-field, you should still prioritise a small f/stop, like f/16 or f/22, to ensure you achieve sufficient back-to-front sharpness. If your DSLR has a depth-of-field preview button or LiveView, remember to use it! Your viewpoint can also help to create a sense of depth – both high and low viewpoints can prove effective, depending on the scene and situation. Also consider the format in which you take your photographs. By simply turning your camera vertically, you will create a greater sense of height. This, combined with good placement of foreground objects, can further increase the three-dimensional feel of your photos.

LEE FROST

2) Picture format

The image format you use to photograph a scene can have a big influence on the way perspective is perceived. To find out for yourself, shoot the same scene in both upright and landscape format, then download the images and crop them to different formats. The landscape format is a solid, reliable format that captures a scene without making a big fuss and produces images that are easy on the eye. Turn the camera on its side, however, and all that changes. Immediately the composition becomes more active and dynamic, as vertical lines are emphasised and the near-far effect is increased because you're able to include more foreground. Crop an image into a square and you'll find that the composition quietens down. It's much more sedate and balanced – boring to some, but beautiful to others and well worth experimenting with, especially on symmetrical scenes such as a landscape that's reflected in a lake. Finally, take one of your vertical shots and crop it into a vertical panoramic. Now you have a real loudmouth image – an eye-catching, confident, brash composition that can't fail to catch the eye. Try it and see how your perception changes dramatically based solely on the picture format.

Foreground interest

Use your wide-angle lens to get close to your foreground. To really enhance the perspective, try and choose something that appears more than once in the image, like these hay bales

ROSS HODDINOTT

3) Quality of light

You may not think light and perspective are in any way connected, but they are.

First of all, the strength and intensity of the light help to emphasise depth in a photograph. On a dull, grey day, the light is soft and scenes tend to look flat because contrast is low, and the shadows that add definition are missing. When the sun comes out it's a different story – shadows are strong and make objects appear three-dimensional, while the effects of an aerial perspective are often more obvious due to an increase in atmospheric haze. Light direction is important too. Scenes that are frontally-lit tend to lack depth because shadows fall away from the camera and out of view. It's the same when the sun is overhead in clear weather. Light the same scene from the side, however, and shadows become much more effective, revealing texture and form and emphasising depth. Alternatively, shoot into the light so shadows appear to rush towards the camera, creating strong lines that lead the eye into the scene.

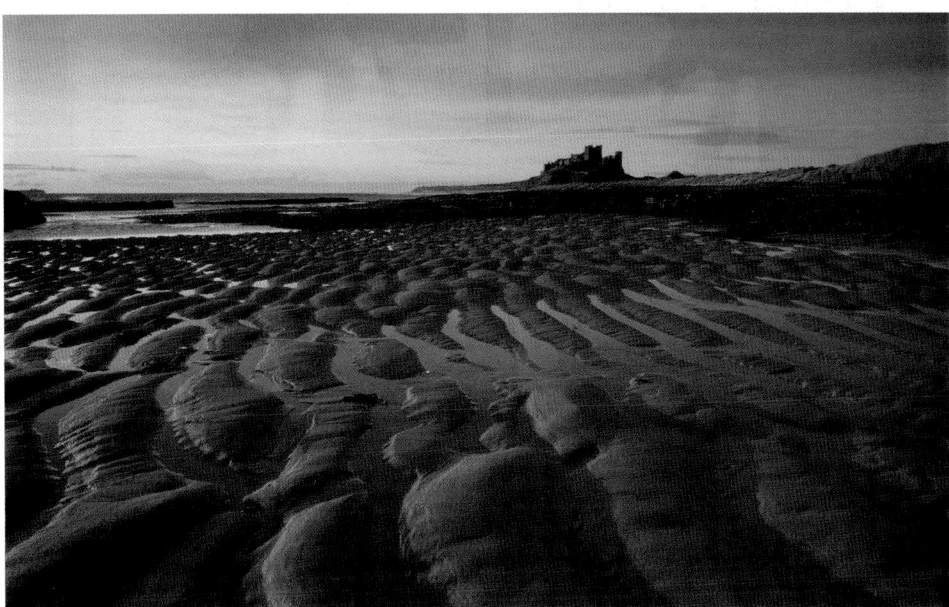

LEE FROST

The basics for shooting water in landscapes

Get prepared to head out into the great outdoors to shoot stunning scenery by ensuring you have the best techniques and the right gear

WE'RE NOT SURE if you've ever noticed, but the majority of stunning landscape images usually have some form of water in the scene. Whether it's as subtle as a small river trickling through, or as obvious as a dominating sea in a coastal seascape, water represents a key element in many landscape images.

One of the main reasons for this is because water is such a photographically pliable element. By using filters and/or manipulating the shutter speed, it's possible to record water in all manner of ways, from freezing its movement so droplets are suspended in mid-air, to using a long exposure to transform it into an ethereal mist. While potentially causing problems with our exposure, the reflective nature of water also plays its part in improving images too. On days where there is little or no wind, by heading to a lake, reservoir or any other large body of water, it's possible to produce a striking result by capturing a clean reflection of the scene on its surface. The possibilities don't stop there – rivers can be used as strong lead-in lines through the scene or, along with the likes of secluded rockpools and meandering streams littered with rocks, can form highly effective foreground interest.

The list is endless, but in this section of our guide, we provide the essentials you need to start going out to shoot water in landscapes and returning with brilliant results. What are you waiting for? Get exploring!

Choosing shutter speeds

The shutter speed you use to capture water will depend on a number of factors: if it's moving, how quickly it's moving, how much of it there is and whether you want to stop it dead or let it blur. For big waterfalls and breaking waves, a shutter speed of 1/1000-1/2000sec will guarantee you freeze every droplet. For fast-flowing rivers and smaller waterfalls like this one, try 1/200–1/500sec, while for slower rivers and streams 1/125–1/250sec should do the trick. When it comes to blurring, one second will have a good effect on big waterfalls or try two seconds for smaller waterfalls. Rivers and streams need a slower speed of two to four seconds, though you can go much slower – 10-20 seconds – if you like. Overexposure can be a problem when large volumes of water are concentrated in certain areas, so keep an eye on the histogram and use a slower speed if you start to clip the highlights. For coastal scenes, one to two seconds will blur waves, while 20-30 seconds will produce a 'milky' effect.

1/60sec

1/20sec

0.4 seconds

Essential gear

Wide-angle zoom: An ultra-wide zoom like a 12-24mm or similar is ideal as it will allow you to fill the foreground with water and deliver plenty of depth-of-field for scenes that are sharp throughout. The Sigma 10-20mm lens is hugely popular due to its excellent performance and value-for-money price tag.

Spirit level: If your tripod kit has a spirit level, use it to ensure horizons are even – you don't want to spend ages in Photoshop levelling them. Otherwise buy a basic £10 spirit level to slip into a hotshoe or treat yourself to a funky £30 Seculine Action Level (www.intro2020.co.uk)

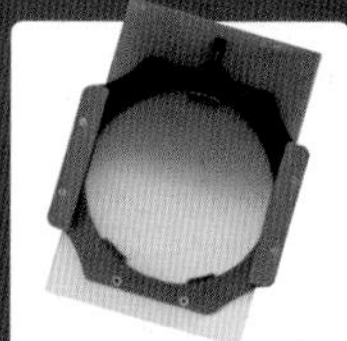

Filters: If you're serious about landscape photography, invest in a slot-in filter system. Cokin's P-system (www.intro2020.co.uk) represent great value for money, while if quality is paramount, look to Lee Filters' superb 100mm system – the choice of the pros. (www.leefilters.com). A polariser helps boost blue skies and deliver clear reflections off the water's surface. A 0.6 or 0.9ND filter (not ND grad!) is also worth considering, as it will allow you to use long shutter speeds in daylight to blur moving water.

Tripod: When shooting water you'll be looking to use small apertures to maximise depth-of-field and the slow shutter speeds require you to keep the camera stable to avoid shake. Check out the gear section later in this guide for advice on the best tripods to buy for outdoor photography.

Photo backpack: When you're walking miles, a photo backpack is a far better option for protecting your kit than a gadget bag. Those with an all-weather cover will offer better protection from water and the elements. Take a look at our website for reviews of some of the best: www.digitalslrphoto.com

Clothing: There's nothing worse than slipping into a river and having to spend the day in wet clothes. Wear decent footwear from reputable brands such as Berghaus and consider waterproof trousers or gaiters from brands such as Paramo, as they allow you to step into rivers and stay dry.

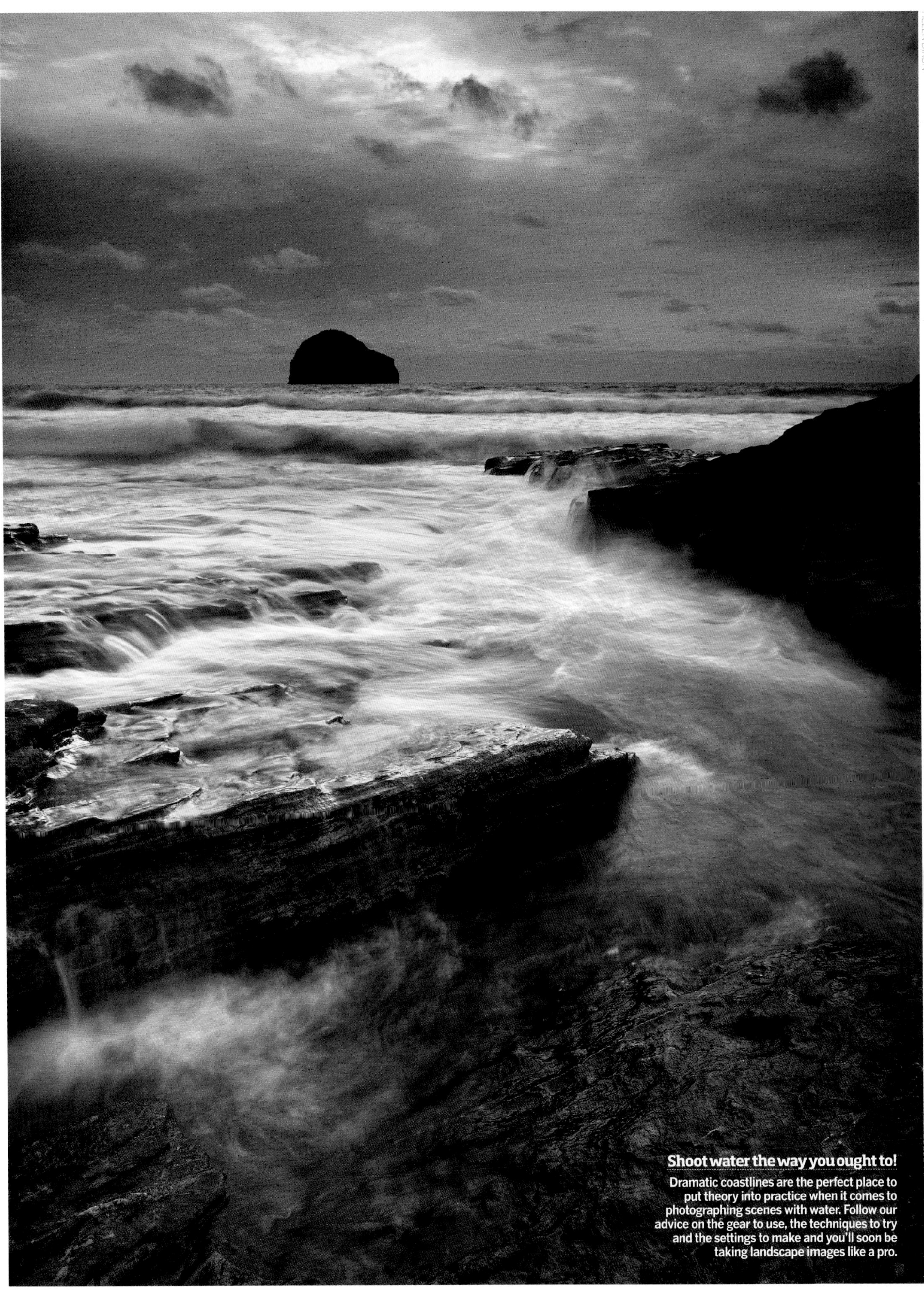

HELEN DIXON

Shoot water the way you ought to!

Dramatic coastlines are the perfect place to put theory into practice when it comes to photographing scenes with water. Follow our advice on the gear to use, the techniques to try and the settings to make and you'll soon be taking landscape images like a pro.

Using water to compose a scene

Not only can water add visual interest or mood to your landscape images, but it can also prove a very useful compositional tool

ON STILL, CALM DAYS, a large body of water, such as a lake or loch, will provide mirror-like reflections, allowing photographers to capture both the landscape and its upside-down reflection in wide-angle views. This type of symmetry is a powerful composition aid, and one of the few occasions when placing the horizon centrally – as opposed to on a dividing third, as per the 'rule-of-thirds' – can actually strengthen composition.

Regardless of whether you are photographing a lake, loch, river, stream, canal, or puddle as part of the landscape, the traditional rules of composition remain. Try to place key elements, such as a cascading waterfall, breaking waves or water crashing on rocks, on a dividing third to create the most interesting and compelling composition.

Scenic photographers, however, most commonly use water as a form of 'lead-in line' that directs the viewer's eye into the image and through the scene. Rivers, streams and canals are particularly well suited to this approach. Regardless of whether the body of water is straight or twisting and turning through the landscape, the effect is the same. By including the water so that it leads from the bottom of the image into the frame, it provides a natural 'entry point' to the photograph. The viewer's eye will then follow the water's journey through the landscape, creating a strong composition.

A river or stream, flowing through the shot, also creates great depth and life, and can provide the impression of motion. Often a slightly elevated viewpoint suits this approach well: if you get too low and close to the water, you will normally begin to lose the water's shape and effect. Shooting from a footbridge above the water will allow you to shoot directly down its length. This can look very striking, with the water disappearing in the distance and creating a 'vanishing point'.

Diagonal lines can also make for strong compositional tools, so try placing a stream or a canal so it cuts from one corner of the frame to the other. Lens focal length will also have a great bearing on how water is recorded in your scene. Wide-angles, in the region of 14-24mm, will stretch perspective, making foreground objects appear larger and more prominent and distant ones look further away. This can work well if you want to place extra emphasis on a specific point, maybe water cascading over an smooth boulder in the image's immediate foreground. Alternatively, attach a longer focal length, upwards of 55mm, to condense perspective, as this can prove useful if you want to photograph a river winding its way through a valley from the hills above.

Without a doubt, water will give your landscape images added depth and interest and can greatly enhance your compositions.

Landscapes in portrait!

Don't forget to turn your camera vertically. An upright composition can help emphasise height or length, so it is particularly well suited to photographs shot down the length of a long river or canal to help emphasise the impression of distance

Top tips for shooting water

1) USE A VARIETY OF FOCAL LENGTHS
Even without changing position, in a windy river scene, it's surprising how many compositions you can find just by changing focal length.

2) WATCH YOUR HIGHLIGHTS Bright highlights on the water can fool your camera's meter into underexposure, so check your histogram and be prepared to add exposure compensation. Bright, reflective highlights will always blow unless you underexpose the shot severely, so ignore them and expose for the rest of the scene.

3) FILTRATION Using the right filters can really improve river shots. Polarisers will help reduce glare off the water, and solid ND filters allow you to use slower shutter speeds to capture a sense of motion. You can use this as a compositional aid by, for example, having streaks of water moving into the frame to lead the eye into the picture.

4) SHOOT IN THE RIGHT CONDITIONS If there is partial cloud at the beginning or end of the day, there's a chance there will be some colour in the sky, which will be reflected in the water, adding impact to the scene.

Mark Bauer uses a river as a lead-in line

I headed to the New Forest near Rhinefield one morning to try and catch the early light reflecting in a stream as it meanders through the landscape. Upon arrival, I soon realise the potential for basing a composition around the stream as it curves gently through the fields. The landscape is quite flat, so I shoot from a bridge, as the elevated position will help to reveal the planes in the landscape.

Set-up

1 **I try shooting in landscape format, which enhances the shape of the river. However, I'm left with the choice of either including quite a lot of bland sky, or chopping the tops off the trees, neither of which is entirely satisfactory. Time for a rethink.**

1

2 **As the sun starts to rise in the sky, it brings with it a touch of colour, and some layering and texture to the clouds, so I change my focal length to around 45mm to include the sky and also make the most of the interesting bends in the stream.**

2

3 **As the colour strengthens in the sky, I decide to switch to portrait format, which allows me to make more of the sky and also include more water in the foreground. These adjustments make the most of the stream as a lead-in line.**

3

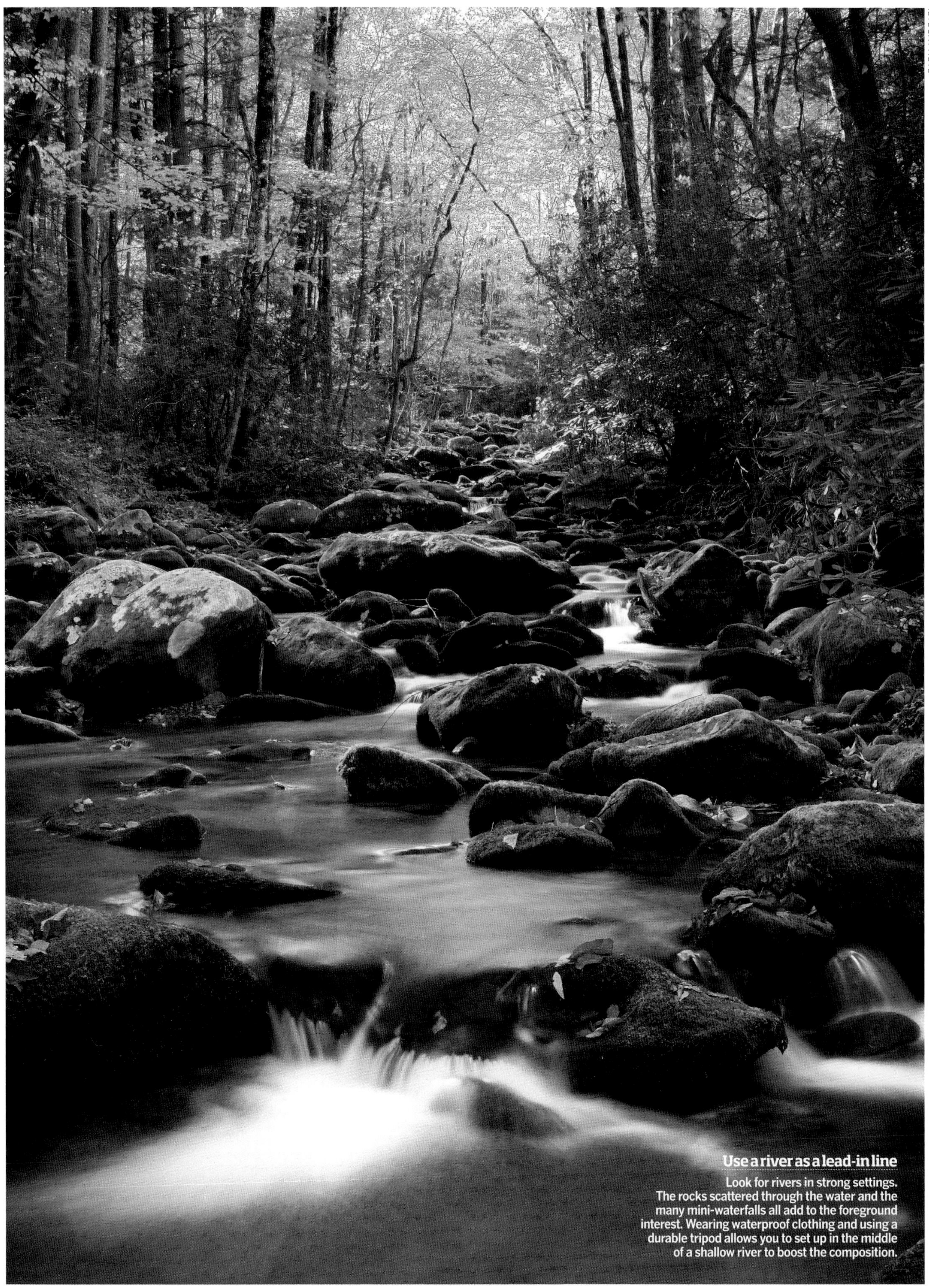

ISTOCK PHOTO

Use a river as a lead-in line

Look for rivers in strong settings. The rocks scattered through the water and the many mini-waterfalls all add to the foreground interest. Wearing waterproof clothing and using a durable tripod allows you to set up in the middle of a shallow river to boost the composition.

Composition by the coast

The same compositional guidelines apply at the coast as they do elsewhere – the rule-of-thirds, the Golden Section, foreground interest and using lines are all relevant. Achieving a basic composition is fairly straightforward – divide the frame into thirds, so that you have an interesting foreground leading to the sea beyond, and the sky occupying the top third of the frame. However, following this formula too slavishly will lead to things looking a little, well, formulaic, and a bit of thought needs to go into setting up pictures if you want to create something a bit more out of the ordinary.

The first thing to remember is that with coastal shots, especially those featuring large expanses of sea, the sky is vital, as it is often reflected or partly reflected in the water, which sets the mood of the shot. The mood can range from calm and tranquil to dramatic and theatrical, but if the sky is bland, with little interest in it, then the chances are that the whole picture will also be pretty plain too.

Foreground interest

The second important point is choosing the right foreground. A good foreground should lead the eye into the picture, but not detract from the rest of the scene. If a foreground is 'busy' or cluttered, the viewer will tend to spend too much time examining detail here, rather than using it as an 'entry point' to the picture as a whole. If the foreground is too cluttered, then the whole composition can end up looking confusing and messy.

Simplicity is usually the key with foregrounds, and indeed with composition as a whole. A single, strong element carefully placed within the frame generally works best. The foreground element should also be sympathetic to the background. One of the nice things about coastal landscapes is that there's often a good selection of suitable foregrounds. Rocks are an obvious choice, especially if the background contains cliffs or rocky headlands, but it's worth remembering that there are other options – ripples or patterns in the sand, seaweed, tidal pools, reflections and the pattern of waves breaking on the shore are just a few of a number of alternatives. Wherever you go to shoot, you should never be short of options!

Effective middle distance

It's also worth paying attention to the middle distance. A wide-angle shot with a big foreground and a wide expanse of empty space behind it usually results in a composition that is 'loose' with nothing for the eye to follow or settle on once it gets past the foreground. If you can't find a composition where there's some interest in the middle distance, taking a lower viewpoint is an effective way of reducing the amount of empty space.

Exploit leading lines

Lines are another effective way of leading the eye into a picture and there are lots of possibilities at the coast – the shoreline, rock ledges, cliff tops, waves, lines of rocks and lines in man-made objects such as rows of beach huts, piers, slipways and so on. Diagonals and converging lines are dynamic and create a sense of perspective, whereas curves, especially 'S' shapes, lead the eye more slowly through the picture, encouraging the viewer to pause and take in details.

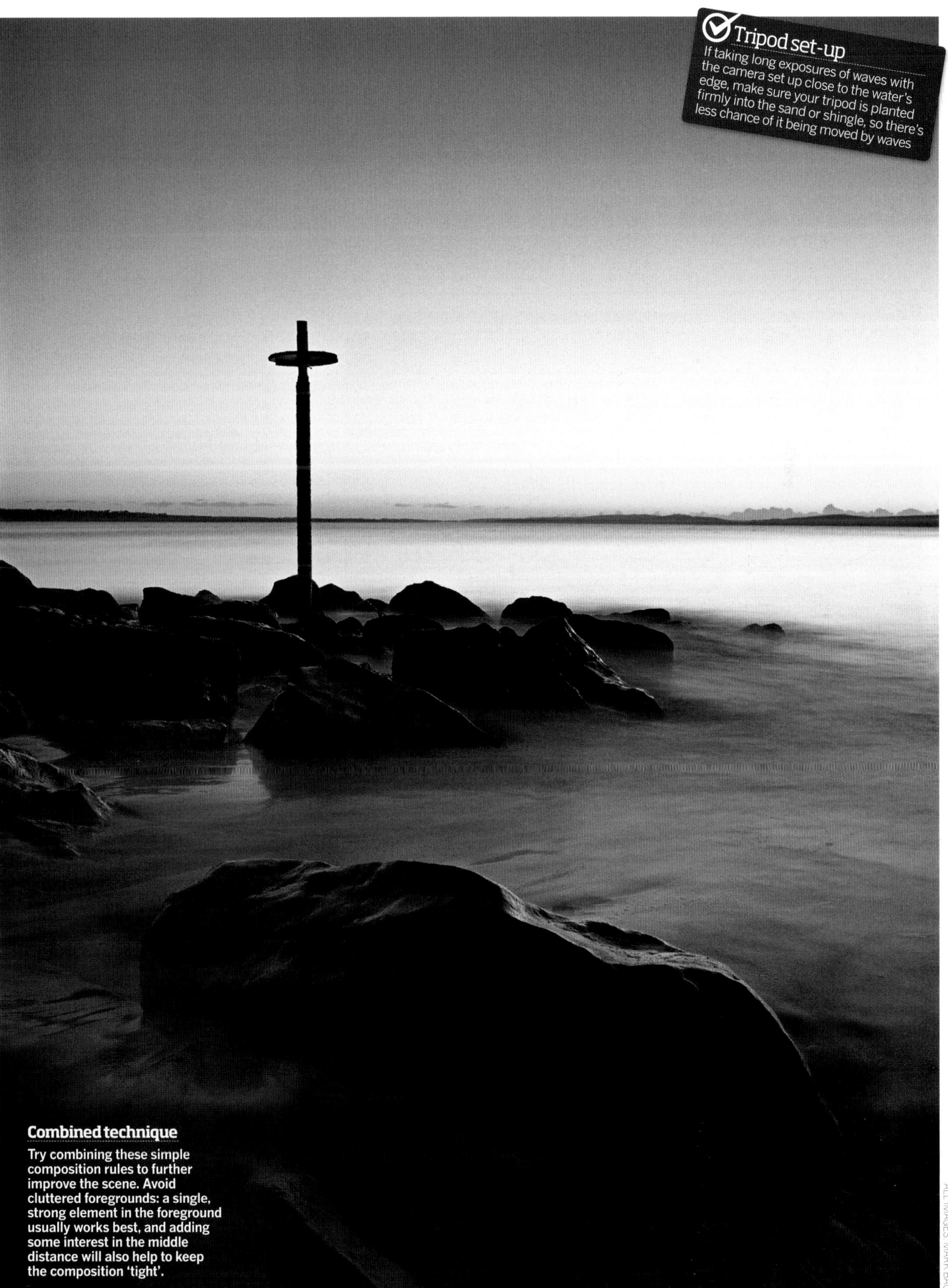

Tripod set-up
If taking long exposures of waves with the camera set up close to the water's edge, make sure your tripod is planted firmly into the sand or shingle, so there's less chance of it being moved by waves

Combined technique
Try combining these simple composition rules to further improve the scene. Avoid cluttered foregrounds: a single, strong element in the foreground usually works best, and adding some interest in the middle distance will also help to keep the composition 'tight'.

ALL IMAGES: MARK BAUER

Exposure and light

Achieving the correct exposure in coastal shots can be a bit trickier than for inland landscapes, as there are several things that can fool the camera's meter: bright highlights on water or bright white foamy waves can lead to underexposure. On the other hand, if you have chosen a large, dark rock for your foreground, this could cause the camera to overexpose. So you need to keep an eye out for any large areas of particularly bright or dark tones and apply exposure compensation accordingly. It is good practice to check the histogram after each shot and be prepared to reshoot if necessary.

There can also be a huge range of contrast within any one scene, with bright skies, dark rocks and bright highlights on water. Neutral Density graduate filters are essential, and depending on the conditions and the brightness of not only the sky but also the sea relative to your foreground, you may need to pull the grad down very low in the frame, below the horizon, to the top of your foreground. If you don't, you could end up with a correctly-exposed sky and foreground with a band of over-bright water in the middle of the picture. So when metering the scene to choose the strength and placement of the filter, remember to take readings from the foreground, sky and sea.

Shooting rocks

If you use a rock, or rocks, as the foreground element, remember they look at their best when they're wet. Consider taking a watering can with you, in case the tide lets you down!

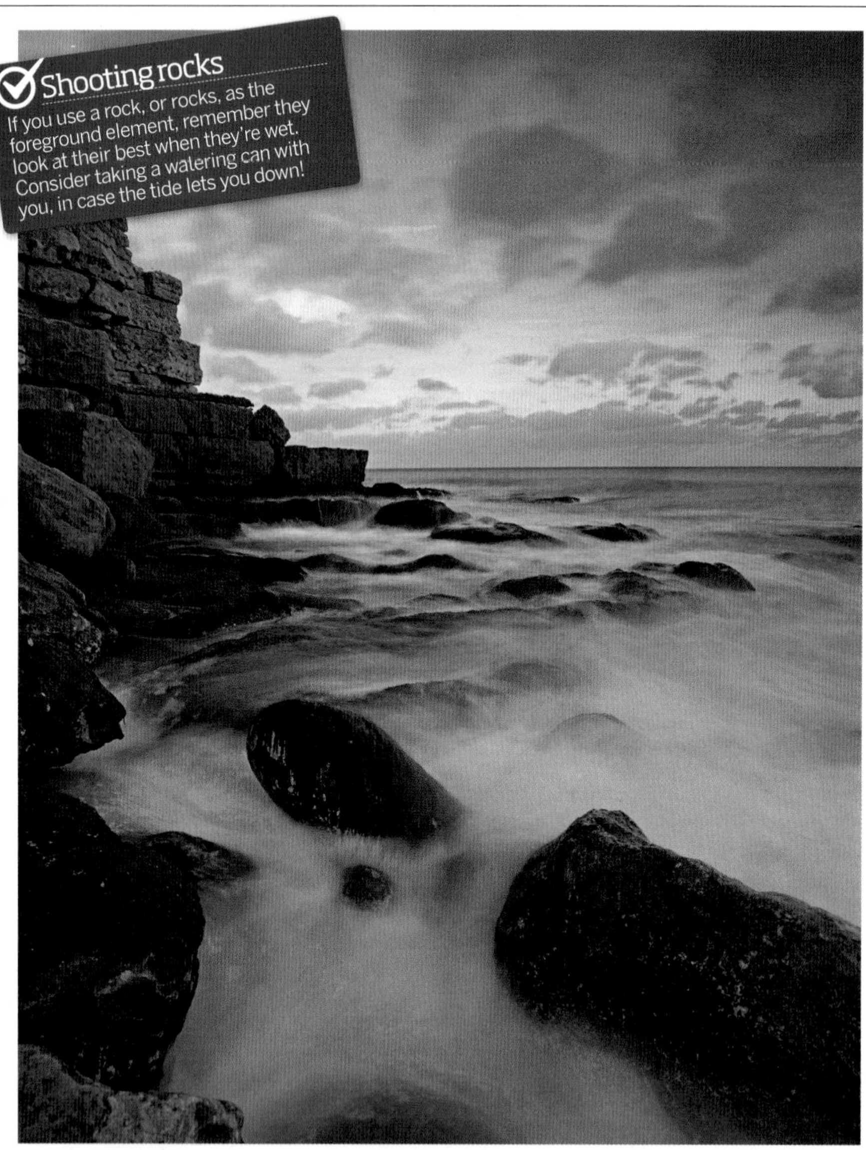

Exposing to capture movement

One of the great things about taking photographs by the sea is the opportunities it gives for capturing the movement of waves and adding atmosphere. In low light, with the lens stopped down to extend depth-of-field, long exposures (ranging from several seconds to minutes, depending on conditions) are a necessity, and as waves wash around rocks or up and down on the shore while the shutter is open, they will record as a mist, giving the scene a romantic, mysterious atmosphere. You may want to capture the drama of waves breaking on the shore, in which case a shorter shutter speed will be needed. However, try not to completely freeze the action, which destroys the sense of movement. I find a shutter speed of around ¼sec is about right for capturing a little motion, while still maintaining the 'shape' of the wave. Of course, this isn't a hard and fast rule, and depends on the size and speed of the waves, so use te camera's LCD monitor to review images and see if you need to change the exposure and reshoot.

Finding the best light

The best times for photographing the coast are at the beginning and end of the day, when the low sun reveals textures in sand, rocks and cliffs. Pre-dawn and post-sunset are also favourites, especially if there are some clouds in the sky, which can be lit from below with dramatic effects by the rising or setting sun. A light sea mist can also be effective at these times of day, as the light will be diffused, creating a calm, tranquil atmosphere.

Try to avoid shooting at the coast in the middle of the day, when the sun is strong and high in the sky. The usual problem of flat lighting is made even worse by glare off the sea and not only will pictures tend to look flat and lifeless, but you are quite likely to have problems with flare as well.

Shooting in changing light

The Met Office had forecast fairly heavy cloud cover, which can result in interesting dawn skies, so I got up early to head to the beach for sunrise. This series of shots was taken within a few minutes, as the light changed rapidly.

5.36am With the sun below the horizon, the clouds were taking on some strong colours. I often like minimalist shots for beach scenes, but it didn't really work here, as the tide was coming in – an outgoing tide would have left wet sand in the foreground, with the opportunity for reflections and ripples in the sand.

5.38am A slightly different approach this time. I decided to use the lifeguard station to add interest to the wide expanse of sand.

5.42am Unconvinced by the effectiveness of the lifeguard station as a focal point, I switched my attention to the sea defences, using the groyne to aid symmetry.

5.45am Shooting in the opposite direction, I thought the buoy would make an interesting foreground. I gave more attention to the sky as there was still an interesting cloud pattern.

5.36am

5.38am

5.42am

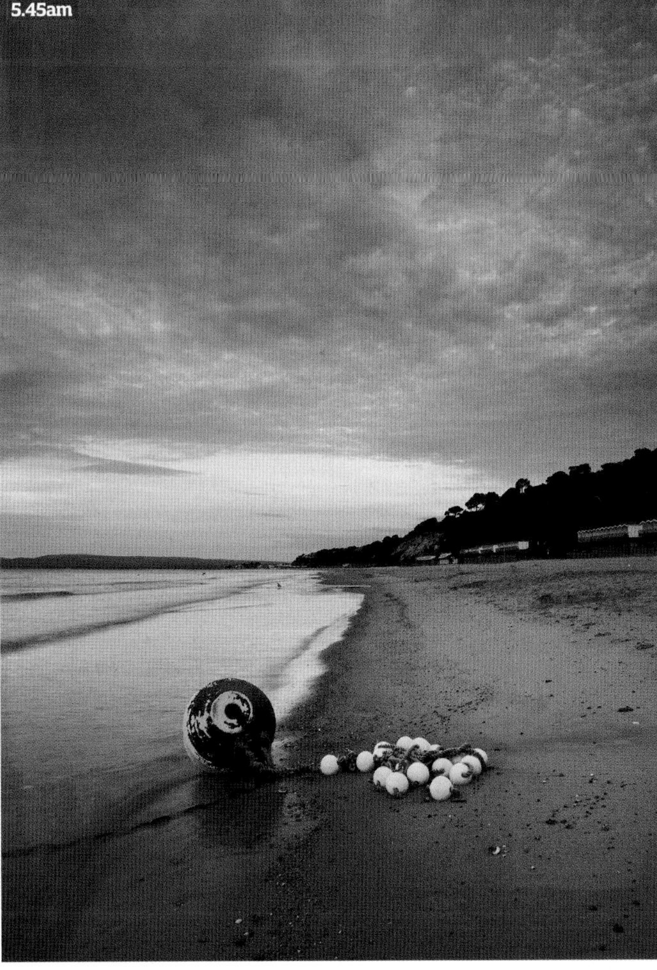
5.45am

Capturing 'natural-looking' waves

Professional photographer Mark Bauer explains the best technique for capturing the movement of breaking waves as they hit the shore

There's a lot of debate about how best to photograph wave movement. Long exposures result in a 'misty' look that is popular with many photographers (see over the page) but is certainly not to everyone's taste as it's not authentic. When we watch waves rolling on to the shore, we see the whole movement – we don't see a moment frozen in time or mist drifting over rocks. One way to truly appreciate wave motion as the eye sees it is to use video rather than a stills camera, but by paying careful attention to shutter speeds, it is possible to record natural-looking waves on your DSLR.

The trick is to record the right amount of movement; if the shutter is open too long there will be too much motion blur, not long enough and the wave will appear too static. You need to find a middle ground where there's misty blur but the waves still keep their shape.

There is no simple recipe for this; the best shutter speed depends on the size and speed of the waves, how they're falling onto the shore, and also personal taste. Experimentation is the key – be prepared to shoot a lot of frames and spend a lot of time looking at the review screen and tweaking the camera controls.

1 I compose the shot so that the waves are falling onto the foreground rocks and then check the exposure for the sky and ground separately using my DSLR's spot meter.

2 As the sky is much brighter than the ground, I added a three-stop ND soft grad filter to balance the contrast. A soft grad means the transition line won't be too obvious.

Controlling shutter speeds

Although there's no 'ideal' shutter speed for capturing a breaking wave, as it depends on the conditions at the time, a shutter speed of between ¼ second and a couple of seconds usually provides the result you'll want.

It's not just a matter, however, of putting the camera into shutter-priority mode and setting the shutter speed. You will also need make sure you're using the right aperture in order to achieve the appropriate depth-of-field and an accurate exposure. For landscapes this is usually between f/8 and f/22 for maximum depth-of-field.

There are other ways you can control the shutter speed too. Apart from waiting for the light to change, for a faster shutter speed, you should increase the camera's ISO rating. Normally this will raise the level of noise, so you do not want to go much above ISO 800 unless you're using a professional DSLR that handles noise well.

For shutter speeds of more than 30 seconds, you will need to set your camera to Bulb mode and time the exposure manually. However this can often result in overexposed shots, so you may need to add a 'solid' neutral density filter to reduce the amount of light falling onto the sensor. ND filters come in various strengths, the most common being one, two and three stops, and you can use several together, along with a polarising filter too, for extremely long exposures.

3 Set to shutter-priority mode, I try 1/100sec but it freezes the movement. For large waves this might convey drama, but with small waves like this it completely fails.

4 In the hope of lengthening the exposure, I wait for the light levels to drop and replace the three-stop ND filter with a four-stop ND filter, giving me a ten-second exposure at f/22.

5 This time the exposure is still not long enough to give an ethereal misty look to the water, but it doesn't capture the drama of the scene by freezing the water either.

6 Opening up the aperture to f/11, and swapping the four-stop ND for a two-stop enables me to shorten the exposure time to 0.3 seconds. The result is almost what I wanted, but the wave is frozen just a little too much.

7 One more attempt, with the light levels a bit lower, I get the shot I want at around 0.6 of a second. There's enough movement to create a sense of drama but the waves still keep their shape.

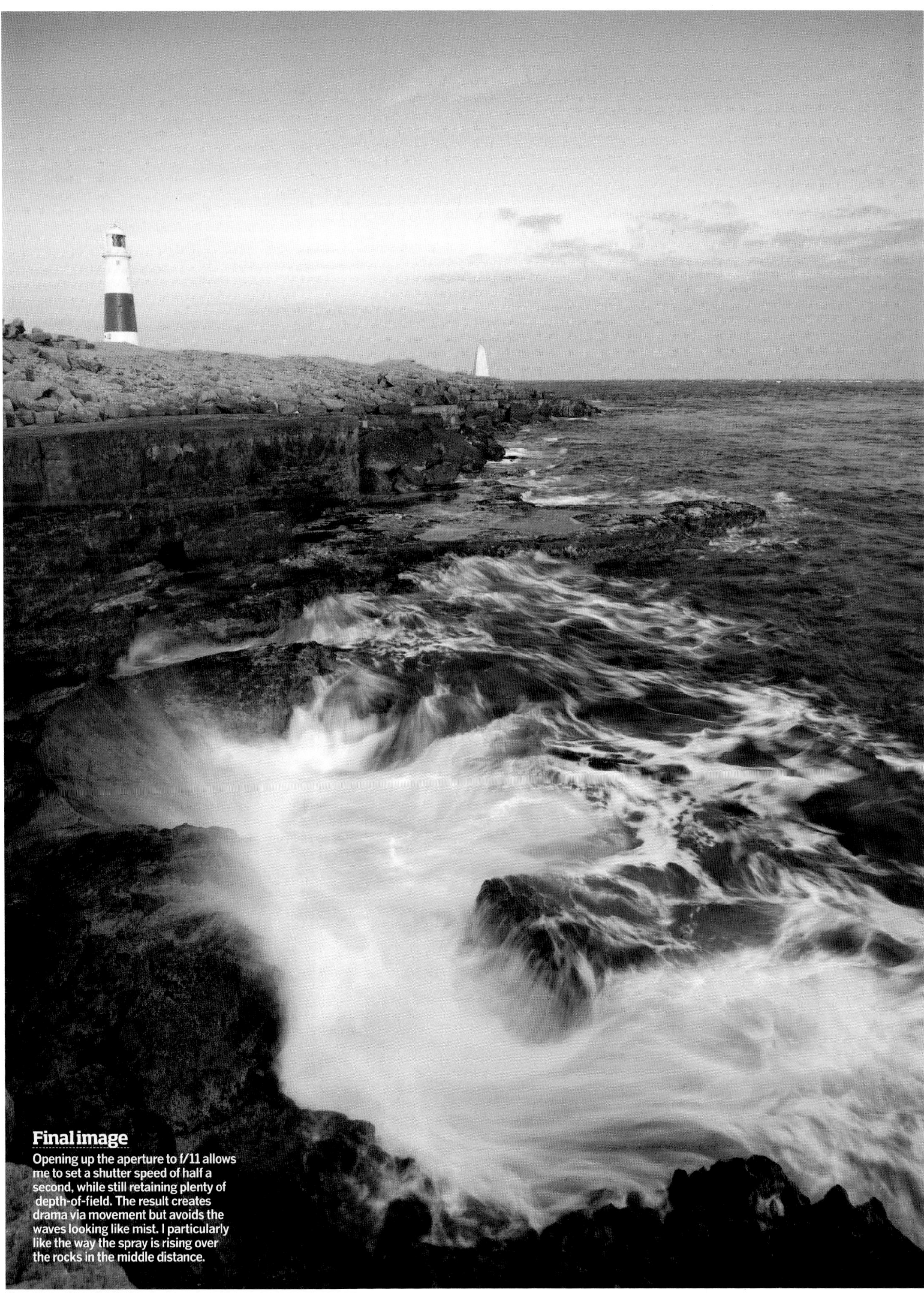

Final image

Opening up the aperture to f/11 allows me to set a shutter speed of half a second, while still retaining plenty of depth-of-field. The result creates drama via movement but avoids the waves looking like mist. I particularly like the way the spray is rising over the rocks in the middle distance.

Blurring motion in water

Regular contributor Ross Hoddinott demonstrates how to render moving water as an atmospheric, ethereal mist for creative effect

Essential kit

Using long exposures to blur water motion is a technique that relies on a sturdy tripod otherwise camera shake will ruin the results. Quite simply, a tripod is essential and not optional

Set-up

Blurry water – you either love it or loath it. I love it.

To render moving water milky, the right exposure time is essential; too fast and the water can look messy. A good rule of thumb is to select a shutter speed of around one second or longer. This should create an attractive level of blur. Even lengthier exposures will create more atmospheric, surreal results.

In order to generate the longest exposure time for the available light, select your DSLR's lowest ISO together with the lens's smallest aperture (eg f/22 or f/32). In low light, achieving a lengthy exposure is relatively easy, with exposure times naturally longer. However, when the light is good, it is not often possible to select a sufficiently slow shutter speed without overexposing the image. The solution is to use a Neutral Density (ND) filter. The stronger the density of the ND filter, the more light it absorbs, the longer the exposure and the greater the level of blur. For extreme effects, Lee Filters' 'Big Stopper' (ten-stops) can generate exposure times of several minutes, requiring the use of your camera's Bulb setting and a remote release. When shooting water's movement using long exposures, every image will be different. Sometimes the difference will be great; sometimes subtle. Take a sequence of images and decide later which one is best.

1 It was evening and the tide was high. To blur the water as it washed over the rocky outcrops and pebbly shore, I carefully arranged my composition, using a tripod to keep my images shake-free. At first, with the camera set to program mode, it automatically set a shutter speed of 1/80sec at f/8 based on the available light – not slow enough to blur water.

2 To blur the water movement, take control from the camera by selecting either shutter-priority mode and the slowest shutter speed available, or aperture-priority mode and opt for the smallest aperture. Either method sets the longest exposure obtainable in the given light. Also, select your camera's lowest ISO rating, typically ISO 100 on the majority of DSLRs.

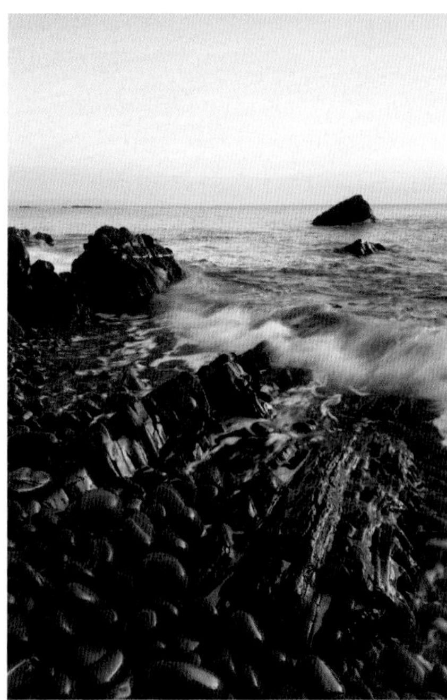

3 Having selected a low ISO rating (ISO 100) and aperture-priority mode, I set the minimum aperture of f/22 and waited for a large wave to wash around the foreground rocks. The exposure of 1/8sec at f/22 was longer, but as the water still didn't render milky, I added a polarising filter to help lengthen the exposure.

4 A polarising filter has a filter factor of two stops, so can be used as a makeshift ND filter by extending the exposure – ideal if you don't own a ND. It also helps remove glare, in this case from the rocks. The result is better, but in this instance, the exposure of 1/2sec at f/22 is still not long enough for the ethereal result I was after.

5 For the blur I want, I had to add a Neutral Density filter. I left the polariser in place and attached a three-stop ND filter. The camera's TTL metering automatically adjusts for the filter, but it also darkens the viewfinder, so you will need to compose and lock the focus for the shot before attaching the filter to your DSLR.

Final image

Thanks to the solid ND filter, and also the lowering light, the exposure time was now six seconds at f/22. Again, I waited for a suitable wave, and released the shutter while the water washed around the foreground rocks. I used a remote release to maximise the sharpness in my image.

Rockpool reflections

Professional photographer Mark Bauer goes paddling among rockpools to show us how to master reflections in water

Framing the shot

Reflections make great subjects for landscape images. There's something unique about the symmetry of a perfect reflection in a still lake, but reflections can work equally well on a smaller scale, in ponds, puddles, or rockpools.

They may not always work as the main subject in a coastal shot, but rockpools make excellent foreground interest in wide-angle landscapes, with reflections creating extra depth in a shot and adding brightness and colour, which can break up dark foregrounds.

You'll find rockpools at any rocky coastline when the tide is low – the trick is to find one that will photograph well. If they're too small, they won't have enough impact, and if they're too shallow or if the bottom is sandy and light, the reflections won't be strong enough. The ideal time to arrive is as the tide is going out, so that you can set up as rockpools are being revealed, and shoot while the surrounding rocks are still wet and shiny. This is also easier than having to rush your pictures before an incoming tide covers up the perfect rockpool.

Weather conditions are also important. It needs to be still enough that there are no ripples on the surface of the water to break up the reflection, and there also needs to be interest in the sky – dramatic clouds or colours – as unless your rockpool is very close to a point of interest such as a lighthouse, it's the sky that will make the reflection. In terms of technique, accurate focusing and depth-of-field are crucial, as this type of image looks best when both the immediate foreground and the reflection are sharp. This isn't as easy as it may seem, as the focal plane of the reflection is much further away than the reflective medium.

One last thing to be aware of is correct filtration, which can be used both to balance the light in the scene overall, and to also enhance the reflection itself.

Equipment for reflections

AN ULTRA WIDE-ANGLE ZOOM will help you get in close and fill the foreground with your rockpool of choice.

A TRIPOD that allows low-level shooting. A low viewpoint will reveal more of the sky in the reflection and make for a balanced shot.

A POLARISING FILTER to enhance the reflection. Contrary to popular belief, polarisers don't simply remove reflections, but reduce glare too, which can actually enhance reflections. You have to be careful to set the correct polarisation, though, because you can kill the reflection if you get it wrong. Look through the viewfinder and rotate the polariser slowly. Stop when you see the effect you want.

ND GRADS help balance contrast in the scene. Take care not to 'overgrad' the scene, however, because in real life reflections are usually darker than the sky and your picture won't look natural if it's the other way round.

SOLID ND FILTERS If conditions aren't still and there are ripples on the water, you can add a Neutral Density filter to lengthen the exposure and 'smooth out' the water.

Exposure and focusing

Reflective surfaces are by their very nature bright, and this can fool your camera's meter into underexposure. Add +0.5 to +1 stops of exposure compensation, and check the histogram after shooting to make sure. You need to be careful when focusing, as the focal planes of the water's surface and the reflection are not the same. If you leave your camera on autofocus, it could focus on the surface of the water, which means the more distant reflection could fall out of focus. To make sure the scene is sharp from front to back, switch to manual focusing and focus a third of the way into the scene and use a small aperture, such as f/16.

1 Arriving at dawn, I look for suitable foreground interest. I quite like the foreground in this shot, but the rockpool doesn't work – it's too small and shallow to reflect the sky properly.

2 This one works a little better, but without any filtration, the highlights in the sky have blown, and the shadows in the foreground are beginning to block up.

3 An ND grad enables me to retain detail in the sky and rays of light are starting to break through in the background, adding drama to the scene. But I feel the reflection can be enhanced.

Composition advice

By taking a low viewpoint, you are able to fill the frame with the rockpool and also include the reflected sky. Landscape-format images usually work better than portraits in these situations

Final image

All the components come together for a perfect image. As you can see, there's always a bit of time for reflection.

4 My next step is to add a polariser. However, as you can see, if you set it incorrectly, you can kill the reflection rather than enhance it. It's time to tweak the polarising effect.

5 Just half a turn of the polariser helps to make the reflection stand out. However, I feel the image can be improved by smoothing out the water in the middle distance.

6 Adding a solid ND filter allows me to increase the shutter speed to ten seconds, which smooths out the sea in the middle distance and improves the look of the water in the rockpool.

Shoot abstract reflections in water

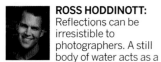

ROSS HODDINOTT: Reflections can be irresistible to photographers. A still body of water acts as a mirror, perfectly reflecting its surroundings. Landscape photographers often use reflections to create symmetry, but water doesn't need to be still for reflections to be photogenic. A slight breeze will create gentle ripples in smooth water, distorting the colour and appearance of reflected subjects. Mundane subjects can be distorted to the point of abstraction, such as a block of flats, a boat's mast or a brightly coloured buoy. By excluding the subject and isolating the reflections, it's easy to take some unusual, arty images. When photographing water and movement, each shot is unique, with the look of the rippled water constantly changing. In order to isolate the reflections, a telezoom is a good lens choice. A 70-300mm lens is ideal, as its focal length range will allow you to achieve a variety of different results. Shutter speed is a key consideration – too slow and the water will blur. For crisp reflections, a speed upwards of 1/250sec is often required. As a result, you can normally work handheld without any great risk of shake. I'd recommend using a polarising filter. This might surprise you, as this filter is often used to reduce reflections, but it can also enhance their colour and intensity. Now all you need is a suitable body of water and a breezy day – not too windy though, or the water will be choppy.

Setup

Get ready!

TIME REQUIRED
30 MINUTES

EQUIPMENT NEEDED
NIKON D300 AND 80-400MM TELEZOOM WITH POLARISING FILTER

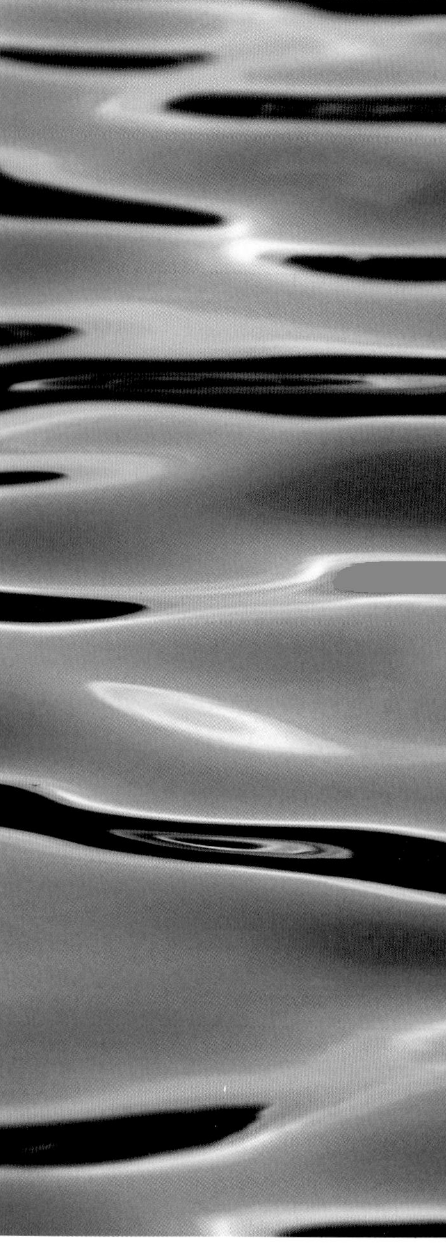

Essential kit

POLARISER: A polarising filter is designed to block light polarised in one plane. By doing so, it can reduce or eliminate reflections and enhance contrast. They are constructed from a thin foil of polarising material, mounted between two circular pieces of glass. By rotating the filter in its mount, you can alter the filter's angle of polarisation and the degree of polarised light that can reach the image sensor. Using a polariser is intuitive – simply look through the viewfinder and rotate the filter until you get your desired effect. Polarisers are one of the most useful filter types and their effect can't be replicated on your computer later. Although designed to reduce reflections, applied correctly, they can also enhance them. By removing the reflective film or sheen on the water's surface, the colours of reflections will be intensified. Apply the effect with care though – the filter will diminish the reflections if you're not careful!

No Polariser

With Polariser

1/30sec

1/250sec

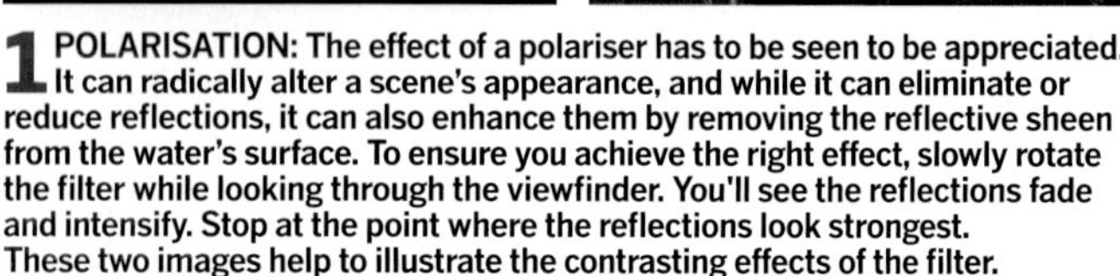

1 POLARISATION: The effect of a polariser has to be seen to be appreciated. It can radically alter a scene's appearance, and while it can eliminate or reduce reflections, it can also enhance them by removing the reflective sheen from the water's surface. To ensure you achieve the right effect, slowly rotate the filter while looking through the viewfinder. You'll see the reflections fade and intensify. Stop at the point where the reflections look strongest. These two images help to illustrate the contrasting effects of the filter.

2 SHUTTER SPEED: Shutter speed is a key consideration when shooting abstract reflections. Too slow and the ripples will blur, which is normally undesirable, as the reflections – and the beautiful, swirly pattern they create – won't be so well defined. A good general rule is to shoot upwards of 1/250sec. Don't worry if you need to select a large aperture to do this – often the narrow depth-of-field this creates will only add to the 'arty' effect. However, this is subjective, so experiment with the shutter speed until you like the effect.

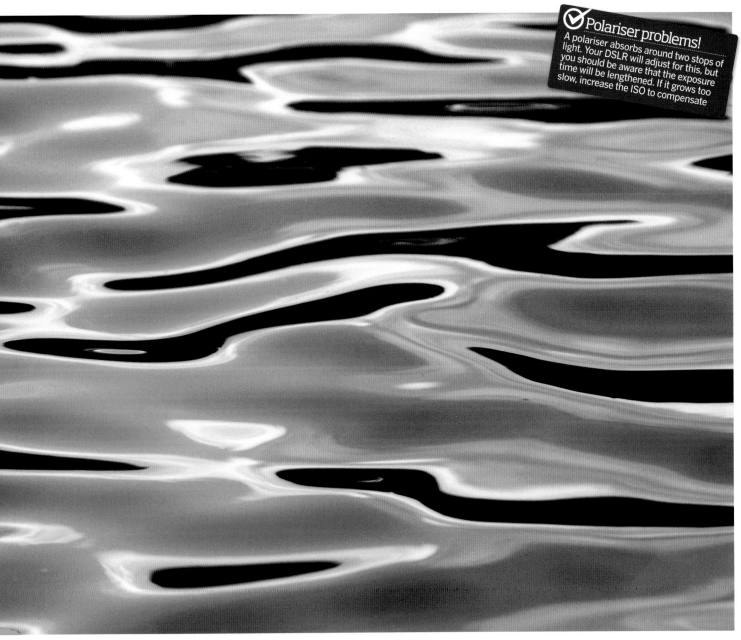

Polariser problems!

A polariser absorbs around two stops of light. Your DSLR will adjust for this, but you should be aware that the exposure time will be lengthened. If it grows too slow, increase the ISO to compensate

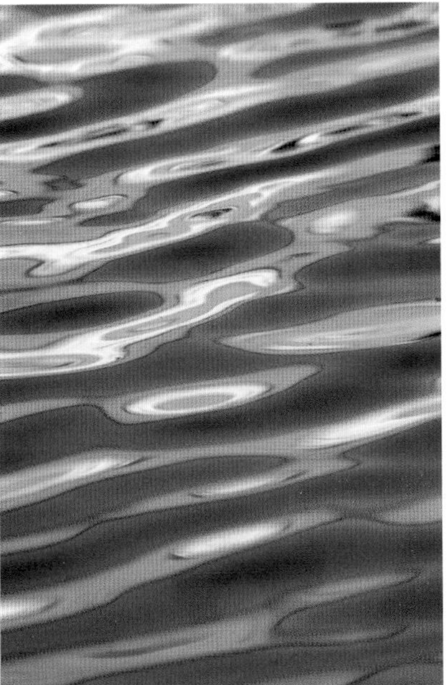

3 COMPOSITION: Don't forget to try both horizontal and vertical format compositions. It is possible to achieve very different-looking results of the same subject by simply turning your camera. If you have a polarising filter attached, remember that switching formats will alter the degree of polarisation, so you will need to adjust the filter accordingly.

4 FOCAL LENGTH: One of the main advantages of using a telezoom to capture arty reflections is the versatility it offers. You can quickly zoom in or out, altering the composition without the fuss of changing lens. The long end of a zoom allows you to highlight specific details, colours or patterns in the water. These shots show the range of an 80-400mm.

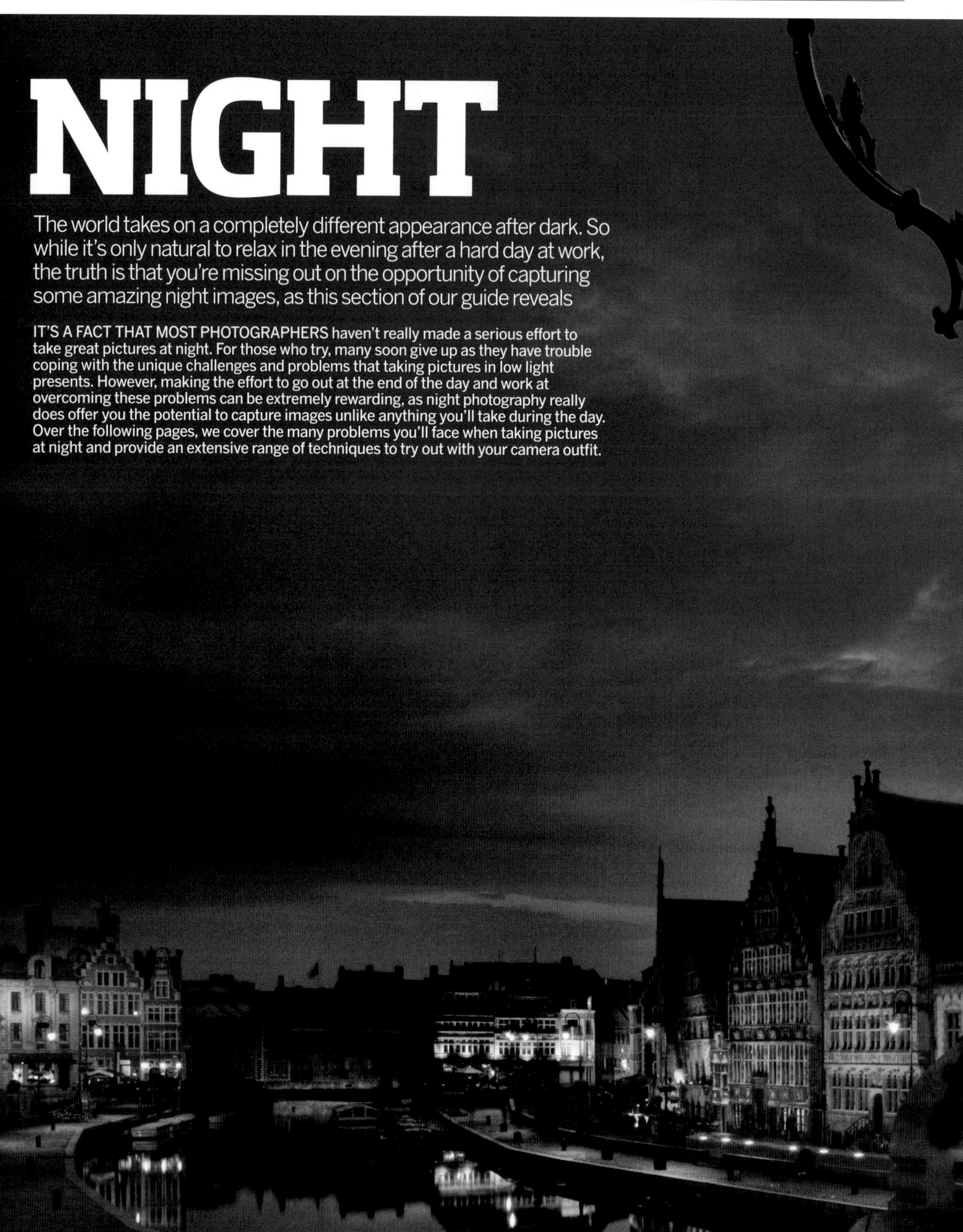

NIGHT

The world takes on a completely different appearance after dark. So while it's only natural to relax in the evening after a hard day at work, the truth is that you're missing out on the opportunity of capturing some amazing night images, as this section of our guide reveals

IT'S A FACT THAT MOST PHOTOGRAPHERS haven't really made a serious effort to take great pictures at night. For those who try, many soon give up as they have trouble coping with the unique challenges and problems that taking pictures in low light presents. However, making the effort to go out at the end of the day and work at overcoming these problems can be extremely rewarding, as night photography really does offer you the potential to capture images unlike anything you'll take during the day. Over the following pages, we cover the many problems you'll face when taking pictures at night and provide an extensive range of techniques to try out with your camera outfit.

JON HICKS

Shooting outdoors in low light

The long nights provide a great opportunity to practice the art of low-light photography. Our major guide is packed with pro advice on essential techniques and key kit to help you take brilliant images

THE SAYING 'LESS IS MORE' could be applied to many things in photography. Equipment is one – you don't need loads of it to take great photographs. Composition is another – the more you cram into an image, the less appealing it's likely to be. Well it's the same with light. You may assume that lots of it is required to produce successful shots, but in reality, the less there is the better.

Sunrise and sunset are universally regarded as the most photogenic times of day, yet light levels are significantly lower than at midday. The urban landscape also looks far more photogenic in the evening, as daylight dies and the colourful glow of man-made illumination takes over. And if you look to the heavens on a starry night, you can't fail to be impressed by the sight of millions of tiny pinpricks of light flickering in the sea of darkness above.

But low light isn't just about the great outdoors – the same rules apply inside as well. Think about it. Does your front room look more inviting with all the lights turned on, or do you prefer the cosy glows of an open fire? Half a dozen halogen spots may stop you tripping over things, but if you want to shoot romantic portraits, a dim room will be far more effective. To show you just how amazing low light can be, we've dedicated a section of this guide to harnessing and mastering it, with a little help from some of our regular contributors. Let's see just how low they can go!

ISTOCK PHOTO

When it comes to light, quality is always more important than quantity. A little special light beats loads of mediocre light any day – or night come to think of it. That's why low-light photography is so rewarding – because whatever the subject or the situation, the light's always good, and when the light's good, the battle to create a great shot is pretty much won.

Outdoors, low-light shooting begins as the day ends and ends as the next day begins – dusk to dawn if you're confused. Sunset kicks things off. As soon as the sun dips below the horizon, day starts its slow transformation into night. Direct light on the landscape disappears and the sky overhead turns into a huge softbox that floods the earth with diffuse illumination, while the sky above the western horizon burns like fire (with any luck). Slot a hard ND grad filter into your filter holder and you can capture the lot in a single exposure – a foreground full of detail and a sky full of colour.

Twilight sees the warmth in the sky dissolve seamlessly into colder purples and blues, while daylight levels fade and scenes visibly darken. This is an ideal time to shoot modern architecture as the colours in the sky are mirrored by its glass and steel surfaces. If you prefer to go wild in the country, head for water so its calm surface can do the same thing. Twilight on a lake's shore or by the sea is hard to beat in the mood stakes and low light levels mean long exposures, which gives blurry water.

The urban landscape comes to life at twilight when daylight fades enough for man-made illumination to cast its technicolor spell, but there's still enough of the natural stuff around to stop those shady spots turning black. The sky – by now a deep blue – also acts like a reflector, bouncing what little light is left into the bits not hit by the streetlamps or floodlights, neon signs and shop displays. This crossover period is the prime time to shoot floodlit buildings, street scenes, traffic trails – any low-light urban scene or subject where sky is included in the frame. Once the sky looks black, it's almost time to stop, although image sensors have a surprising ability to keep pulling colour from the sky long after your eyes have stopped seeing it, so don't be in too much of a hurry to head home.

Actually, you don't need to bother heading home at all, because once night arrives, you can turn your attention to the heavens. How about shooting landscapes in moonlight? Again, put water in the foreground so it picks up the shimmering silver ribbon of moonlight dancing on the inky-black surface. That contrast alone can make great shots.

Or keep the camera's shutter open for ten minutes or longer and turn night into day. This produces surreal effects because scenes look like they've been shot in broad daylight, but instead of being lit by the sun, they're lit by the moon. Whatever takes your fancy, low light offers you lots of photo opportunities.

Essential accessories

Tripod The easiest way to avoid camera shake in low light is to attach your camera to a decent tripod. If you haven't got one, then buy one! Look to spend around £100 for a decent model.

Remote release A very useful aid to help avoid camera shake. As well as own-brand remotes, you'll also find compatible remotes from the likes of Seculine, Hahnel and Hama. Ask your photo dealer for details on what's available for your model of camera.

Torch It's worth keeping a small torch handy if you're setting up in very low light. Any torch is suitable, but you may want to check out the Gorillatorch, from the makers of the Gorillapod, which can be wrapped around objects to free up both your hands.

Low-light seascape

While most people head to the seaside on a hot summer's day, enthusiast photographers prefer visiting at dawn to capture stunning seascapes.

LEE FROST

Five outdoor techniques to try...

ISTOCK PHOTO

1) TRAFFIC TRAILS

Find an elevated viewpoint overlooking a busy road or roundabout, mount your camera on a tripod and use an exposure of 30-60 seconds to record moving traffic as colourful light trails. Include floodlit buildings or the dusk sky for added interest. This is the ideal time of year as dusk and rush hour coincide. Just take care with the traffic!

LEE FROST

2) FLOODLIT BUILDINGS

Another classic low-light subject that's accessible to all. Churches, castles, cathedrals, monuments; every town and city has its fair share of floodlit buildings. For best results, shoot at twilight while there's still colour in the sky and enough daylight to stop the shadows blocking up – but the colourful floodlighting stands out.

ISTOCK PHOTO

3) STAR TRAILS

Get as far away from civilisation as you can on a clear night and use a long exposure to record stars in the sky as trails of light. Point your widest lens towards the northern sky so you include the Pole Star (Polaris), lock your camera's shutter open on Bulb for two hours at f/4 on ISO 200 and see what happens. You'll be amazed by the results.

DANIEL LEZANO

4) PAINTING WITH LIGHT

Find an old building that's unlit, then as it begins to get dark, use repeated bursts from a handheld flashgun set to manual to illuminate the exterior, while your camera's shutter is locked open on Bulb. Use filters to colour the light if you like. Instead of using a flashgun you could use a powerful torch and see what results you can produce.

LEE FROST

5) COASTAL LANDSCAPES

Head to the coast either before sunrise or just before sunset and capture stunning sea views at the fringes of the day. Light levels are low so use long exposures to record motion in the sea, while wet sand and rocks reflect the rich colours in the sky. Remember to be careful with the tides, pack a mobile and let someone know where you are.

Get prepared for the night ahead

Taking pictures at night presents a number of challenges. However, your DSLR is equipped to be able to cope with them all. We provide the best settings and techniques for ensuring you're ready to cope

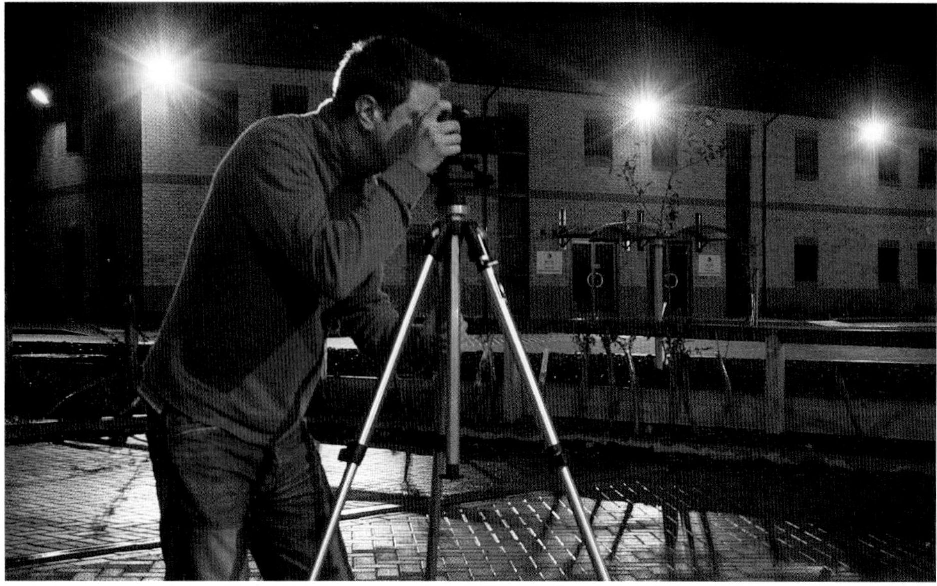

How to reduce the risk of shake without a tripod

1) INCREASE THE ISO RATING By setting a faster ISO rating, you can increase the top shutter speed available to you. The main drawback with this method is that an increase in the ISO rating also sees a gradual degradation in the image, with higher levels of noise and less realistic colours being recorded. That said, the current generation of DSLRs produce excellent images up to ISO 400 and in some cases ISO 800, so it's only beyond these speeds that you'll notice a major drop in quality. We'd only recommend increasing the ISO rating if you're shooting handheld or have placed the camera on an unstable support. If you have your camera on a stable surface, like a tripod, then we'd use a low ISO (100-200) to ensure the best possible quality.

The following set of images shows how noise becomes progressively more evident as you increase the ISO rating. The amount of noise will vary from camera to camera – try shooting the same scene at different ISO ratings to check the noise of your camera.

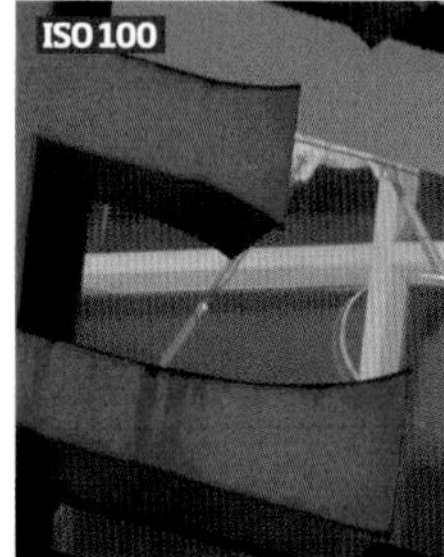

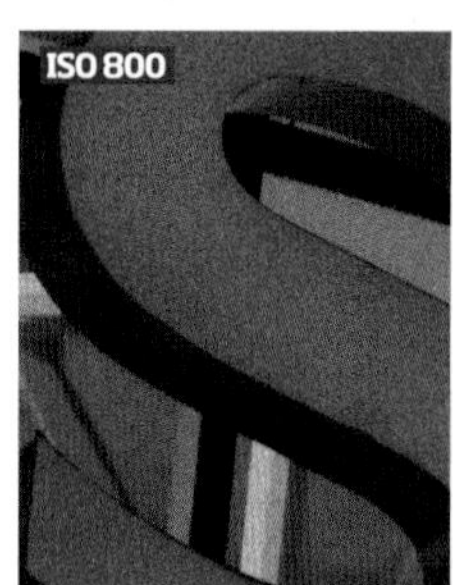

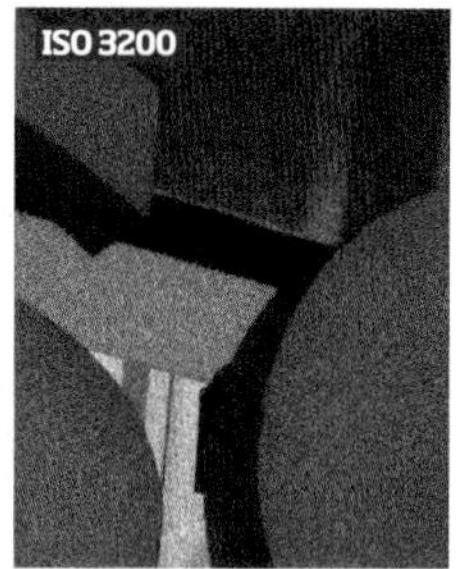

2) IMAGE STABILISATION Depending on which camera you use, you'll find that either your camera body or certain lenses in the range offer image stabilisation (also referred to as shake reduction or similar). If you haven't placed your camera on a stable tripod, it's well worth activating this feature, as it can allow you to use a shutter speed three to four stops faster than without stabilisation.

3) REST THE CAMERA You'll find that leaning against a tree or resting your camera on a wall offers better stability than handholding it, so look for objects that you can rest your DSLR on.

Reciprocal law

Unsure what shutter speed you can get away with when handholding? The easiest way to remember is to ensure that the shutter speed you use is a reciprocal of the focal length you use. So, if you're shooting at 100mm, ensure your shutter speed is at least 1/100sec etc

Gear up for night!

It's essential that you use some form of support for your camera and a decent tripod should be top of your list. Models like the Slik Pro 400DX or Manfrotto 190X Pro B are worth considering – check out the gear section in this guide for further options.

If for whatever reason you can't use a tripod, there are other supports available, including beanpods, mini tripods and suction cups. Another accessory we'd recommend is a remote release for firing the shutter without having to touch the camera. Also, depending on what you're shooting, you could find a flashgun or a torch useful. Finally, make sure you're wrapped up nice and warm.

Camera shake

The most obvious problem that you'll have to overcome with night/low-light photography is that of long exposure times, which create the very real risk of camera shake ruining your images. You'll most likely be looking at shutter speeds running into seconds, so your biggest challenge will be to ensure that your pictures are shake-free. The ideal scenario is to support your camera on a stable platform, such as a tripod, as this will keep your camera steady and give you complete freedom with exposures. It's vital that your camera is totally still during the exposure, so ensure you set up your tripod to be as stable as possible.

AVOID SHAKE AT THE START!

What many newcomers to DSLRs do not realise is that camera shake is often caused by two actions at the start of the exposure. One is from movement caused when you press the shutter button, the other is caused by the action of the mirror inside the camera body flipping up at the start of the exposure. The following are easy ways to eliminate these problems.

✔ **USE A REMOTE RELEASE** Almost every DSLR allows a remote release of one type or another to be used. These useful accessories allow you to take a picture without having to press the shutter button, so reducing any risk of camera shake caused by when you push down on the button. Some remotes work via infrared, while others connect into a socket on the camera body.

✔ **SELF-TIMER** An alternative to using a remote is to fire the shutter using the self-timer. The interval between pressing the button and the shutter firing (two or ten seconds, depending on your DSLR) is enough time for any vibration to stop.

✔ **MIRROR LOCK-UP** This facility isn't one that's often spoken about, but it's well worth using if your camera has it. It works by raising the mirror prior to the exposure being taken, to avoid any risk of shake from its action.

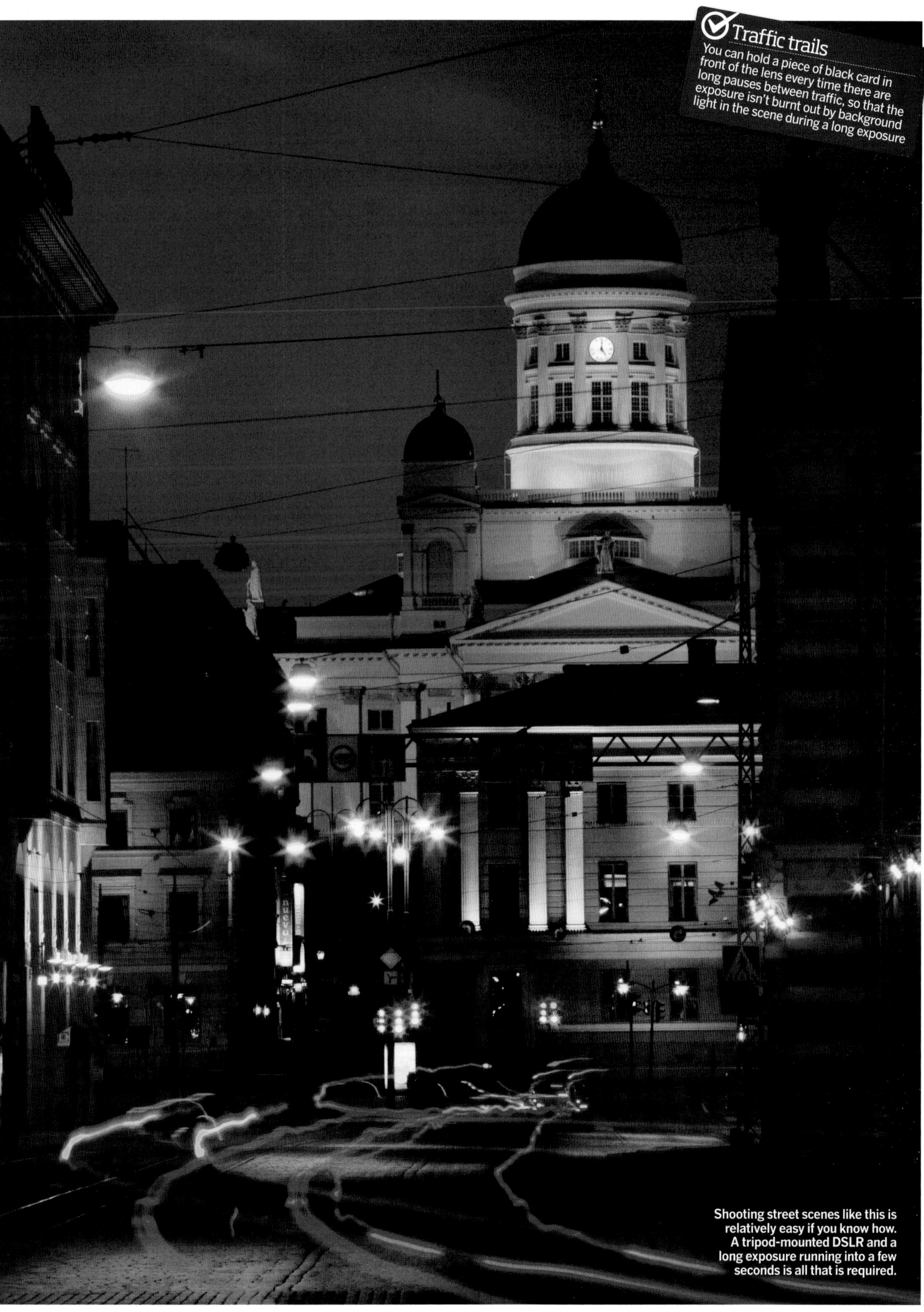

Traffic trails

You can hold a piece of black card in front of the lens every time there are long pauses between traffic, so that the exposure isn't burnt out by background light in the scene during a long exposure

Shooting street scenes like this is relatively easy if you know how. A tripod-mounted DSLR and a long exposure running into a few seconds is all that is required.

JON HICKS

What mode should you use?

This will depend what you're trying to shoot and the technique you're using. For outdoor scenes, traffic trails or painting with light techniques, most people begin by using aperture-priority or shutter-priority, and setting an aperture of f/8 or a shutter speed between one and eight seconds. However, neither of these two modes is ideal – you'd be far better off setting your camera to manual (M), setting a mid-aperture like f/8 for optimum quality, then experimenting with shutter speeds and checking results on the LCD monitor. You'll get a better idea of how to do this by following our guides and trying the techniques out for yourself.

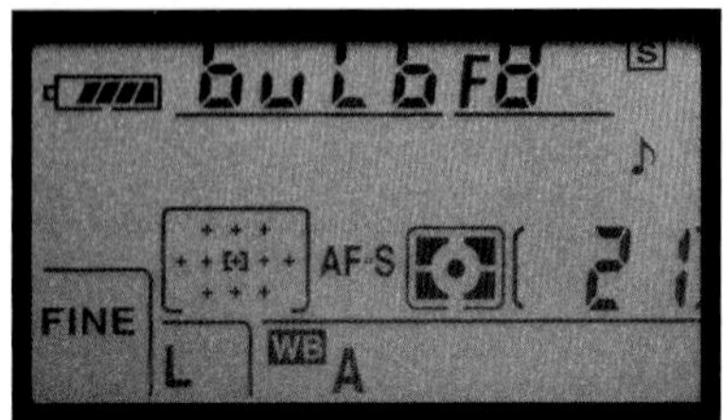

BULB MODE: Run through the shutter speeds and beyond the slowest setting (usually 30 seconds) you'll come across the Bulb mode. This mode allows you to shoot images where you determine the length of the exposure, so for instance, you can shoot at 23 seconds, three minutes etc. With some DSLRs, you press the shutter button once to activate the Bulb exposure and again to end it. With others, you need to keep your finger depressed on the button during the whole exposure – this latter method seriously runs the risk of shake, so a remote is recommended.

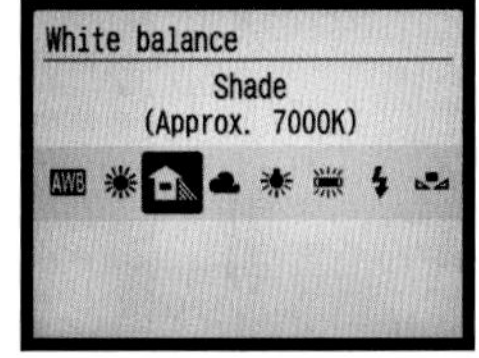

WHITE BALANCE: When shooting at night, you need to be prepared for images exhibiting very unusual colours due to the use of artificial lighting. You'll find most street lighting will produce an orange cast, while floodlit buildings like cathedrals or churches often record with a bluish-white cast. We'd recommend you shoot in Raw and try out different White Balance settings on your computer to see which works best. If you're shooting in JPEG, take a sequence of exposures set to different White Balance presets and compare the results.

Night photography: Ideal settings

If you can set up your camera as below, then you'll be fully prepared for taking great night images

- ✔ Digital camera on a sturdy tripod
- ✔ Set to Raw (+ JPEG if available) so that colour casts can be easily managed
- ✔ ISO rating at 100 or 200 for optimum quality
- ✔ Set to Manual, a mid-aperture (f/8 or f/11) and Bulb
- ✔ Mirror lock-up activated and shutter fired by self-timer or remote control

Prepare your DSLR for night shooting

If you're unsure of how to set your camera so that it's optimised for night shooting, follow our quick help operation guide

CANON EOS SERIES

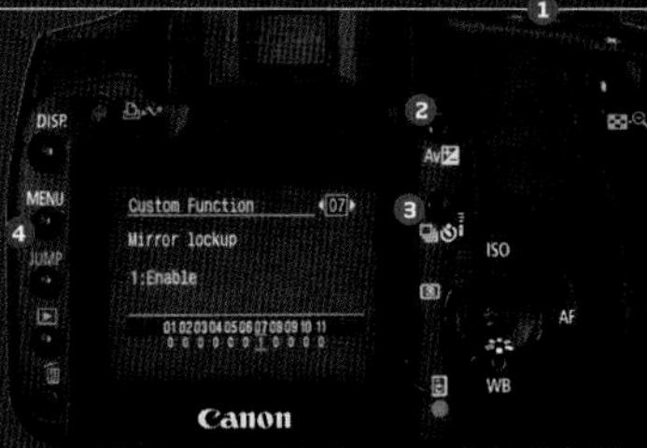

(1) Turn the mode dial to M (manual mode). To set a shutter speed, turn the dial behind the shutter button. (2) To set an aperture, press and hold the +/- button, then turn the dial. (3) To use the self-timer or remote control, press the drive button and choose the appropriate icon. (4) To use mirror lock-up with suitable cameras, press MENU, go to Custom Functions and choose the appropriate number. Press Set, select 1: Enable. When you want take a picture, press the shutter button once to raise the mirror and again to take the picture.

NIKON DSLRS

(1) Turn the mode dial to M (manual mode). To set a shutter speed, turn the rear dial. To set an aperture, turn the dial at the top of the handgrip. (2) To use the self-timer or remote control, press the drive button and choose the appropriate icon. (3) To use mirror lock-up with suitable models, press MENU, go to Custom Setting and choose the appropriate number.

OLYMPUS E-SERIES

(1) Turn the mode dial to M (manual mode). To set a shutter speed, turn the dial on the top-plate. (2)To set an aperture, press and hold the +/- button on the top-plate, then turn the dial. (3)To use the self-timer or remote control, press OK, move to the drive icon on the LCD, press OK button and select the appropriate icon.

PENTAX K-SERIES

(1) Turn the mode dial to M (manual mode). To set a shutter speed, turn the rear dial. (2) To set an aperture, press and hold the +/- button, then turn the dial. (3) To use the self-timer or remote control, press the Fn button, press the up button on the four-way control and select the appropriate icon, then press OK to set. You'll find that selecting the two-second self-timer also engages a mirror lock-up facility.

SONY ALPHA SERIES

(1) Turn the mode dial to M (manual mode). To set a shutter speed, turn the dial in front of the shutter button. (2) To set an aperture, press and hold the +/- button, then turn the dial. (3) To use the self-timer, press the drive button and choose the appropriate icon. You'll find that selecting the two-second self-timer also engages a mirror lock-up facility.

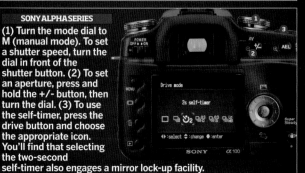

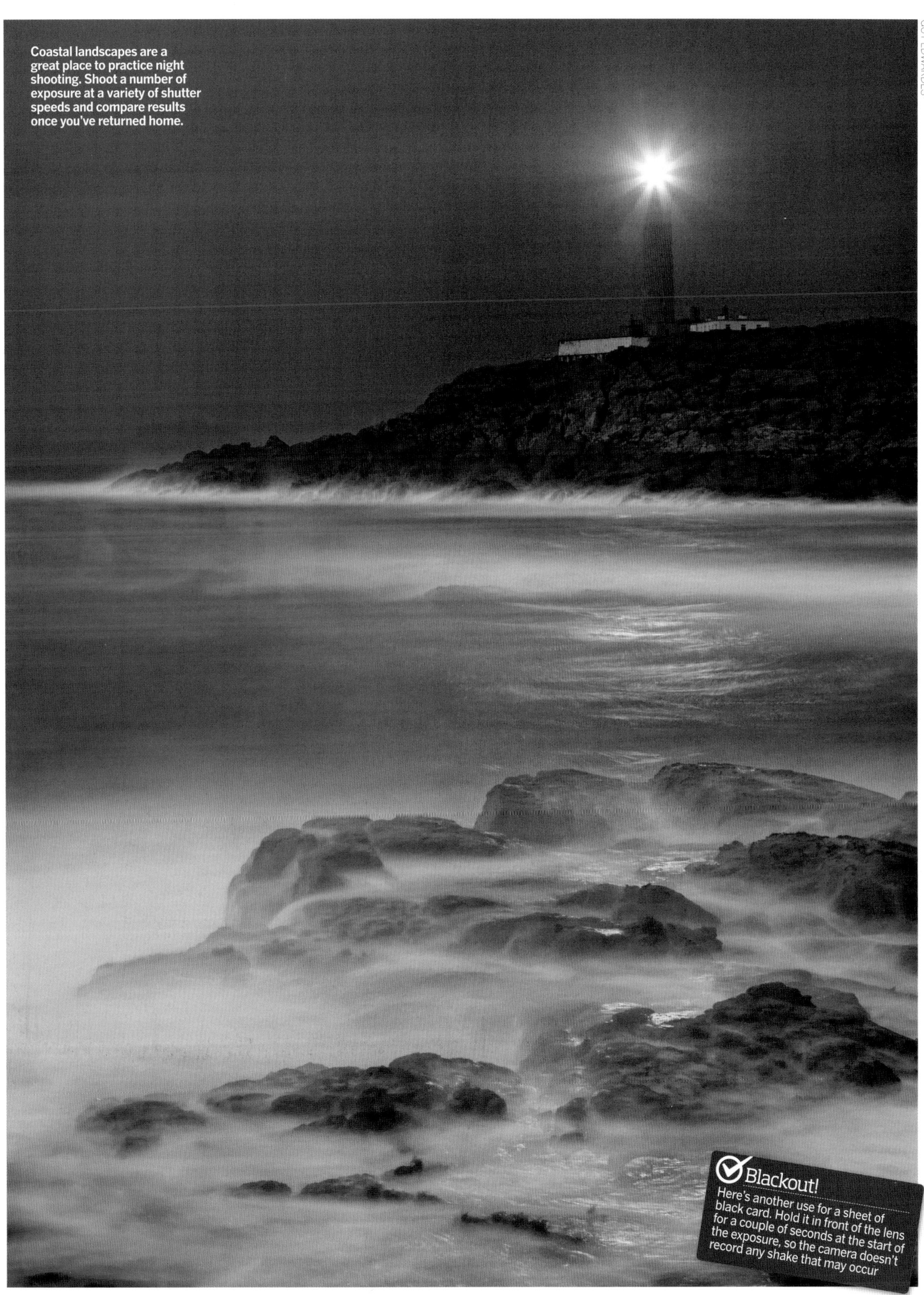

Blackout!
Here's another use for a sheet of black card. Hold it in front of the lens for a couple of seconds at the start of the exposure, so the camera doesn't record any shake that may occur

Coastal landscapes are a great place to practice night shooting. Shoot a number of exposure at a variety of shutter speeds and compare results once you've returned home.

GUY EDWARDES

Urban night scenes

From your local street corner to modern city skylines, we show you how to get your urban shots glowing in the dark

MANY TOWNS CAN LOOK rather boring and uninteresting by day, but come nightfall and it is a different story. As the light begins to fade you start to get a beautiful mix of the ambient daylight and artificial glowing lights. Wait for dusk to arrive and you will be rewarded with some great opportunities once ambient and artificial lights balance out. This is often referred to as the 'crossover' period and it occurs about twenty minutes after sunset. The sky should be a lovely dark blue colour, which compliments the warm street lighting perfectly. It is this contrast of warm and cold colours that helps make night photography so exciting.

Getting into a good routine increases your chances of successful night shots. First, you must arrive at your chosen location early. If you don't know the area then get there a good hour before sunset so you can scout around for a selection of good viewpoints. You can even grab a nice sunset into the bargain! It is no good turning up at the last minute and hoping all will be well – preparation is key to success.

You should be setting up your tripod as the sun sets. It is possible to run around and shoot several different angles but to begin with just concentrate on getting one shot perfect and let your confidence grow. Now take a series of bracketed shots as the light changes.

There are many different bright light sources that can fool the camera's meter, usually into underexposing, so look out for areas that can be accurately metered from. If necessary, you can use a pavement to take an exposure reading from. Pavements are close to mid-grey, so will give you a decent starting point. For distant views a spot meter reading taken using a telephoto lens may be the best option. Use your LCD monitor to check how accurate your measured reading is.

Bracketing your exposures (ie taking a set of shots at + and – the indicated exposure) is highly recommended as night shots can be tricky to get right. The contrast between light and dark areas is among the worst you will encounter in photography, so to cover all bases you must take extra bracketed shots above and below the metered reading.

Your camera's meter reading is often a good starting place for the first exposure. You should now add extra overexposed shots to capture shadow detail and underexposed shots to record highlights. A three stop bracket is usually fine for most situations. To do this, shoot a fame at the indicated exposure reading, then set exposure compensation to +1 to overexpose and follow this by shooting another frame at -1 to underexpose. On many cameras, you can set the autobracketing facility to fire a sequence of three different exposures automatically.

CHANGE YOUR VIEWPOINT: Adopting alternative viewpoints can produce very different results. A low viewpoint close to buildings exaggerates converging verticals, while high positions produce stunning nightscapes.

You should also bracket the 'period of time' by taking a series of bracketed shots every ten minutes or so and every five minutes when you think things are looking good. By doing this you are guaranteeing that you will get that perfect shot when the different lights are perfectly balanced, usually halfway into the shoot.

Finally, make sure to try out different viewpoints and lenses. Wide-angles are the best choice for urban scenes as they allow you to capture wide scenes. As well as shooting from ground-level, consider gaining permission to shoot from the upper floors of buildings – multi-storey car parks are a good place to try. Telezooms are useful for isolating details and zooming in on distant buildings.

Night light

This series shows how Tim Garside shot the changes in light as the sunset fades to dusk and then to night. "I arrived early to grab a nice sunset and kept taking shots as the light changed. By around 19.45 you might be tempted to think the day is over as the light is looking flat and boring. By hanging on an extra fifteen minutes I could see that the city lights were beginning to have an impact on the feel of the shot. By 20.00 the light was beginning to reach that point where everthing was in balance and by 20.15 I had the picture in the bag. You can stay on longer to get a black sky which can work really well when transformed into black & white images."

19.45

20.00

20.15

21.00

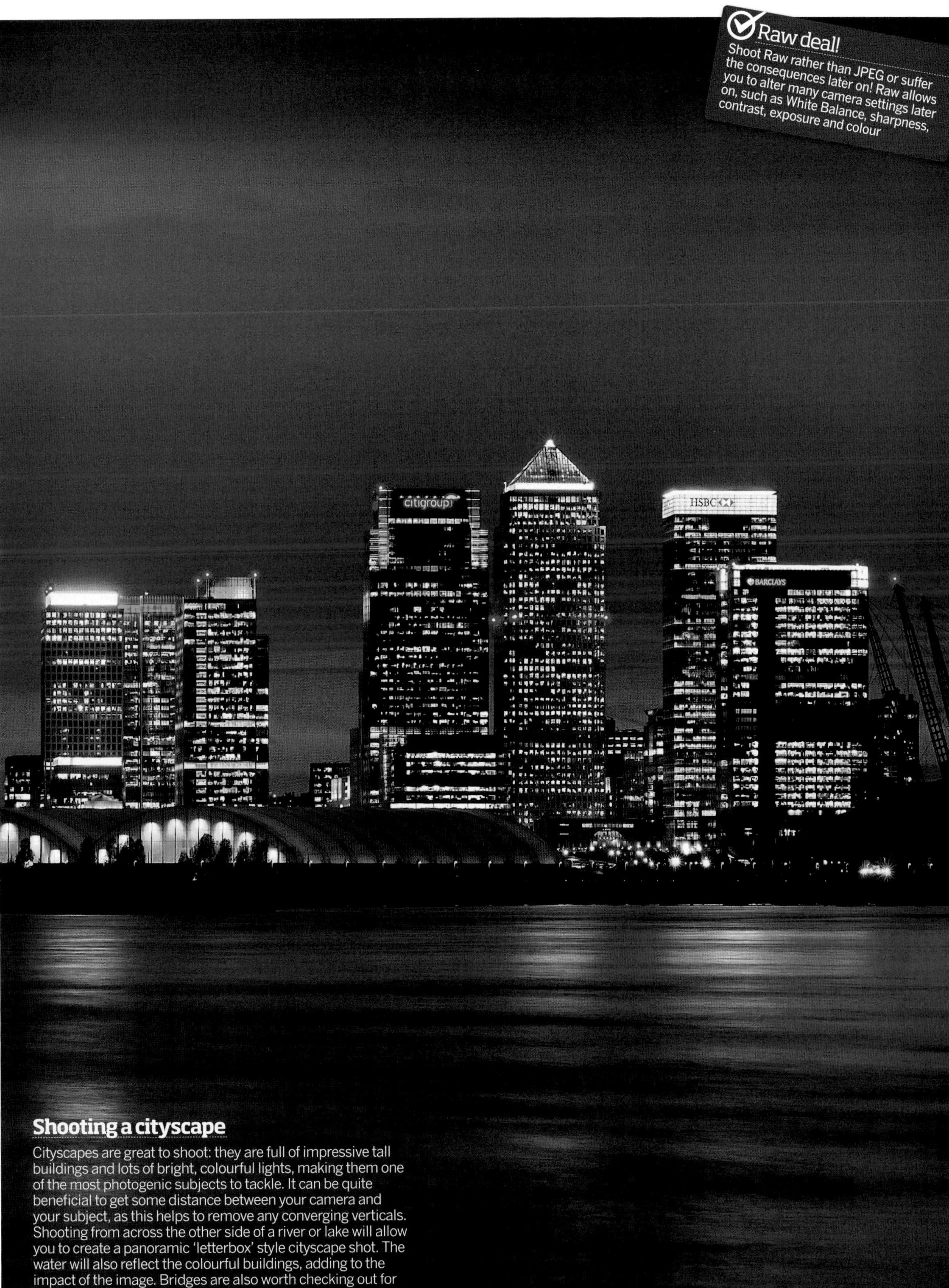

Raw deal!

Shoot Raw rather than JPEG or suffer the consequences later on! Raw allows you to alter many camera settings later on, such as White Balance, sharpness, contrast, exposure and colour

Shooting a cityscape

Cityscapes are great to shoot: they are full of impressive tall buildings and lots of bright, colourful lights, making them one of the most photogenic subjects to tackle. It can be quite beneficial to get some distance between your camera and your subject, as this helps to remove any converging verticals. Shooting from across the other side of a river or lake will allow you to create a panoramic 'letterbox' style cityscape shot. The water will also reflect the colourful buildings, adding to the impact of the image. Bridges are also worth checking out for great vantage points. They very often have a river or busy road running under them which can be successfully used.

ALL IMAGES: TIM GARTSIDE

TIM GARTSIDE

Shoot a street scene

Shooting street scenes and small groups of buildings is a much more intimate affair than shooting a cityscape from across a river. It is not always possible to shoot a town from a distance and be guaranteed to get a good viewpoint, so moving in close is the only option. Although static scenes are great, try adding some action to your shots by introducing movement. Try to get some shots with people in – rush hour is a particularly good time. Alternatively, cars, buses and trains can add extra impact. Try shooting from a bridge looking down onto a busy road and use a long shutter speed of several seconds to blur the traffic trails.

It is possible to experiment with quite a few different focal lengths and get results that are quite different. Wide-angles allow you to include a lot of foreground and allow you to move in close to shoot one building. Converging verticals may be a problem but rather than trying to fix them, use them to create dynamic angles. Telephotos are useful as they allow you to move back and keep verticals correct, if there is enough space.

Turn down noise!

With shutter speeds of 30 seconds or more, image sensors begin to generate increased levels of noise. Your camera's long exposure NR (Noise Reduction) facility can reduce its effects but take care as it can soften results

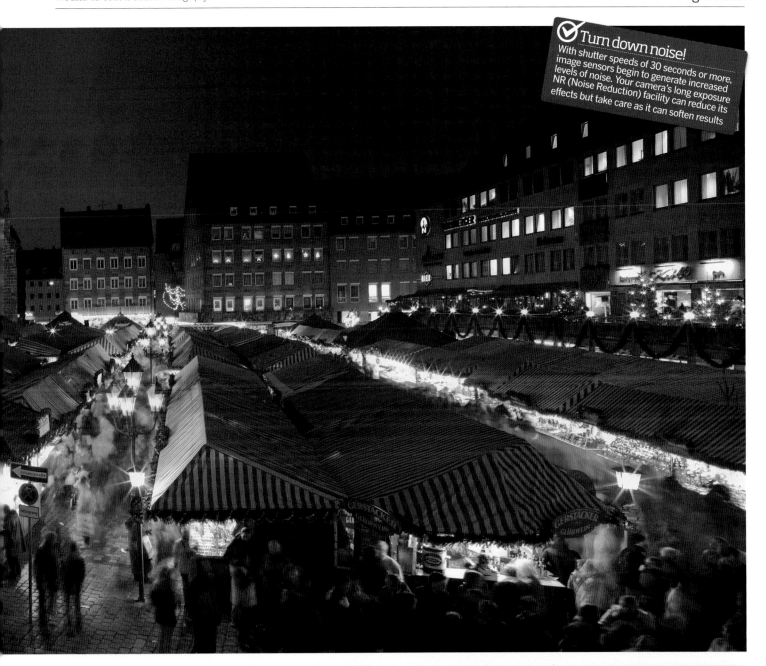

Problems associated with night photography

✗ FLARE: Flare is a major concern, so keep checking images on your LCD monitor for any problems. It is best to zoom in on the image and carefully check for flare as it can cause very subtle loss of contrast that is difficult to see at first glance. Flare is caused by light scattering inside the lens during the exposure. It is usually a strong light source just outside the frame that causes the problem, so look out for things like a lamp-post or neon sign. You will often have to recompose your shot and move slightly to eliminate this problem. For more serious flare a black card or even your hand placed between your lens and the light source should do the trick. It can be a tricky technique to master as the card must remain relatively still during the long exposure.

✗ BRIGHT HOTSPOTS: Burnt-out windows and other bright lights like lamp-posts can be problematic, particularly if in the foreground. If you must include bright lights in your shot, try shooting them at the beginning of the crossover period. Their impact will be lessened considerably as your exposures will be much shorter. The longer your exposure the more brightly-lit areas will blow out and there comes a point where your exposures are so long that such bright areas flare uncontrollably and ruin the shot. The only ways around this are to shoot several different exposures and merge them later, make the lights smaller in the frame or exclude them from the composition.

TIM GARTSIDE

FLARE & HOTSPOTS Scenes like this can cause problems. Ensure your lens optics are spotless to help avoid flare ruining the image.

Get creative: Traffic trails

New to night photography and want to practise your techniques? Then head to a main road near you and set your digital camera on a tripod

FOR ANYONE LOOKING TO DEVELOP their skills at night photography, there are few subjects as accessible and relatively straightforward to photograph as traffic trails. The technique behind it is simple: you set up your camera so that it's aimed at a road and you fire a long exposure while the traffic zooms by. The aim is to capture the lights from the passing traffic as streaks of white (headlights) and red (tail lights). It's one of the easiest night techniques that you can try, so you should really give it a go.

Set your camera on a tripod and compose the scene so that the road is prominent in the frame. You then have a choice of which exposure mode to use. We'd recommend you select manual (M), rate the ISO at 100-200 and set a mid-aperture like f/8 or f/11 to give the optimum quality. Then, it's simply a case of deciding how long you'd like the exposure to be. You can set particular shutter speeds, or you can set Bulb and use whatever length of exposure you like. We'd suggest you shoot in sequences that increase/decrease in one-stop intervals eg 2 secs, 4 secs, 8 secs, 15 secs etc, as you can compare the results on the LCD monitor and determine which works best. Bear in mind that the speed of the traffic will greatly influence this – slow-moving vehicles will produce shorter trails than traffic moving at speed. You should also consider different viewpoints to shoot traffic trails from. While setting up the camera at normal working heights is an obvious start, you should also try shooting from a higher vantage point (eg the upper floor of a building, or a footbridge) as well as getting down low to make it appear as if trails are streaking through the air. Our step-by-step below provides a beginner-style approach to trying out traffic trails.

White Balance

Shooting at night is going to give you strong colour casts. Our advice is to leave your DSLR set to AWB and shoot Raw, then tweak colours once you've downloaded images on to your computer

Set-up

Test shot

1 BEANBAG TEST This test shot was taken with the camera resting on a beanbag on the railings. As you can see, the vibration of the traffic has travelled through the railings and beanbag and caused serious camera shake. There is no doubt that you can't beat the trusty tripod.

Four seconds

2 FOUR SECOND EXPOSURE The first of our shutter speed sequence is a four second exposure. A quick review of the LCD monitor shows that when shooting cars within a 40mph speed limit, we're going to need much longer exposure times to capture traffic trails that extend through the entire frame.

Final image

When you've got some experience with shooting traffic trails, look for unusual and striking viewpoints that allow you to produce very striking images where trails provide an added dimension.

PAUL WARD

3 15 SECOND EXPOSURE A much longer exposure time has allowed the traffic trails to extend through the entire frame and the colours of the trails are nice and punchy. The ambient light levels are well controlled too, so there are no burnt out areas of the frame.

4 30 SECOND EXPOSURE While the extra time allows more light trails to be recorded, there is a point where too much light starts to burn out the traffic trails. If this happens, either select a smaller aperture, shorten the exposure time or lower the ISO rating (or combine two or more of these methods).

Painting with light: Flash

Ross Hoddinott shows how any external flashgun can be used to paint subjects with bursts of light

THE WORD PHOTOGRAPHY quite literally means 'painting with light', so it is an apt title for this unusual technique. Painting with light is a method that involves using a long exposure, up to a minute or more, in near or total darkness. Then, whilst the shutter is open, the photographer manually illuminates the subject using an artificial light source – like a flashgun or torchlight. The resulting images have a surreal, atmospheric feel to them, created by the uneven illumination of the artificial light source combined with any ambient light.

At first, the concept of painting with light might sound bizarre, but it is great fun to try and the results can be striking. Also, whilst this technique might rely heavily on trial and error, it is not difficult to attempt. First, you need to identify a suitable subject. Practically anything can work, big or small. However, larger subjects, like trees and buildings, often create the most eye-catching results. Old ruins, dilapidated buildings and – if you're not easily spooked – gravestones work especially well.

The technique relies on it being dark. However, arrive at your location while it is still light, so you can easily compose your shot. This will also help you familiarise yourself with your surroundings – after all, you will be wandering around in the dark and don't want to be tripping over. Whilst it can be tempting to begin shooting immediately after sundown, don't – if there is too much ambient light, the effect of your torch or flashgun will be diluted and ineffective. Instead, wait patiently until it is sufficiently dark, remembering to wrap up warm, and keep a torch with you at all times for safety.

Generally speaking, it is best to shoot around an hour after sundown, when there is still some colour in the sky. There is no set rule regarding the length of exposure required; it is a hit or miss affair. Begin by using a 30 second exposure, combined with a small aperture of f/16 or f/22. However, you may find that the best results are achieved at a minute or longer. To shoot exposure times this long, it will be necessary to employ your camera's Bulb setting. Be prepared to experiment and review images after every frame; you can then adjust settings accordingly. With your camera set up on a sturdy tripod and exposure set, release the shutter using either a remote release or the self-timer. By doing so, you can be in position ready to begin painting. A flashgun is ideal for illuminating larger, outdoor subjects. You will need to fire the flash on full power several times to create a decent exposure. Walk around the subject directing the flash burst toward the areas you want lit. You can emphasise certain regions by giving them repeated flashes. To minimise being recorded in the shot, make sure to wear dark clothing and keep moving as you paint!

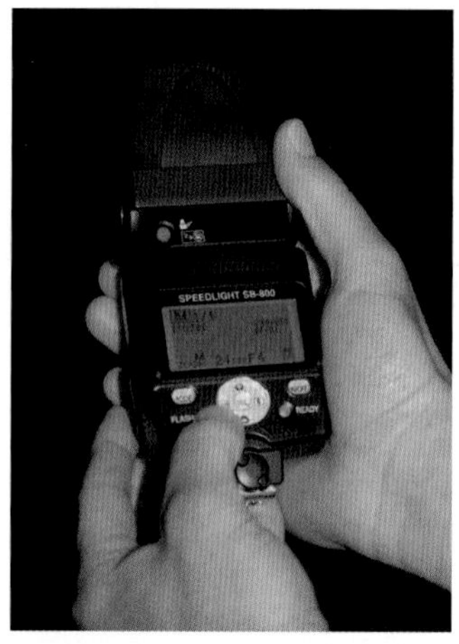

Bulb setting

Most digital cameras usually has a maximum automatic exposure of 30 seconds. For exposures longer than this, the camera needs to be set to Bulb or 'B'. Using this setting, the shutter will remain open for as long as the shutter release button is depressed – either manually or via a remote. The term 'Bulb' refers to old-style pneumatically-actuated shutters – squeezing an air bulb would open the shutter and releasing the bulb would close it again. When using the bulb setting, exposure has to be timed manually, meaning a degree of trial and error is required.

1 The sun might have set, but there is too much ambient light to begin 'painting'. However, it gives me time to set up the camera on a sturdy tripod, arrange composition and take a test shot whilst it's still light.

2 The first attempt was taken using an exposure of 15 seconds. However, this didn't allow sufficient time to allow me to illuminate the ruins of this folly properly and the effect of the flash isn't obvious enough.

Get flashing!

Flashguns can be fired manually by pressing the test button. To paint effectively, it should be fired repeatedly in the direction of your subject. Therefore, insert new batteries beforehand to ensure flash recycle time is rapid, and take along spares

Final image

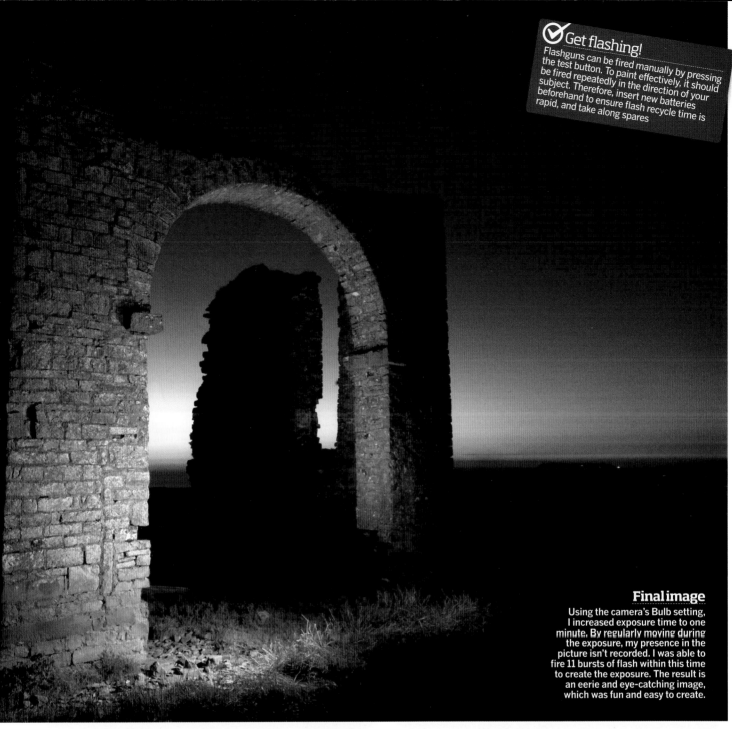

Using the camera's Bulb setting, I increased exposure time to one minute. By regularly moving during the exposure, my presence in the picture isn't recorded. I was able to fire 11 bursts of flash within this time to create the exposure. The result is an eerie and eye-catching image, which was fun and easy to create.

3 An exposure of 30 seconds allowed time for twice as many flash bursts as the previous image. The folly is far better illuminated, but by remaining still in one position, my outline has accidentally been recorded.

4 Achieving the correct exposure is hit and miss. Although now an hour after sundown, the light is still growing steadily darker. This affects exposure time so if you don't adjust regularly, images may underexpose.

Put your subject in the spotlight

MARK BAUER: Dull weather and a lack of light are no excuse to pack up your camera gear and leave a perfectly good landscape behind. Go equipped with your own light source and you won't miss a shot. A powerful torch, for instance, can shed some light during a long exposure on subjects that would otherwise be too dark for a camera to record well, thus making them stand out from a night scene. The colour contrast between the cool ambient light and the torch's warm light can also add impact. So, with this in mind, on a dull evening, I took a trip to Poole Harbour in Dorset to try out this technique on the boats on the sand at low tide.

Get ready!

TIME REQUIRED
30 MINUTES

EQUIPMENT NEEDED
CANON EOS 5D MKII & ZEISS 21MM F/2.8

EQUIPMENT NEEDED
A TWO-MILLION 'CANDLE-POWER' TORCH, TRIPOD & REMOTE RELEASE

Shed some light on the matter!

It's surprising how many different types of torches there are, and some are better suited to this technique than others. The brightness of torches is often expressed in 'candelas' or 'candle power'. If you're painting a large object, such as a building, you might want to use a more powerful torch, perhaps one that's ten million candle power. The type of bulb is important too as they have different colour temperatures altering your White Balance – another reason why it's best to shoot in Raw.

1 First, I tried to find the right boat. After a couple of test shots, I realised I needed a boat that wasn't too tatty and that leaned towards the camera. While this boat had the streetlights of Sandbanks twinkling in the background, the boat wasn't particularly photogenic or at the best angle. It was a little too early in the evening too as everything was grey – I waited until it got darker.

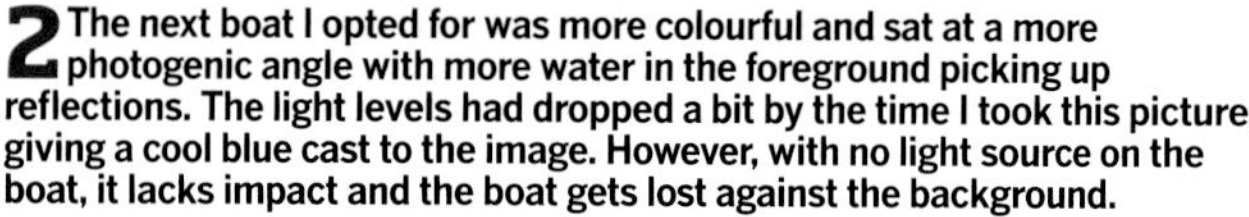

2 The next boat I opted for was more colourful and sat at a more photogenic angle with more water in the foreground picking up reflections. The light levels had dropped a bit by the time I took this picture, giving a cool blue cast to the image. However, with no light source on the boat, it lacks impact and the boat gets lost against the background.

3 I took a spot meter reading from the sky so it would record as a mid-tone. My initial settings were ISO 100 and f/16, which resulted in an exposure of 24 minutes! This was way too long and increased the risk of the tripod sinking into the wet sand and ruining the shot. So I increased ISO to 200 and set f/8, then, using the Bulb setting, set an exposure of three minutes.

Final image

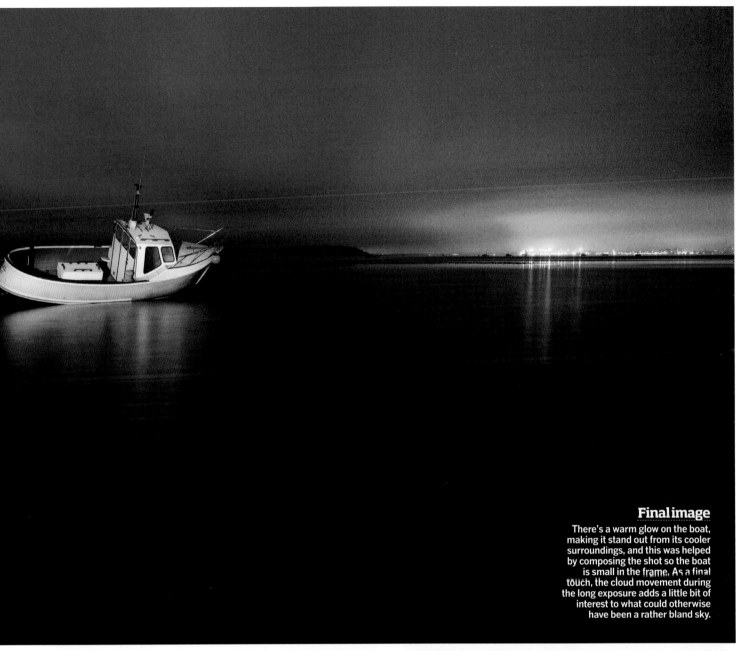

There's a warm glow on the boat, making it stand out from its cooler surroundings, and this was helped by composing the shot so the boat is small in the frame. As a final touch, the cloud movement during the long exposure adds a little bit of interest to what could otherwise have been a rather bland sky.

4 I then started painting the boat with light. How long you need to do this for depends on several factors: how powerful your torch is, how close you are to the subject you're illuminating and how reflective the subject is. I kept the beam of the torch moving during the exposure, while I stood out of frame, making sure that I lit the boat evenly.

5 Getting the right amount of light on the boat was a matter of trial and error. As you can see from the review image on the LCD monitor, I overcooked this one by shining the torch on the boat for around two minutes during a three-minute exposure. I reshot, this time 'painting' the boat for 90 seconds – probably a good starting point for most images of this type.

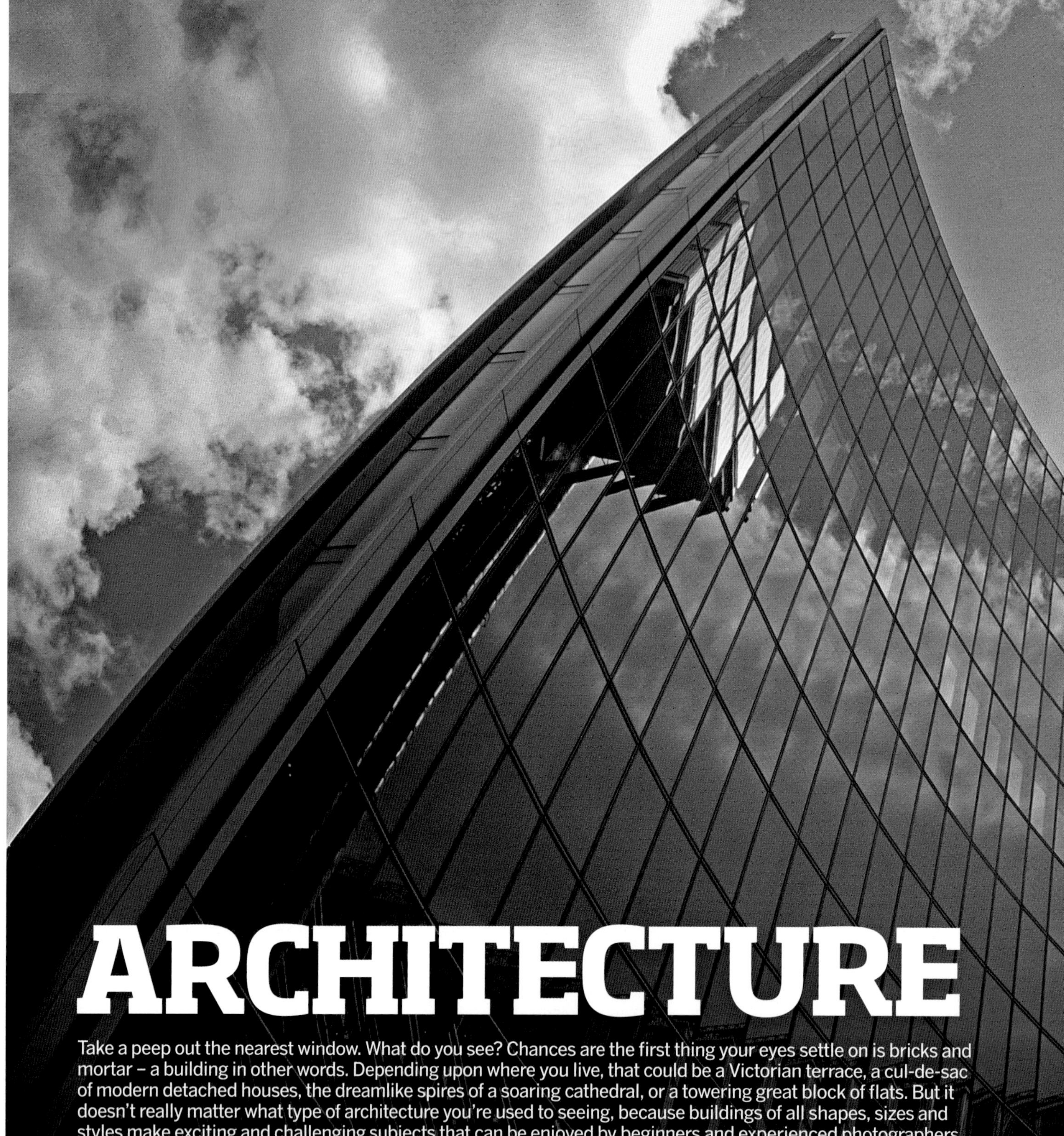

ARCHITECTURE

Take a peep out the nearest window. What do you see? Chances are the first thing your eyes settle on is bricks and mortar – a building in other words. Depending upon where you live, that could be a Victorian terrace, a cul-de-sac of modern detached houses, the dreamlike spires of a soaring cathedral, or a towering great block of flats. But it doesn't really matter what type of architecture you're used to seeing, because buildings of all shapes, sizes and styles make exciting and challenging subjects that can be enjoyed by beginners and experienced photographers alike. From crumbling castles and magnificent cathedrals to state-of-the-art skyscrapers, suitable subjects can be found literally everywhere you go. Even better, you don't need the communication skills of a portrait photographer, the expert knowledge of a nature photographer, or the lightning-quick reflexes of an action photographer to make the most of them – just an appreciation of light and composition, a little patience and lots of imagination.

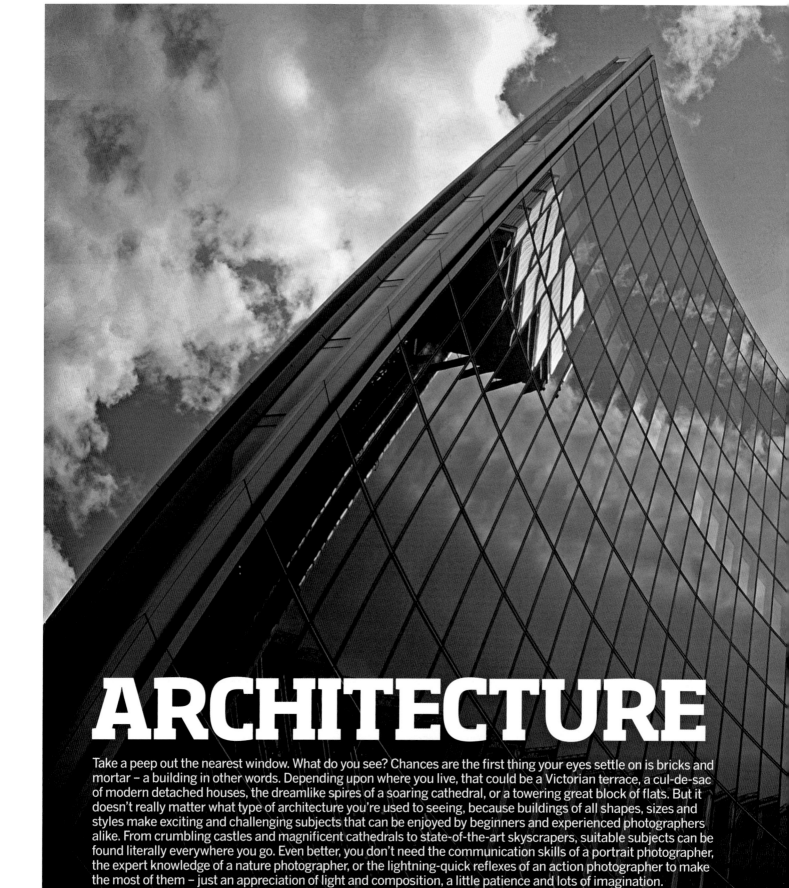

ISTOCK PHOTO

Building blocks to success

Buildings come in all shapes and forms, and make for very interesting subjects. Our expert advice will help you capture them at their best

ARCHITECTURE IS AN ART FORM, and the more creative architects are artists, designing buildings that will not only survive for centuries but still make people gasp in awe and delight. We take ancient buildings like cathedrals and castles for granted because they've always been there, but there was a time when they were new and at the cutting edge of architectural style, in the way that amazing structures like London's 'Gherkin' are today. Imagine how people will perceive them in 200 years – assuming they're still standing – and how architecture will change over the next two centuries given the advances made over the last two. When you photograph a building, you're celebrating the individual who designed it, so rather than just snap away, think how you can capture it to bring out its character.

The viewpoint you shoot from can make all the difference, so always spend a little time looking at the building from different positions and angles until you find the most successful one.

Pay particular attention to rivers, streams and ponds, which may feature an interesting reflection of the building that you could use as foreground interest. Trees can be used to frame the building and fill out unwanted sky or hide ugly details such as parked cars, lamp posts and other features you'd rather not include, while flower beds, paths, hedges and gardens can be used to add interest to the foreground.

Professional architectural photographers put a lot of effort into this planning and groundwork so they can get the best possible pictures. You should do the same, by asking around to see if there are any interesting viewpoints available.

Wherever you're shooting, look for alternative angles, especially if the subject building is popular with photographers. Holes in walls, a gap between other nearby buildings – things like this can give your pictures an unusual twist. Alternative viewpoints also work well – get really high off the ground if possible by heading to the top of a multi-storey car park, or get down low, perhaps shooting from ground level with a wide-angle lens to exaggerate converging verticals and produce powerful compositions.

ISTOCK PHOTO

CAPTURE THE ENVIRONMENT: Taking a wider shot can place your building in context. This can work well with a lone building, such as this lighthouse.

ISTOCK PHOTO

CONSIDER THE VIEWPOINT: Keep an eye to the ground when walking around urban areas because you may well find inspiration literally at your feet.

One factor to bear in mind is that city centres are much quieter on weekends because all the offices are closed. This makes it much easier to take pictures without people or traffic getting in the way, though it also means you won't be able to enter any of the buildings to gain a better view, as the vast majority will be closed. Another reason for shooting at weekends is you're less likely to be hassled by security. Thanks to the rise in global terrorism, it's getting harder and harder to use tripods in our city streets without being approached and asked to move on.

Ideal kit for architecture

While there are specialist lenses developed for architectural photography, the truth is that you can get great results using a modest outfit. In built-up areas your choice of viewpoint may be restricted due to the close proximity of other buildings, traffic, street furniture and so on, in which case you will have to make the most of what you've got – a wide-angle lens is ideal as it allows you to shoot from close range. The wide end of your standard 18-55mm kit lens may be suitable, although an ultra-wide zoom like an 11-18mm is far better. It's also the perfect choice when shooting interiors, where you may need to work in tight spaces. A telezoom like a 55-200mm is perfect for tight shots of detail, or when you want to back off to compress perspective. The other essential accessory is a tripod, which allows for careful composition as well as shooting in low light.

Buildings don't have to be the main subject – they can occupy a small part of the image area, acting as a focal point. Showing a building as part of a wider view is worth it when its environment is significant to its story. For example, if a lighthouse is perched on rocky coastline, it will look far more impressive when captured in its environment, complete with waves washing over the shore, than if you were to move in close and exclude all traces of its surroundings. Including the surrounding environment adds a sense of context to the shot.

Correcting converging verticals

If you photograph a building from close range, using a wide-angle lens, you might get 'converging verticals' (where vertical lines appear to lean inwards). To avoid this, keep your camera back parallel with the subject, but if you do this you will usually find that the top of the building is cut off and you end-up with lots of unwanted foreground.

Perspective control or 'shift' lenses can be used to overcome this because they have an adjustable front section – all you do is compose the shot with the camera level and square, then move the front of the lens up until the top of the building is included. Shift lenses are expensive, so use in-camera techniques or Photoshop as a cheaper alternative. Below is a short step-by-step to correcting converging verticals in Photoshop.

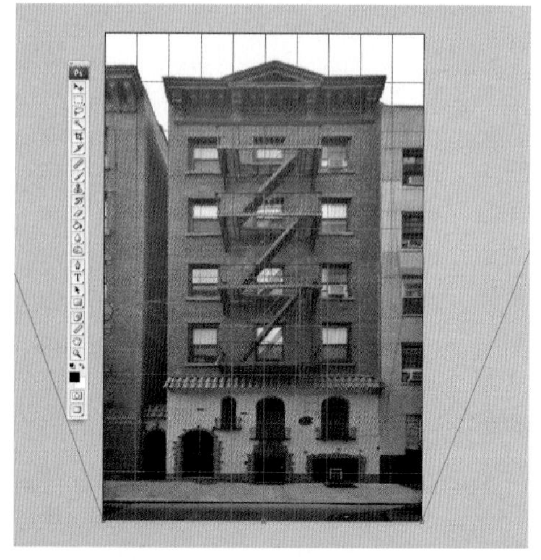

Step 1. Open your image in Photoshop then choose ***Select All*** to place a dashed line around it.
Step 2. Go to ***View>Show>Grid*** to display a grid over the image, which will aid the correction process.
Step 3. Go to ***Edit>Transform>Distort***, then drag the top left corner of the picture out to the left until that side of the picture begins to straighten, then repeat for the right side. Step 4. Hit Return to process the transformation then turn off the grid by going to ***View>Show>Grid***. Step 5. If the image looks squat, select ***Image>Image Size***, uncheck the Constrain Proportions box and increase the height of the image by 5-10%.

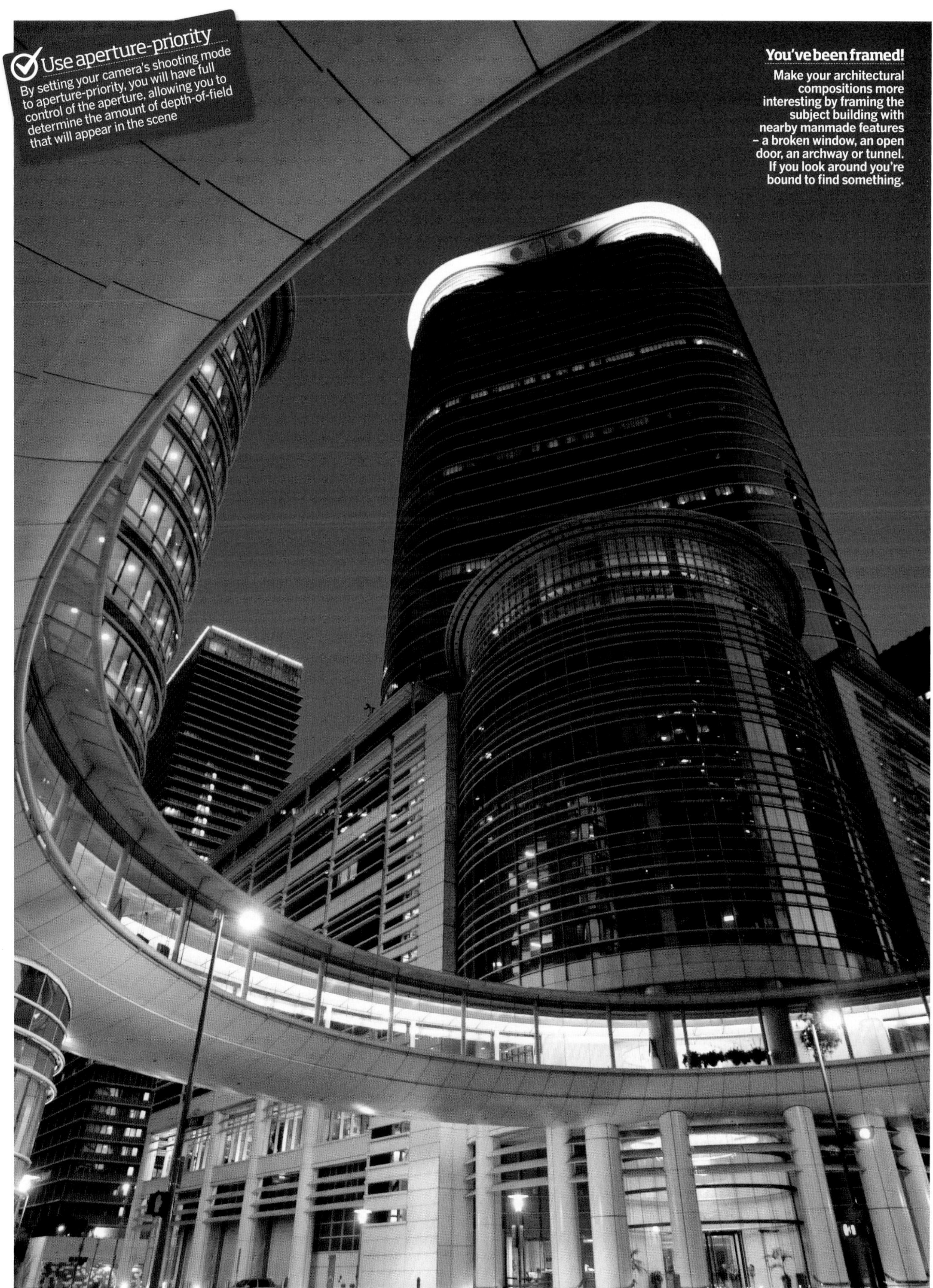

Use aperture-priority

By setting your camera's shooting mode to aperture-priority, you will have full control of the aperture, allowing you to determine the amount of depth-of-field that will appear in the scene

You've been framed!

Make your architectural compositions more interesting by framing the subject building with nearby manmade features – a broken window, an open door, an archway or tunnel. If you look around you're bound to find something.

ISTOCK PHOTO

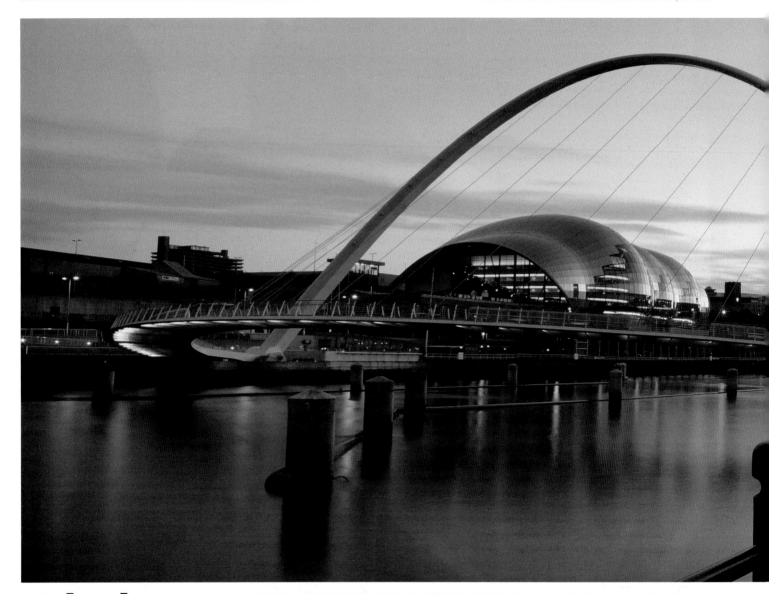

Make the most of light

Planning your shoots is vital as the time of day and the sun's angle play a vital role in architecture shots

QUALITY OF LIGHT is vitally important when shooting architecture because it not only helps to define the physical shape of a building, but also its character. The best time of day to photograph a particular building depends upon its aspect – the direction in which it faces – as this will determine whether or not it's in shadow. Buildings that face east will be lit in the morning, while west-facing facades will be at their best in the afternoon and a southerly aspect will receive light through most of the day. If you're lucky, the light may be perfect when you arrive, but often you'll have to wait for a while, or return the next day either earlier or later, to catch it at its best.

Warm light from a low sun enhances the mellow stonework or worn brickwork of old buildings, while side-lighting reveals texture in the coarse surface of the masonry. If you want to shoot churches, castles, cottages or other types of old building, early morning or late afternoon are generally regarded as the best times of day.

Modern architecture can look more dynamic when it's bathed in bright sunlight against a clear blue sky, as this heightens the graphic shapes and bold lines of the subject building. For the best results, use a polarising filter to deepen the sky, remove reflections from non-metallic surfaces such as windows and make the building stand out more boldly. The same applies when photographing whitewashed buildings, of the type you see in Mediterranean countries such as Spain and Greece – the stark whiteness will be enhanced if it's captured against a rich blue sky.

Dusk is another great time to photograph modern architecture and grand cityscapes. Once the sun has set, the sky turns into a huge softbox and produces soft light suffused with pastel colours, which are mirrored brilliantly by glass-fronted buildings. Midday generally isn't the best time to shoot unless you're going for an abstract effect – the light is too contrasty and lacks character. However, in built-up urban areas, you may have no choice but to shoot at midday, as at any other time the building you want to shoot might be shadowed by nearby buildings.

Shadows can also be a problem when photographing street scenes in the morning or afternoon, with the sun to one side of the camera. It's not uncommon for one half of a street to be bathed in sunlight, while the other half is shaded. In such situations you could wait

LEE FROST

Deal with harsh light!
If you're shooting in harsh lighting conditions, use your camera's spot or partial meter and lock a reading from an a mid-toned subject, such as a grey pavement or some brown brickwork

ISTOCK PHOTO

SHOOT SILHOUETTES: Buildings, landmarks and monuments look great when captured in silhouette because it really emphasises their bold shape. Aim to shoot at sunrise and at sunset as the colourful sky forms a dramatic backdrop.

until the whole scene is in shadow, and the contrast reduced, but a more practical option is to use a Neutral Density graduated filter at an angle, so it covers the sunlit part of the scene and you can give more exposure to the shady area to get an even exposure throughout the scene.

Alternatively, take two shots – one exposing for the shadow side of the scene, and one for the sunlit side – then combine them using HDR software such as Photomatix Pro, or Photoshop.

Buildings at night

Many buildings are floodlit at night, giving you the chance to take totally different pictures that are full of vivid colours, created by the mixed artificial lighting. The best time to shoot this is during the cross-over period between sunset and nightfall when there's still colour in the sky but ambient light levels have dropped sufficiently for the artificial lighting to be clearly visible. Exposure times can run into seconds, so you'll need a sturdy tripod to steady the camera and remote release (or self-timer) to trip the shutter. Start out with your camera set to Auto White Balance (AWB) but don't be afraid to experiment with other presets for some unusual results. In terms of exposure, shoot using aperture-priority and multi-zone metering. Keep the ISO low for optimum image quality – with your camera on a tripod there's no need to shoot any higher than ISO 100 or 200. As well as floodlit buildings, also photograph neon signs outside clubs, bars and tourist attractions, and add foreground interest to town and cityscapes by shooting near busy roads, so passing traffic records as light trails.

LIGHT UP: Waiting for the light to fade and the building lights to come on can really transform an image, even on an overcast day.

Bridges & structures

Don't restrict your pursuit of great architectural images to buildings – other structures are worth shooting too

ARCHITECTURAL PHOTOGRAPHY doesn't just include buildings – any structure from bridges and piers, statues and monuments to fountains and follies counts, so don't be afraid to cast your creative net a little wider than normal – you could be very surprised by the images that result.

Road and rail bridges make fantastic subjects, simply because they're so big and bold. Old bridges like the famous Tyne Bridge in Newcastle-upon-Tyne or the Forth Rail Bridge in Edinburgh are incredibly photogenic, thanks to their graceful shape, while modern bridges, such as the Millennium Bridge across the Thames in London or the suspension bridge at Salford Quays in Manchester, have a fantastic sci-fi look about them. There are no hard and fast rules when it comes to photographing bridges, as each has to be shot on its own merits. For some, shooting from a distance with a telezoom lens will be the best option, while with others, a wide-angle lens from close range will work better. In many cases, you could go to both extremes, and try everything in between too!

Shoot at dawn or dusk, to capture the structure against a colourful sky, or wait until the sun has gone down and colourful man-made illuminations take over; but don't avoid the middle of the day – when the sun is high and the light harsh, you can produce some amazingly graphic images, not only of the whole structure, but the details as well. And, if the bridge crosses water, the addition of reflections can give your compositions a real boost.

Piers hold a similar appeal. You can shoot them side-on from the beach; you can shoot down the pier itself, to make a feature of the converging lines created by the railing and floorboards, creating striking compositions that make good use of perspective; or why not get underneath the pier and concentrate on the criss-crossing of the legs and beams supporting it?

As well as capturing the whole structure with a wide-angle lens, also look for interesting patterns and details. Pleasure piers often have a funfair at the end, for example. Repetition is a common theme in all piers too – in the shelters that often run down the centre, the rows of ornate lamps and the deckchairs fluttering in the breeze. Dawn and dusk are the most atmospheric times of day to photograph piers. Dawn is especially good because there will be very few people around to spoil your shots, while in the evening, artificial illumination will add colour and interest to the scene.

One technique you must try is to take a long exposure of 30 seconds or more to blur the motion of the sea, so the pier stands out in stark 3D – again, this is easiest to achieve at dawn or dusk when light levels are low.

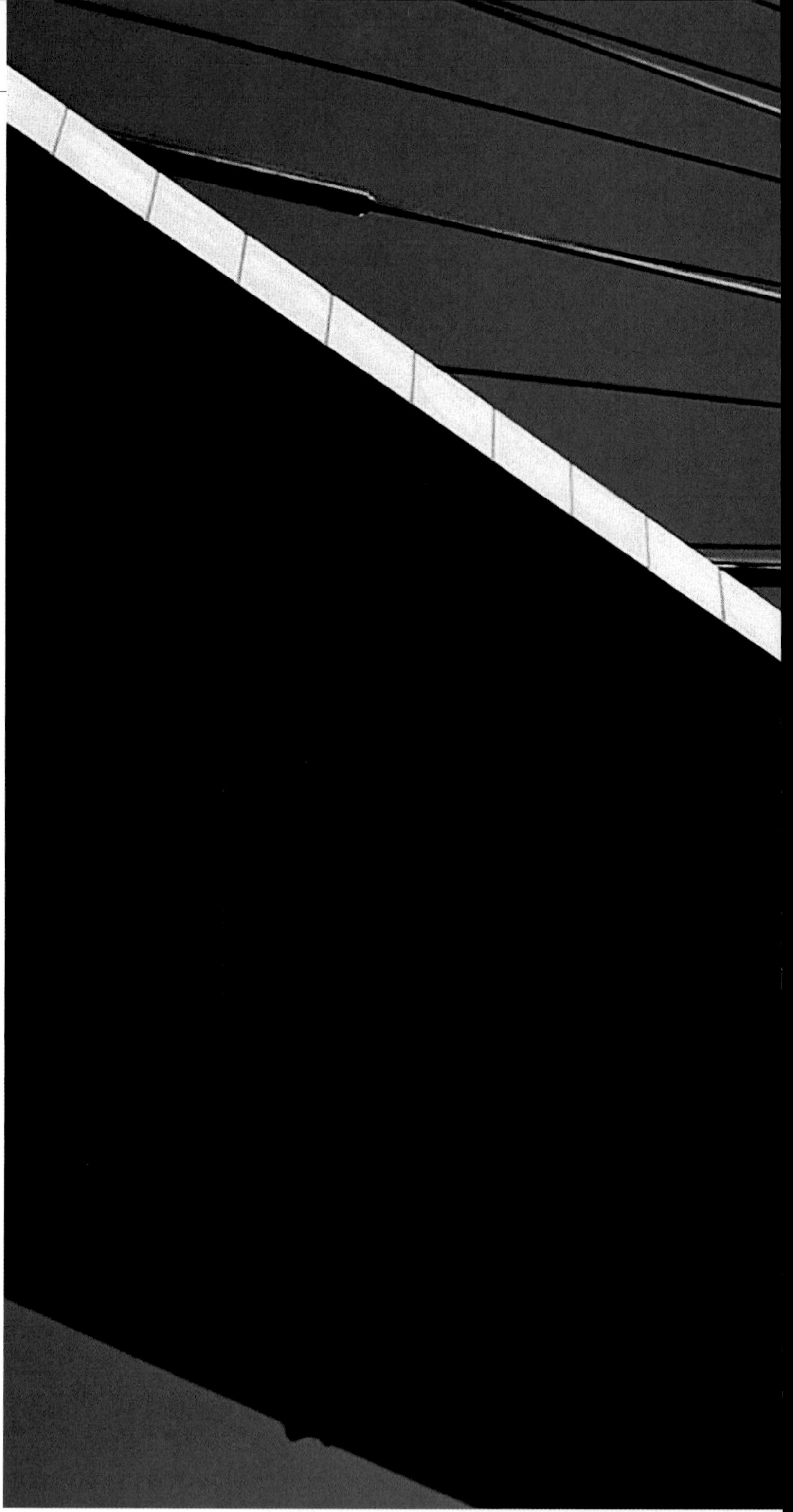

Mirror images

LEE FROST

Bridges and piers usually boast a symmetrical design, so why not take advantage of this and create eye-catching mirror images? Here's how... Standing in the centre, look down your subject's structure and take a shot. Once the image is downloaded to your computer, crop the image down the central line, so only one half of the original image remains (the well-lit half). Next, make a copy of the image and flip it over by going to *Image>Rotate Canvas>Flip Horizontal*. On the original cropped image, go to *Image>Canvas Size* and double the width of the canvas in the direction you intend to add the reflection to. Then, select the Move tool in your toolbar, now click and drag the flipped image onto the enlarged canvas. The final stage is to carefully move the flipped image until it joins up with the image on the extended canvas and you'll have a perfect mirror image!

ABOVE: Create stilt-like legs by getting low and close to subjects with an ultra-wide zoom. A bright sunny day can help add a graphical contrast to the shot.

FROM LEFT TO RIGHT: Statues can have huge impact when shot from below, against an interesting sky. Getting underneath a pier can reveal some interesting patterns and shapes, either with the pillars or in the details. Use structures as silhouettes and try adding people to give a sense of scale.

ISTOCK PHOTO

Success with LiveView

By using the LiveView facility rather than the viewfinder, you'll be able to preview the changes to the focus and aperture, allowing for more control over the depth-of-field (area of sharp focus)

ISTOCK PHOTO

LEE FROST

ISTOCK PHOTO

FILTERS

No other accessory offers more creative possibilities for making the most of your camera than the humble filter

We're all aware that digital cameras are a great way of capturing wonderful images, but many are still oblivious or unsure of how filters can dramatically improve results. Take a look at the work of established photographers and you'll see most have used filters like polarisers or ND Grads to capture the best possible results. In this section, we cover the main filter formats, which types of filters you'll find most useful and explain how you should use them

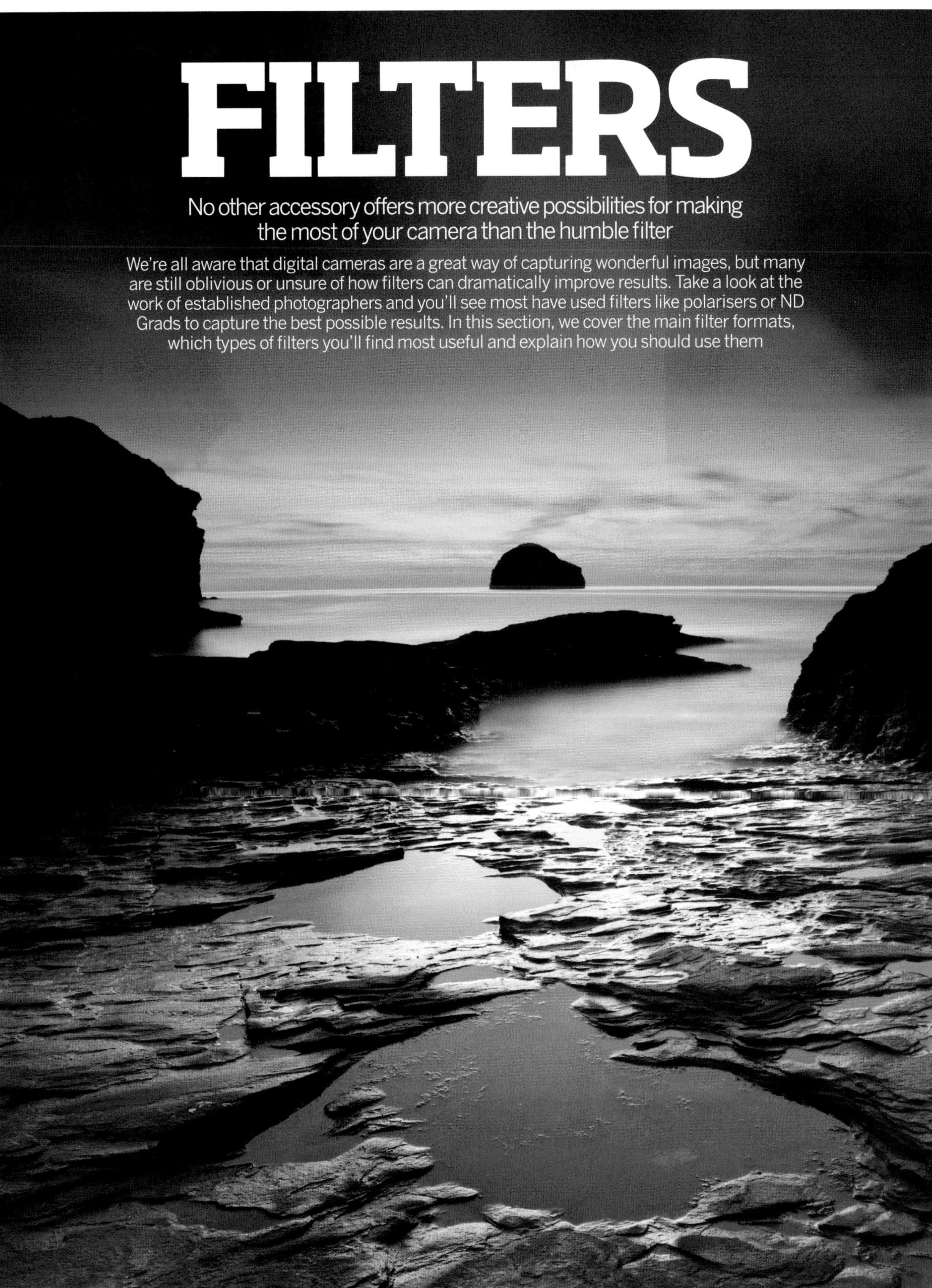

ROSS HODDINOTT

Filter systems

Filters have long been the simplest and most inexpensive way to improve or alter your images in-camera. Even in the digital age, they have their place in every photographer's kit bag. We explain the main types of filter systems, our recommended filter types and the major brands to consider...

THE WORTH OF FILTERS, now that we have Photoshop, is a topic that still divides opinion amongst amateur photographers. But for those that like to get it right in-camera, filters are still invaluable tools, in particular with outdoor photographers.

While some filters can give an image a colour cast, other popular types are neutral in tone and instead enable photographers to balance bright and dark areas of a scene, or have more scope for their choice of apertures and shutter speeds. There are many different uses for filters to suit all types of photography and in this section, we help you decide which types of filter, as well as what filter system, is right for your photographic needs.

Filters come in two main types: screw-in, which attach directly to the filter thread at the front of your lens barrel; and slot-in, which slip into a holder held in place on the front of your lens by adapter rings screwed on to the filter thread. Both have their pros and cons, which you should consider before deciding which to buy. As you'll no doubt discover as you read on, a combination of both types is often the best solution for most photographers.

Screw-in filters

These are quick and easy to attach and remove from your lens, so are a very convenient choice. As they're made from glass, they are of high optical quality and more difficult to scratch. Screw-in filters come in various sizes, with 52mm to 77mm being the most common. If you own a number of lenses, each with different filter threads, you will either need a filter in each size or take the more affordable option of a stepping ring (see tip below). Another negative point worth considering is that grad filters aren't well suited for use as a screw-in, which will be off-putting for landscape photographers in particular. You also need to take care when using more than one screw-in filter at a time, as you run the risk of vignetting (darkening at the image corners), especially with wide-angle lenses. Another disadvantage is that occasionally you may find a filter won't budge, in which case you'll need a filter clamp to help remove it.

TOP TIP: STEPPING RINGS
A cheaper option than buying the same type of filter in various sizes is to buy the largest size you need and a step-down ring, which allows you to fit a large filter on a smaller thread. For instance, if you have a 72mm filter and buy a 72-67 ring, you can screw the filter to the ring, which attaches easily to the lens. Don't go for a step-up ring for attaching smaller filters to larger lenses, as these can cause vignetting.

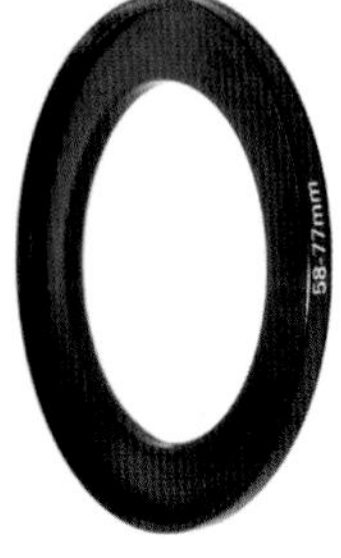

Slot-in filters

With these systems, you only need to buy one filter even if you have several lenses of different sizes. This is because the filter slips into a holder, which attaches to the lens via an adapter ring. So, instead of needing costly screw-ins in various sizes, you can simply buy affordable adapter rings in the sizes you need and swap the holder between them. It does mean the initial investment is higher but over time, it proves to be far more economical, especially if you have several lenses. You'll find there is an extensive range of filters available, in particular graduates, but if you're a macro enthusiast, you'll need to look to screw-ins for close-up filters. Unlike screw-in filters, slot-in filters are made from optical resin, which is incredibly tough and lighter than glass, although more prone to scratches. Optically, they offer excellent quality, with little discernible difference in quality to screw-ins.
For the ultimate quality, look at pro-brand filters such as Lee Filters, which use the very best materials.

TOP TIP: COMPATIBILITY
You'll find most brands make more than one size of slot-in system to suit different types of DSLRs. The standard size is 67mm but if you have wide-angle lenses, we'd recommend you consider the 85mm or 100mm formats. Note that as these sizes are standard, similarly sized holders will accept filters from other brands.

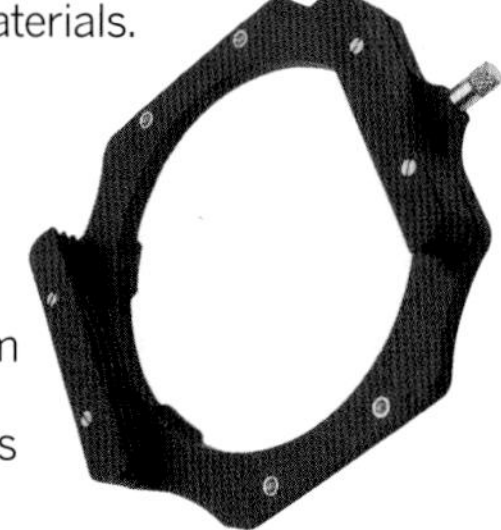

How to use slot-in filters

1) Screw in the appropriate adapter ring

2) Attach the filter holder to the adapter ring

3) Slide in the filter and start shooting!

Don't want to fork out for a system holder? No problem. There are two alternatives

1) USE *BLU-TAC* A favourite trick of the trade with the pros, this is a fast and effective method if you don't want to fumble with the holder. It's worth keeping a lens cleaning fluid and cloth in your gadget bag to clean up the filter after use, although you'll find Blu-tac leaves very little mess in practice!

2) HOLD THE FILTER Simply holding the filter in place is good for most filters, though keeping a grad level and at the right height is difficult and, when using long exposures, there's a chance of knocking the camera and ruining your image. Works best if your camera is tripod-mounted.

Filter factors

The amount of light a filter absorbs and allows through varies and is indicated by its filter factor. Your camera's metering automatically compensates, but it's worth noting the filter factor, as it will affect the choice of apertures and shutter speeds available to you. Our table provides an easy reference guide.

Filter	Filter Factor	Number of stops
UV	1	0
82C	1.5	2/3
1B Sky	1	0
ND 0.3	2	1
ND 0.6	4	2
ND 0.9	8	3
Polariser	4	2

Need protection?

It's advisable to leave a UV or Skylight filter attached to your lens to prevent your front element being damaged. Both the Skylight and UV filter subtly reduce the effects of UV, with the pinkish tint of a Skylight also reducing blue light on sunny days. Alternatively, you could fit a clear protective filter.

Problems with vignetting

Vignetting refers to the effect of dark shading at the corners of the frame and is more prominent in wide-angle lenses. It's caused by the lens's field-of-view being obstructed at the edges of the frame, for example using multiple screw-in filters or if a hood is fitted on top of a filter. If you're using a wide-angle or the wide-angle end of a zoom, check for vignetting via the viewfinder or review screen. It's normally not obvious at wide apertures, so set the aperture you plan to shoot at, then use the depth-of-field preview facility (if your camera has it) to check for dark corners.

The easiest ways to avoid vignetting are:

- ✔ Avoid using more than one screw-in filter at the same time.
- ✔ **Don't use a hood with filters attached**
- ✔ Use a suitable square filter system
- ✔ **Buy a step-up filter ring**

Screw in filters

Guide prices for popular brands

	UV	Polariser	ND
B+W			
52mm	£32	£68	£22
55mm	£32	£77	£25
58mm	£35	£79	£25
62mm	£38	£83	£28
67mm	£45	£99	£35
72mm	£53	£114	£40
77mm	£70	£129	£55
Hoya			
52mm	£16	£35	£20
55mm	£18	£40	£30
58mm	£20	£45	£35
62mm	£27	£50	£35
67mm	£34	£55	£40
72mm	£40	£60	£55
77mm	£45	£65	£65
Jessops			
52mm	£15	£32	-
55mm	£16	£34	-
58mm	£20	£38	-
62mm	£20	£44	-
67mm	£26	£52	-
72mm	£32	£54	-
77mm	£36	£62	-
Kood			
52mm	£8	£18	£12
55mm	£8	£21	£13
58mm	£8	£22	£15
62mm	£9	£30	£15
67mm	£9	£30	£19
72mm	£10	£36	£28
77mm	£12	£38	£29
Tiffen			
52mm	£12	£30	£23
55mm	£12	£30	£25
58mm	£15	£35	£30
62mm	£15	£40	£30
67mm	£18	£45	£35
72mm	£25	£55	£50
77mm	£25	£60	£50

Filter brands

There aren't too many brands of filter but the choice they offer can be confusing. We've highlighted the tried and tested filter brands that offer great value as well as high-quality products

B+W

www.daymen.co.uk

This prestigious German brand is renowned for producing screw-in filters with optimum quality, both in terms of the metal filter ring and the manufacturing process behind its premium optical glass. It's a very popular brand with pros but it does cost around twice as much as other brands. If you need the ultimate in quality from a screw-in filter, then B+W is the option for you, otherwise, Hoya is a great choice. One string in its bow is the ten-stop ND filter, which has proved incredibly popular for daytime long-exposure photography.

Hoya

www.intro2020.co.uk

Hoya produces around 60 percent of the world's optical glass, so you can be assured it offers excellent quality and value. Hoya offers the most extensive range of any screw-in filter system, with literally every type of filter you can imagine. What's more, for popular types of filter such as polariser or UV, it has a number of options to suit all levels of photographer from amateur through to pro. Its filters boast several cutting edge technologies, for instance the HD series boasts hardened glass and several layers of multi-coating to improve contrast and reduce flare, while the Pro 1 Digital series has been exclusively designed for use with digital cameras. The extensive Super HMC series covers the majority of filter types and provides fantastic quality at a great price. It's worth downloading Hoya's filter brochure to get a better idea of the full range of filters on offer.

Cokin

www.intro2020.co.uk

For many photographers over the decades, the search for high-quality and affordable slot-in filters started and ended with Cokin. This isn't a surprise, because this manufacturer was the innovator of creative filters for amateur photographers and has led the way ever since. Cokin offers four filter sizes as follows: 67mm (A-series); 84mm (P-series); 100mm (Z-Pro) and 130mm (X-Pro) . The A-series is aimed more for use with compacts or camcorders, so the P-series is the best introductory option. If you use wide-angle lenses with a focal length wider than 28mm, you should consider the Z-Pro range, while the X-Pro is more for medium-format photographers. All the ranges offer plenty of options but the P-series has everything the DSLR photographer may ever need, with over 140 filters to choose from, including polarisers and a variety of ND grads. Filter rings are available for threads up to 82mm and the P-holder accepts up to three filters at a time. The Z-Pro series is a better choice for landscape photographers, in particular those with ultra-wide zooms. Adaptor rings are available from 49mm to 96mm and filters are 100mm square, except for the grads which are 100x150mm.

All the filters are made from CR39 optical resin and deliver high-quality results and because it's such a popular range, filters are very well priced. The ND Grad Kit for the P-series is affordable at £50 and consists of a Cokin P filter holder, one P121L ND2 Light Grad, one P121M ND4 Grad and one P121S ND8 Soft Grad filter. The Cokin P164 circular polariser is around £80 while for the Z-Pro, you're looking at around £275 for the Z164!

Adapter rings cost as follows: A-series: £8; P-series: £11; X-Pro: £52 and Z-Pro: £22.

Jessops

www.jessops.com

Its range of screw-in filters may be limited to 21 protection and polarising filters, but with prices starting at £15 for a 52mm Skylight or UV, it's a good place to start your filter collection. They're well made too, so you won't have to worry about quality. Most filters are kept in stock in-store as well as being available for home delivery.

Lee Filters

www.leefilters.com

Lee Filters is the ultimate choice for the discerning photographer. Loved by pros and relished by enthusiasts, Lee Filters are as good as it gets in terms of optical quality, but due to the stringent manufacturing processes involved, they command high prices. The brilliant 100mm system is the cornerstone of Lee Filters' success, with a high quality versatile holder that can be made to your own specification to hold varying numbers of filters. The filters themselves are brilliant quality and are manufactured from a number of materials, including glass, resin and polyester. Various kits are available and we'd recommend the £187 Digital Starter kit, which comprises an assembled holder, 0.6ND ProGlass ND hard grad, 0.6 ND and cleaning cloth, all packed neatly into a pouch. The other kit is the £132 Starter kit, which includes an assembled filter holder, 0.6ND grad, cleaning cloth, Coral 3 grad and pouch. Its ten-stop 'Big Stopper' ND (around £100) is the best on the market. Adaptor rings from 49mm to 77mm cost £17, 82mm and 86mm are £36 while 93mm, 95mm and 105mm rings are £52. The filter holder (the Foundation kit) is £50.

If you intend making a living from photography and investing in expensive lenses, then these are the filters you should aspire to own.

ROSS HODDINOTT

Filter aid
Do not underestimate how filters can be used to improve your images, especially if you're keen on shooting landscapes.

Formatt (Hitech)

www.formatt.co.uk

Formatt makes a range of filters for movies and stills photography. Its Hitech filters are aimed specifically at digital SLR photographers. They're made from optical resin and are manufactured in the UK to extremely high standards to provide excellent optical quality. The 67mm, 85mm and 100mm filter systems are compatible with other slot-in brands and include an extensive range of graduates. As well as hard- and soft-edged ND grads (from 0.3-1.2), it offers a huge choice of colour grads, as well as the Blender, which graduates the effect through the entire length of the filter. Hitech isn't as well known or as widely available as Cokin, but is a good alternative. An ND grad kit with 0.3, 0.6 and 0.9 ND grads costs £30 (85mm); £65 (100mm) and £85 (100x150mm). The circular polariser costs £106 (85mm) or £110 (100mm). A plastic holder costs under £10 and plastic adaptor rings costs around £5 from 49mm to 77mm.

Kood

www.kood-international.com

Kood has its own range of filters, with screw-in filters imported from Japan and slot-in filters manufactured in the UK. The range of screw-in filters isn't too large but includes polarisers, protection and close-up filters, as well as various special effect items such as starburst and colour correction filters. Kood also has a good range of stepping rings too. Kood offers four sizes of slot-in filters: 67mm, 84mm, 100mm and 130mm, so its filters are compatible with all the major slot-in brands. Made from CR39 optical resin, they offer decent quality and are a good budget buy. Kood isn't available from all high street outlets, so visit its website for your nearest stockist. Kood Circular Polariser and ND grad in sizes 84mm to 130mm cost between £20 and £30 and can be purchased from Kood direct as well as a number of camera dealers.

Unknown brands

Search the web and you'll find filters from little known brands like Helios. Most stem from China and as there are no official UK importers, it's hard to qualify how good the optics are, although in the April 2010 issue's *Budget Photo*, we found a £20 close-up set produced very good results

Tiffen

www.tiffen.com

Tiffen is an American brand that has been around for decades and is particularly popular in the movies industry. Its range of screw-in filters isn't as comprehensive as Hoya's, but it does cover all the key types including protection filters, polarisers and Neutral Density filters. It also has a number of special effect filters, in particular lots of diffusion filters including soft-focus, mist and fog, but these aren't filters you'd use on a regular basis. While the range is relatively small, quality is high and Tiffen filters come with a ten-year guarantee. You'll also find that prices are competitive too, making them a decent alternative to brands like Hoya, although the latter is more likely to be stocked by your local photo dealer.

Polarising filters

There is only one photographic filter whose visual effect can't be recreated digitally and that's the polariser. Here's how it works

If you only ever buy one filter, buy a polariser. It is like no other filter – by simply rotating it in its mount you can bring your images to life. A polariser is designed to eliminate glare, minimise reflections and enhance saturation.

To understand how polarisers work, it's necessary to get a little technical. Basically, light is transmitted in wavelengths. Light travels in straight lines, vibrating as waves in all directions – side to side, up and down and at all other angles. When light strikes a surface, a portion of the wavelengths are reflected while others are absorbed. It is the absorbed wavelengths of light that define the colour of the surface it's striking. For example, a red-coloured object will reflect red wavelengths of light whilst absorbing others. Similarly, green foliage absorbs all wavelengths of light other than the ones forming the green, and so on. Polarised light is different, though. It occurs due to the reflection or scattering of light waves and only travels in one direction. It is these wavelengths that create glare and reflection, reducing colour intensity. A polarising filter is designed to block polarised light, thus restoring contrast and saturation.

Polarisers are made from a thin sheet of polarising material, sandwiched between two circular pieces of glass and screwed onto the front of your lens. The front part of the mount can be rotated, affecting the angle of polarisation. As a result, the amount of polarised light passing through the lens can be altered to control the amount of polarisation. Looking through the viewfinder while rotating the filter, reflections will come and go and the intensity of colour will strengthen and fade again. Simply stop rotating the filter when you feel the effect is at its best for the scene or subject. Polarising filters are best known for their ability to darken blue skies. However, they are equally useful for reducing reflections from non-metallic surfaces, and also the glare from wet or dry foliage.

Not only does an enriched blue sky look appealing as part of a landscape photograph, but a polarised sky can also create an attractive backdrop. Try shooting buildings (modern or old), people, trees or flowers contrasted against a polarised sky – the results will be bursting with impact. This is just one reason why a polariser is a must-have filter – regardless of the type of subjects you enjoy shooting.

One last thing. A polariser has a two-stop filter factor and, while your camera's automatic metering will allow for this, it's worth bearing in mind how this will affect the range of shutter speeds and apertures you have available. However, once you start to recognise the benefits of a polariser, you'll find yourself using it regularly.

Polariser choice

LINEAR OR CIRCULAR?

There are two types of polarising filter on the market – linear and circular – and this choice has a nasty habit of causing confusion. However, if you're not sure which type to buy, fear not, the answer is simple. Only the circular type will work properly in combination with your digital SLR. Although both varieties are physically circular in shape and similar in appearance, the design of the linear variety will affect the accuracy of your camera's metering system. This is because digital SLRs polarise some light inside the camera. If this light has already been polarised by a linear polariser, a false meter reading is given. Circular polarisers are constructed with a wave-retardation plate, allowing the light waves passing through to rotate and appear unpolarised to the camera's metering system. So, when you buy a polariser, ensure you're choosing a circular polariser and you've nothing to worry about.

Uneven polarisation

Natural light polarisation is uneven across the sky; its maximum effect is when facing 90° to the sun and its minimum is at 180°. Therefore, when taking pictures at certain angles, you may find that the colour of the sky will be irregular. For example, you might find that the sky in your photograph darkens more noticeably in just one area, due to this region of the sky containing more polarised wavelengths. This effect can look odd and is best avoided. Ultra wide-angle focal lengths (10-14mm) are most prone to it. To try and side-step this problem, use a lens with a long focal length or adjust your shooting angle. However, if this just isn't practical, you could try positioning a Neutral Density graduate filter at an angle so that it filters the lighter region of the sky. Although this isn't a faultless solution, an ND grad can greatly reduce the effect of uneven polarisation.

Uneven polarisation

With polariser

Plan your angle!

The polarising effect is at its greatest at around a 90º angle to the sun. An easy way to find this angle is to make a 'gun' with your forefinger and thumb, point it at the sun and then rotate your thumb 90º left or right

polarising results

You can see increased saturation and the greater contrast levels created by the polariser. This is one of the reasons why it's a must-have for landscape photographers

ALL IMAGES: ROSS HODDINOTT

Reflections

Reflections can either be good or bad. For example, rolling hills or snowy mountain peaks will be enhanced if they're mirrored in the still, reflective surface of water. But the light and glare reflecting from shiny non-metallic surfaces or glass, in a cityscape or on a skyscraper, can be ugly and distracting. A polariser can be used either to emphasise reflections – by reducing surface glare – or to eliminate them. However, the strength of the effect will depend on the camera angle in relation to the reflective surface. The maximum effect is at 30-45º.

Over-polarisation

BEWARE! Whilst the look of a deep blue, polarised sky may be appealing, it is possible to overdo the effect. In some situations, a polariser isn't needed at all – or only partial polarisation is required – to produce the best-looking result. If the effect is too strong, the sky can appear almost black in colour. This will look unnatural and degrade the aesthetics of the image. So use image playback to check the effect and adjust the rotation of the filter accordingly.

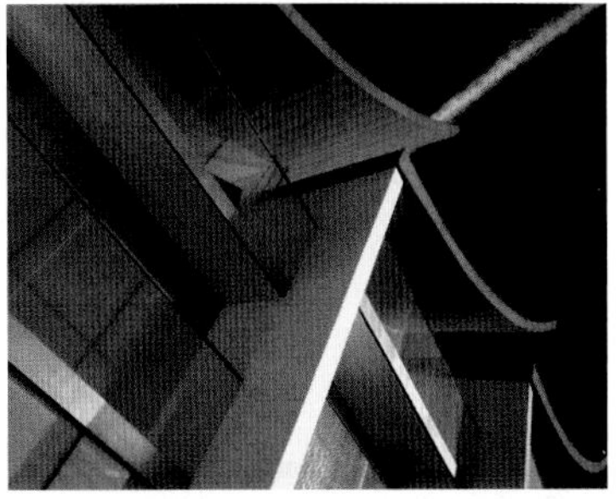

Graduated filters (Grads)

Next to a polariser, graduates should be at the top of your list of filters to own if you're serious about landscape photography

Graduates are one of the most important and widely used filter types. They are half-coated, half-clear, with a transitional zone where the two halves merge. There are two distinct types: Neutral Density (ND) and colour grads. ND graduated filters are designed to darken bright skies and lower contrast levels, whilst the coloured variety are intended to add a splash of colour to otherwise dull, nondescript skies.

ND grads work by absorbing all the colours in the visible spectrum in equal amounts, with no colour cast. This is necessary as the contrast in light between sky and land is often greater than the dynamic range of the sensor – making it impossible to capture a correctly-exposed scene. They are available individually or in a set in a variety of strengths to suit different conditions. Their strength, or density, is indicated on the filter; 0.3 equals a one-stop exposure reduction, 0.6 a two-stop and 0.9 equates to three stops. ND grads are also available in both hard- and soft-edged transitions. Soft NDs are designed with a feathered edge, providing a gentle change from the coated portion of the filter to the clear area, whilst a hard ND grad has a more sudden transition. Both types are useful; soft grads are better suited to shooting landscapes with broken horizons as they don't noticeably darken objects breaking the horizon, like buildings or trees. Hard grads are designed so that the full strength of their specified density is spread over a greater proportion of the coated area, allowing you to reduce the brightness of the sky with greater accuracy.

Whilst colour grads are not as useful on a day-to-day basis, they shouldn't be overlooked. To an extent, they also lower contrast, but instead of having the practical role of an ND grad, colour grads are designed for creative effect. There is a wide variety of different colours available, from subtle-looking shades of blue, coral and orange, to the artificial look of red, pink and tobacco. Some, like the sunset filter discussed below, lack a clear area. Instead the whole filter graduates from a strong to weak colour tint.

Colour grads may not be for the purists, but combined with a suitable scene, they can help produce eye-catching results. However, a quick word of warning. They should be used with care and in moderation. Only employ a colour grad when its effect genuinely enhances the image you are about to capture – if you have any doubts, take an unfiltered shot as well. You also need to ensure accurate placement; if you push the filter too far down in the holder, the coated area of the grad will stray over the foreground, ruining the result.

Grad filter options

ANGLE YOUR GRAD: When using graduated filters, a slot-in filter holder – like the Cokin P system – is a must-have accessory. Whilst circular, screw-in graduated filters are available, they are hugely restrictive because, unlike a slot-in filter, the position of the graduation zone can't be adjusted up or down to suit your composition. Another advantage of using a holder is that, if the scene you are photographing has a sloping horizon, it is possible to adjust the orientation of the holder to match. This will avoid the graduated area of the filter overlapping your foreground, which will either artificially darken or colour part of your scene. You may also wish to position a grad at an angle to help alleviate uneven polarisation, although this does carry an enhanced risk of vignetting with wide-angle lenses, so check images via your LCD monitor.

Sunset filters

Have you ever stayed out late with your camera in anticipation of a spectacular, colourful sunset, only to be disappointed? To avoid future frustration and wasted time, why not attach a sunset filter to mimic the effect? Sunset filters are designed to simulate the colours of the setting sun. They're best used in the evening, but can also be used in the early morning or even during the day. Although the full length of the filter is tinted, the density of the colour is graduated to replicate the feel and appearance of a real setting sun. They are the perfect filter for adding colour, warmth and atmosphere to your shots.

Without sunset

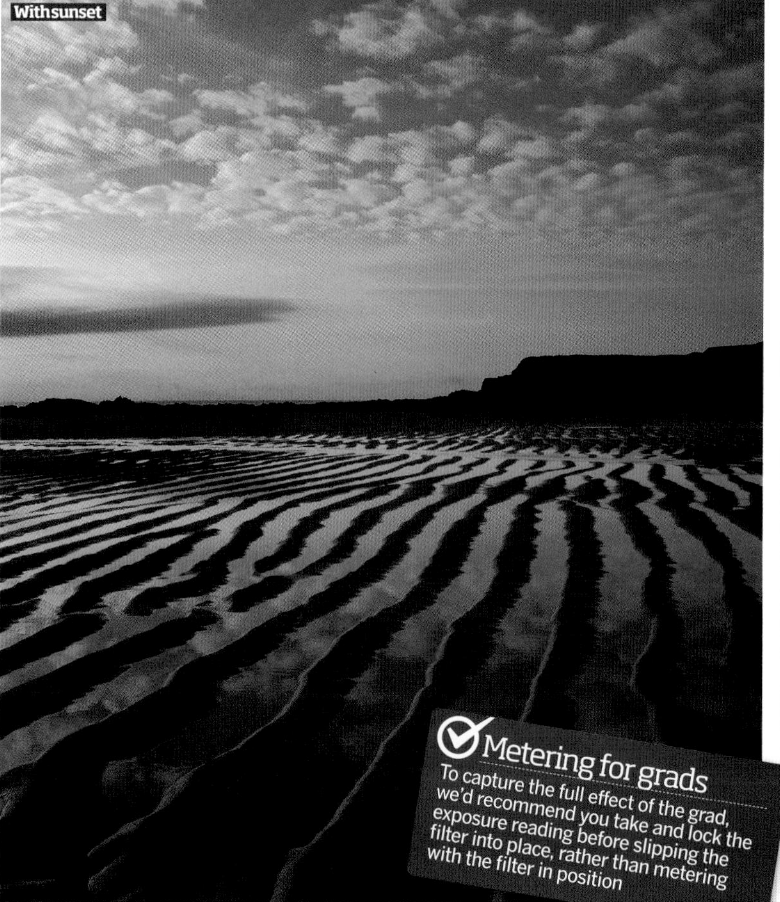

With sunset

Metering for grads

To capture the full effect of the grad, we'd recommend you take and lock the exposure reading before slipping the filter into place, rather than metering with the filter in position

ND Grad results

These four images show the effects of the most common Neutral Density filters compared to an unfiltered scene. As you can see, the grads only affect the sky.

Diffusers & Neutral Density filters

Why we'd recommend you consider using these two important filters

Check out the brochures of the leading filter brands and you'll find literally hundreds of filters on offer. Many have their uses, but we've limited our selection in this beginner's guide to those that we strongly recommend you consider buying, regardless of whether you're good at Photoshop or not. We've covered grads and polarisers, and the final two filters that we'd suggest you add to your shortlist are the diffuser and the Neutral Density. Soft-focus images are still popular in photography, and ideally suited for portraits of subjects of all ages, and we don't think that recreating the effect in Photoshop is anywhere near as good as using a diffuser. A Neutral Density filter is another that you won't need every day, but the usefulness of its light-reducing properties is not to be underestimated.

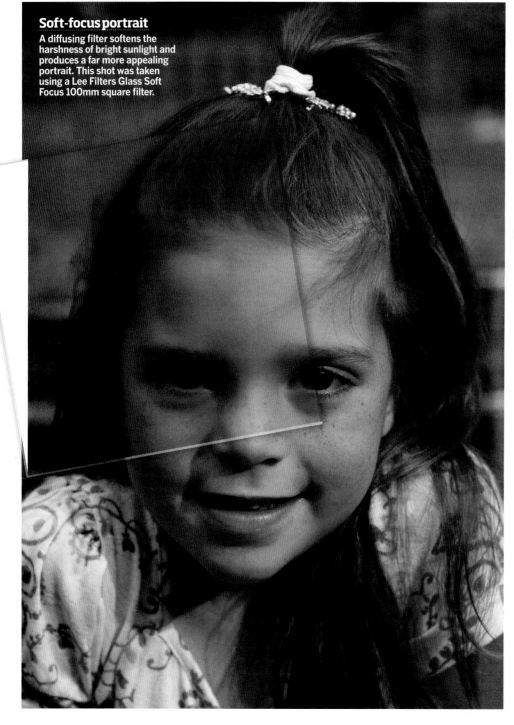

Soft-focus portrait

A diffusing filter softens the harshness of bright sunlight and produces a far more appealing portrait. This shot was taken using a Lee Filters Glass Soft Focus 100mm square filter.

Neutral Density

Neutral Density filters work using a similar principle to a graduated ND. However, unlike a grad, the entire filter is coated. They are designed to limit the amount of light passing through the lens. Therefore, if after adding the filter the shutter speed is kept the same, a larger aperture must be selected to obtain the correct exposure. Alternatively, if the f/stop is maintained, a slower shutter speed must be selected to achieve the right exposure. ND filters are available as both slot-in and screw-in types and also in progressive strengths (densities).

Whilst they can be employed to compensate for too much light – in situations where you'd like to increase the aperture more than the light or camera capabilities permit – an ND filter is more often used to emphasise movement, especially water.

Diffusing filter

So you've spent all your hard-earned cash on buying a camera with several million pixels and lenses with computer-designed optics to ensure the best possible quality. So what do you do next? Go out and buy a diffusing filter (also known as a soft-focus filter or diffuser) that sits on the front of the lens and works at reducing sharpness and creating a soft, diffused result. While doing this might not seem sensible at first, it has to be said that diffusers have maintained their popularity as a creative filter with many photographers. Ideal when shooting portraits, whether of subjects that might look worse for wear if pin-sharp, or when adding an artistic element to landscapes. Diffusers can also have the effect of adding a romantic mood to images, as well as producing an appealing glow in highlights, making them a popular choice for portrait photography. For the best effect, use them with a wide aperture setting.

Diffused glow

When forced to shoot portraits in bright sunlight, you'll find a diffuser can help to not only reduce the harshness of the strong, directional light, but also create a diffused glow around highlights

Neutral Density filter
An ND filter is ideal when you want to use slower shutter speeds to blur movement in bright lighting.

Close-up filters

These useful accessories offer an affordable way to shoot great close-ups

CLOSE-UP FILTERS OFFER a great introduction to the world of macro photography, without the need to spend hundreds on a dedicated macro lens. Technically speaking, they're not actually a filter, but a dioptre. However, they are commonly regarded as one and produced by the majority of the major filter brands. They are a screw-in type filter, attaching to the front of the lens and acting like a magnifier. By doing so, they reduce the lens's minimum focusing distance. Typically, they are of a single element construction and manufactured in a range of four strengths: +1, +2, +3 and +4. The higher the number, the nearer it is possible to focus and therefore the greater the magnification. Some brands also offer a powerful +10 dioptre, which is normally a two-element construction to help optimise image quality.

It is possible to couple close-up filters together to create a greater level of magnification. If you decide to do this, attach the most powerful one on your lens first and the weakest last. However, combining three or more filters will degrade image quality and exaggerate any optical flaws, which is why it is recommended that you attach a maximum of two at any one time. They can be purchased in a set or individually. Expect to pay around £20 for a single filter. Naturally, at this price, it is unrealistic to expect them to match the optical quality of a macro lens, or extension tube, and they are prone to spherical aberration (softening of the image). However, this can be kept to a minimum by selecting a mid-range aperture of f/8 or f/11 and, considering their price tag, they are capable of excellent results. They are best combined with a prime focal length lens, as opposed to a zoom. A standard 50mm lens is an ideal focal length, but short telephoto lenses, up to 135mm, are also well suited. That said, it's possible to get decent results when used with standard zooms, so if you like close-ups, give them a try.

"Close-up filters offer a great introduction to the world of macro photography"

A close-up filter has much the same effect as a magnifying glass and is ideal when you want to increase the size of a small object, like a flower, in the frame.

Distortion

Close-up filters can sometimes exaggerate lens distortion at the edges of the frame, so avoid using them with wide-angle lenses whenever possible

In-camera filtration

Try using your DSLR's White Balance settings for creative filtration

THE COLOUR TEMPERATURE of light is measured in degrees of Kelvin (K) and is handled by your camera's White Balance system. Light is considered neutral at around 5500K, with lower temperatures appearing warmer and higher temperatures getting cooler. By intentionally mismatching the WB setting with the available light, it's possible to creatively play with how colours are recorded. For example, shooting a sunlit landscape with the WB to Cloudy produces a warm hue. In contrast, select a lower setting, for example 3000K – or the Tungsten WB preset – and the photo will look cooler. Once you understand the creative potential of WB, you can begin using it as a form of convenient in-camera filtration – available at all times at the simple flick of a switch. Most DSLRs allow you to set the WB value manually for added control, so don't feel you have to rely on the camera's preset values. Whilst often the best effect will be subtle, don't be afraid to experiment – sometimes the most pleasing result will be one boasting a strong, artificial tint. Some images benefit from a little extra warmth – especially portrait and scenics. However, a blue cast can convey a sense of coolness and mystery and, while fewer subjects suit a colder colour temperature, it's an effect

Candle light | Tungsten | Daylight | Flash | Cloudy | Shade

2000K | 3400K | 4000K | 5200K | 5500K | 6000K | 7000K | 8000K | 10000K

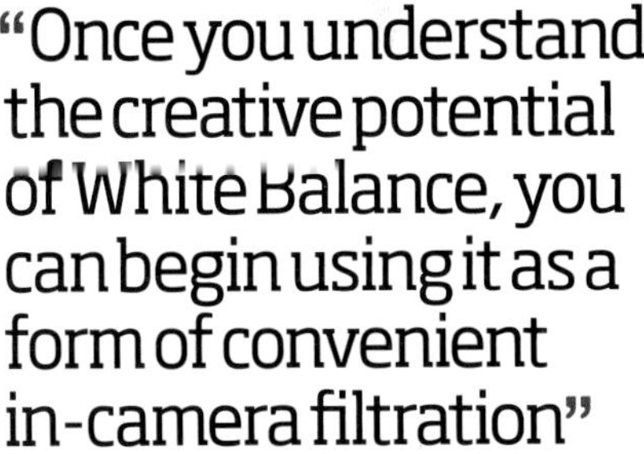

"Once you understand the creative potential of White Balance, you can begin using it as a form of convenient in-camera filtration"

WHITE BALANCE COMPARISON
A colour cast will greatly alter the feel, mood and look of a scene or subject. Digital SLR photographers can 'filter' their images quickly and easily, by simply mismatching the White Balance setting with the ambient light. Different scenes will suit different colour shifts. For example, in the first sequence (water and rocks) a cool blue hue works best; whilst in the second (geese at sunrise) a warmer hue is better suited. In both instances, a technically inaccurate White Balance preset suits the image far better than the correct White Balance setting.

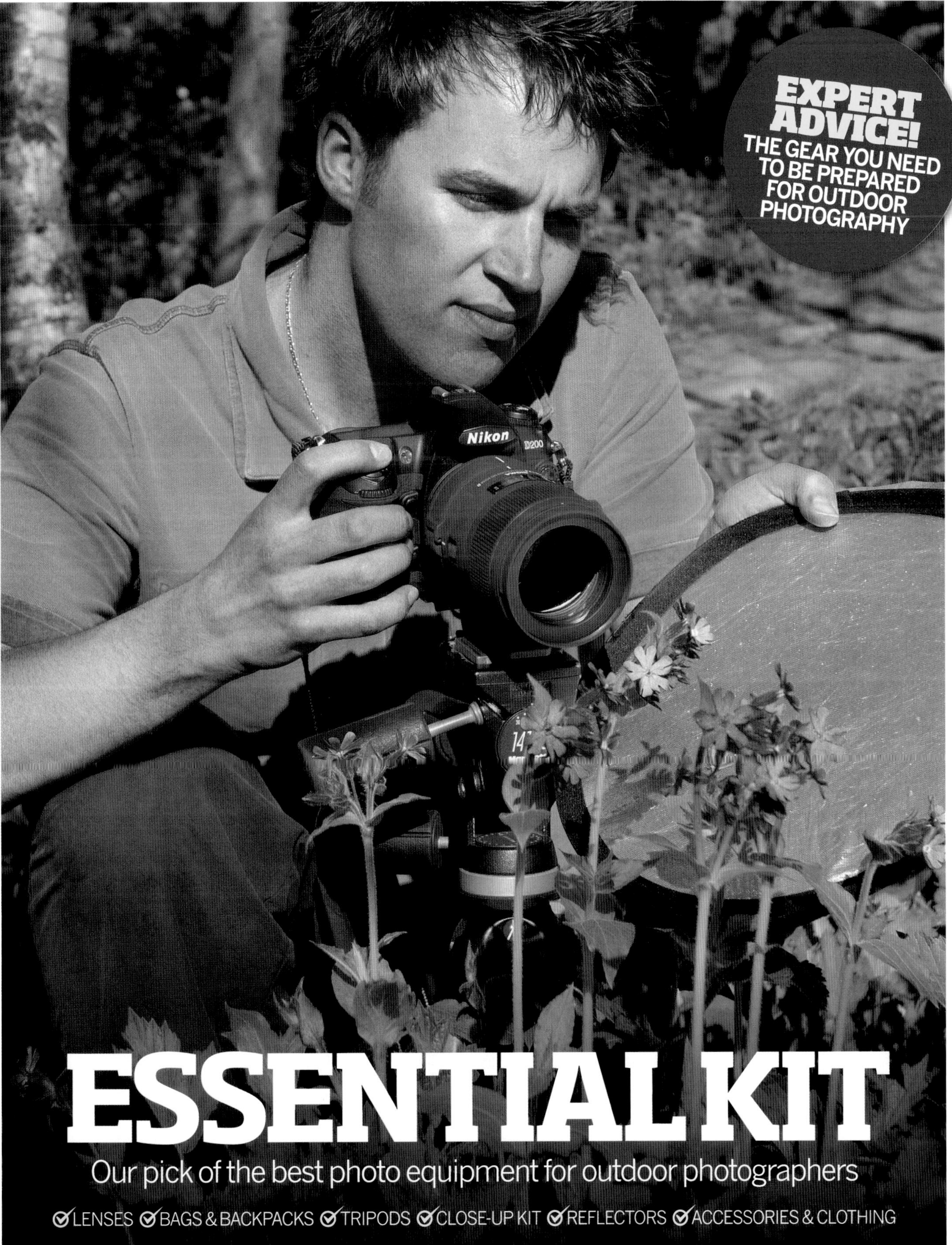

EXPERT ADVICE!

THE GEAR YOU NEED TO BE PREPARED FOR OUTDOOR PHOTOGRAPHY

ESSENTIAL KIT

Our pick of the best photo equipment for outdoor photographers

✓LENSES ✓BAGS & BACKPACKS ✓TRIPODS ✓CLOSE-UP KIT ✓REFLECTORS ✓ACCESSORIES & CLOTHING

Lenses

Outdoor photography demands the use of different types of lenses depending on the type of subject that you're photographing. Here we offer some basic advice and a number of recommendations on which lens is best for you

It doesn't matter what type of camera you own – fit the wrong lens and you'll struggle to make the most of the photo opportunity in front of you. Choosing the best lens therefore is one of the most important decisions you'll make when preparing to take pictures. The choice is relatively straightforward though.

For landscape photography, your first choice should be a wide-angle lens. An ultra wide-angle zoom represents the best value and will allow you to capture fantastic scenics.

With nature photography, the emphasis is filling the frame with subjects that are either close-by or at a distance. Macro lenses with a life-size (1:1) reproduction ratio are perfect for small subjects like insects and are ideal for photographing flowers too. They're specialist lenses so if you're on a budget look for used lenses or consider a close-up accessory (turn over the page for more details).

Wildlife photographers wishing to take great images of animals should add a telezoom to their equipment arsenal. A 55-200mm or 70-300mm are good budget choices, while those who can afford it will benefit from the additional pulling power and superior optics of bigger zooms like the 120-400mm.

Use the information provided on these pages to help you make the right choice.

Prime or zoom lens?

It is the age-old question – why buy a fixed lens, with only one focal length, when a zoom is much more versatile? Here we have listed the 'pros and cons' to both lens types to help you decide which suits your photography best.

FIXED 'PRIME' LENS

- ✔ Simpler optical design means sharper results with better contrast
- ✔ More robust, compact construction
- ✔ The faster maximum aperture provides a brighter viewfinder, shallower depth-of-field and better low-light capabilities
- ✔ Will often boast a closer focusing distance than a zoom
- ✘ Restricted to just the one focal length
- ✘ Cost – prime lenses are typically more expensive than zoom lenses

ZOOM

- ✔ Covers a range of focal lengths, so provides greater versatility
- ✔ Replaces the need to carry several different fixed lenses, meaning that there is less for you to carry around
- ✔ Most zooms offer very good quality
- ✔ Lots of flexibility at a very good price
- ✘ Not as good optically as a fixed lens, particularly towards the edges of the frame
- ✘ The maximum aperture is usually slower than on a fixed lens
- ✘ Paradoxically, zooms can offer too much choice – complicating framing and composition

Teleconverters

A teleconverter is an optical component that fits between camera and lens and increases the focal length without altering the minimum focusing distance. They are most commonly made in 1.4x and 2x versions – although 1.7x and 3x versions are also produced. Therefore, a 200mm telephoto combined with a 1.4x converter would be equivalent to 280mm, while the same lens coupled with a 2x multiplier would be transformed into a 400mm lens. Converters are relatively inexpensive, light and compact, so are a convenient and economical way to expand the overall flexibility of your kit, making them a great choice for nature photographers in particular. However, there are disadvantages to using converters. Firstly, they reduce the amount of light entering the camera by one stop (1.4x) or two stops (2x) respectively. This can prove a problem in low light, when the risk of camera shake is increased, and when photographing fast action, when subject blur is more likely due to the resulting slower shutter speed. The other drawback of attaching one is that image quality is slightly degraded, with zoom lenses being affected more than fixed focal lengths. They can also lead to problems with autofocus too. Generally speaking, though, the benefits of using one outweigh the disadvantages. For best quality, opt for one with more elements in the construction. Nikon, Canon and Sigma are among the camera manufacturers with teleconverters in their range, but check compatibility as some are designed for use with specific lenses. Look at independent brands like Tokina, Tamron and Kenko for teleconverters with more universal compatibility – your local photo store can offer expert advice.

Understanding focal lengths: Wide-angles

The focal length stated on a lens relates to SLRs using 35mm film and full-frame sensors. If your camera has an APS-C-sized sensor (most have), then you're effectively cropping the image and increasing the focal length of the lens (by 1.5x with Nikon, Pentax and Sony; 1.6x with Canon). The chart below shows popular wide-angles and the change in effective focal length.

Focal length on lens	Sensor size Full-frame 1x	APS-H 1.3x	APS-C 1.5x	APS-C (Canon) 1.6x	Four-Thirds & Micro Four-Thirds 2x
14mm	14mm	18mm	21mm	22mm	28mm
15mm	15mm	19mm	22mm	23mm	30mm
20mm	20mm	26mm	30mm	32mm	40mm
24mm	24mm	31mm	36mm	38mm	48mm
28mm	28mm	36mm	42mm	45mm	56mm
10-17mm	10-17mm	13-22mm	15-25mm	16-27mm	20-34mm
10-20mm	10-20mm	13-26mm	15-30mm	16-32mm	20-40mm
10-22mm	10-22mm	13-29mm	15-33mm	16-35mm	20-44mm
11-18mm	11-18mm	14-23mm	16-27mm	18-29mm	22-36mm
12-24mm	12-24mm	16-31mm	18-36mm	19-38mm	24-48mm
16-35mm	16-35mm	21-45mm	24-53mm	26-56mm	32-70mm
17-40mm	17-40mm	22-52mm	25-60mm	27-56mm	34-80mm

Understanding focal lengths: Telephotos

As with the wide-angle lenses above, if your digital camera has an APS-C sized sensor – as the majority do – then you are effectively cropping the image and increasing the focal length of the lens. While this isn't welcome with wide-angles, the extra pulling power is a benefit with telephotos as it helps fill the frame with the subject. Our table lists below the most popular telephotos and how the effective focal lengths change with different sensor sizes.

Focal length on lens	Sensor size Full-frame 1x	APS-H 1.3x	APS-C 1.5x	APS-C (Canon) 1.6x	Four-Thirds Micro Four-Thirds 2x
50mm	50mm	65mm	75mm	13mm	16mm
100mm	100mm	130mm	150mm	160mm	200mm
200mm	200mm	260mm	300mm	320mm	400mm
300mm	300mm	390mm	450mm	480mm	600mm
400mm	400mm	520mm	600mm	640mm	800mm
500mm	500mm	650mm	750mm	800mm	1000mm
55-200mm	55-200mm	72-260mm	83-300mm	88-320mm	110-400mm
70-300mm	70-300mm	91-390mm	105-450mm	112-480mm	140-600mm
100-300mm	100-300mm	130-390mm	150-450mm	160-320mm	200-600mm
80-400mm	80-400mm	104-520mm	120-600mm	128-640mm	160-800mm

Our shortlist of the best value lenses

These lenses have been highlighted as they offer great value and excellent performance

Tamron 10-24mm f/3.5-4.5 Di II LD

www.intro2020.co.uk

Guide price: £500
Street price: £400

MAIN SPECIFICATIONS
Lens construction: 12 elements in nine groups
Aperture range: f/3.5-4.5 to f/22
Filter thread: 77mm
Dimensions: 83.2 x 86.5mm
Weight: 406g
Fittings: Canon, Nikon, Pentax and Sony

Tamron's 11-18mm has proved popular for years, but this addition, with its very wide focal length range, is even more versatile. It's compact and lightweight with good handling and an internal focusing system that will please filter users. Optical quality is good, thanks to the inclusion of aspherical and low-dispersion elements.

Tamron AF55-200mm f/4-5.6 LD Di II

www.intro2020.co.uk

Guide price: £180
Street price: £120

MAIN SPECIFICATIONS
Lens construction: 13 elements in nine groups
Aperture range: f/4-5.6 to f/32
Filter thread: 52mm
Dimensions: 71.6x83mm
Weight: 300g
Fittings: Canon and Nikon

Normally sharpness falls off as you zoom through the focal lengths, but this lens retains good sharpness throughout. Its wide zoom ring is very easy to use. The autofocus turns in a good performance – it's not the quickest or quietest but is accurate and performs well in low light. It's light and compact and is a great budget telezoom.

Tamron AF18-270mm f/3.5-6.3 Di II VC

www.intro2020.co.uk

Guide price: £600
Street price: £400

MAIN SPECIFICATIONS
Lens construction: 18 elements in 13 groups
Aperture range: f/3.5-6.3 to f/22
Filter thread: 72mm
Dimensions: 79.6x101mm
Weight: 550g
Fittings: Canon and Nikon

The Tamron 18-270mm boasts an incredible 15x zoom range, giving an effective focal length of 28-419mm, making this suitable for almost every type of subject. The addition of image stabilisation gives it a four-stop benefit, so it can be used handheld in low-light conditions or at longer focal lengths, with a reduced risk of shake.

Tamron SP AF60mm f/2 Di II L Macro

www.intro2020.co.uk

Guide price: £550
Street price: £400

MAIN SPECIFICATIONS
Lens construction: 14 elements in ten groups
Aperture range: f/2 to f/22
Filter thread: 55mm
Dimensions: 73X80mm
Weight: 400g
Fittings: Canon, Nikon and Sony

Designed for exclusive use with DSLRs with APS-C sensors, this lightweight lens holds an ace card in the form of its maximum aperture of f/2, which gives a couple of big advantages over its rivals. As well as a brighter viewfinder image, it creates a very shallow depth-of-field – highly desired by macro photographers.

Voigtlander 20mm f/3.5 Color Skopar SL II

www.robertwhite.co.uk

Guide price: £475
Street price: £450

MAIN SPECIFICATIONS
Lens construction: Nine elements in six groups
Aperture range: f/3.5 to f/22
Filter thread: 52mm
Dimensions: 63x28.8mm
Weight: 205g
Fittings: Nikon and Pentax

This manual focus lens is one of the most affordable prime lenses on the market and one of the smallest and lightest. The manual focus action is smooth and the barrel boasts a clear hyperfocal scale. Optically, this lens is a very good performer with excellent sharpness once stopped down. A great budget prime lens.

Sigma 120-400mm f/4.5-5.6 DG OS HSM

www.sigma-imaging-uk.com

Guide price: £749
Street price: £700

MAIN SPECIFICATIONS
Lens construction: 21 elements in 15 groups
Aperture range: f/4.5-5.6 to f/32
Filter thread: 77mm
Dimensions: 92x203mm / **Weight:** 1,640g
Fittings: Canon, Nikon, Pentax, Sigma and Sony

Despite its focal length, this high ratio zoom is relatively compact and includes an Optical Stabiliser (OS), a rear focusing system and HyperSonic Motor (HSM) for quiet, high-speed focusing. Its minimum focusing distance is 150cm with a magnification of 1:4.2 – something that is sure to appeal to nature photographers.

Equipment for close-ups

Many standard zooms boast a useful reproduction ratio of around 1:4 – quarter life-size. This is ideal to get you started, but if you want to get even nearer to your subjects, you may need to invest in a close-up attachment or dedicated macro lens. Here, we look at the most popular and widely used options and cover the merits of each type

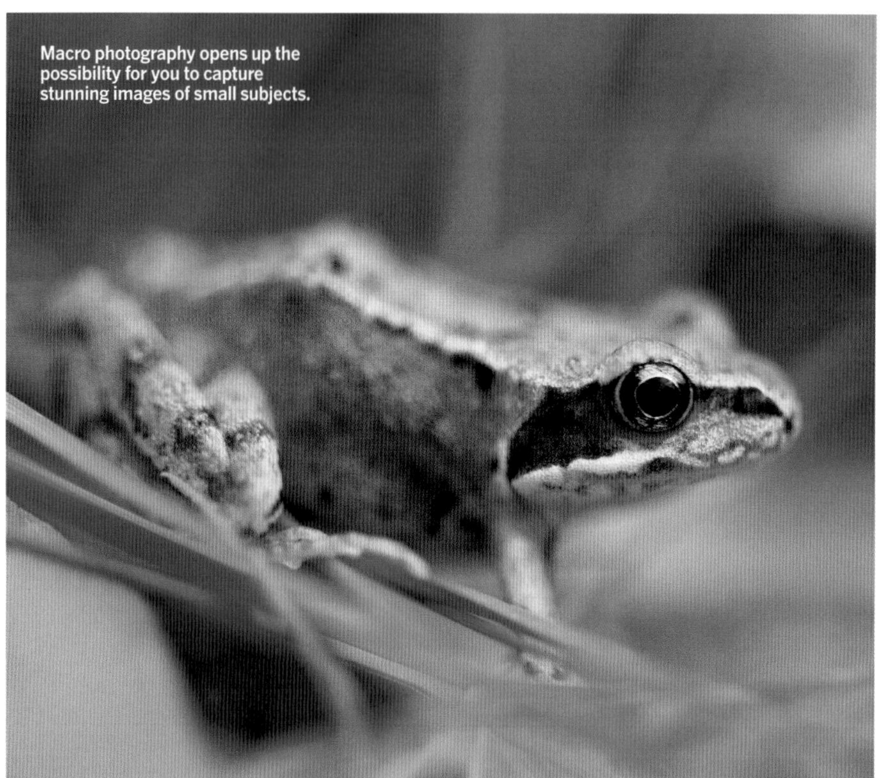
Macro photography opens up the possibility for you to capture stunning images of small subjects.

Useful close-up accessories

TRIPOD: At high magnification, the effect of camera movement is exaggerated. A tripod is the best form of support. A flexible design is best suited to shooting close-ups as it lets you get low.

REFLECTOR: Small, collapsible reflectors can be angled to bounce light accurately onto your subject. The intensity of the light can be adjusted by moving the reflector closer or further away.

PLAMP: The Plamp is an articulated arm with a clamp fixed at either end. One end can be attached to a tripod leg, while the other can be used to hold a reflector.

RING-FLASH: A ring-flash is designed specifically for close-up work. It attaches directly to the front of the lens, so the burst can illuminate close-up subjects. Twin flash units work in a similar way.

REMOTE RELEASE: Depressing the shutter release button while using at high magnification, and a slow shutter speed, can cause slight camera vibration. A remote release allows you to trigger the shutter without any fear of camera shake.

Close-up filters

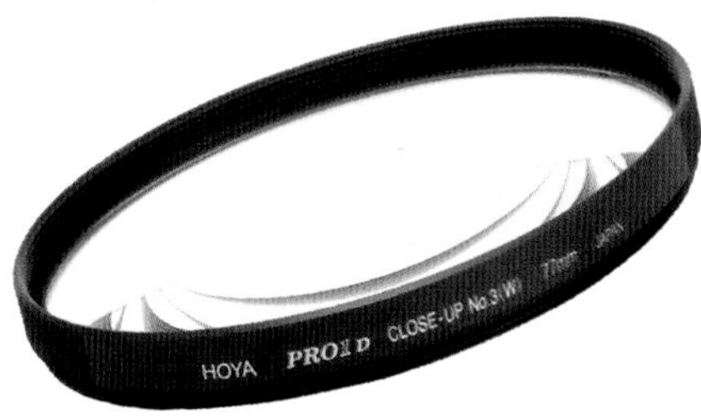

Close-up filters screw to the filter thread of your lens and work like a magnifying glass. Depending on the brand and size, they can cost as little as £10. They are normally of a single element construction and available in progressive strengths, stated in dioptres. +1, +2, +3 and +4 are the most popular, although a two-element +10 dioptre is also available. The higher the number, the nearer the lens can focus and the higher the magnification. Although they can be used in combination, image quality will degrade if you attach more than two at one time. Close-up filters do not affect normal camera functions, so are easy to use and well suited to giving beginners a taste of close-up photography. Despite their modest price, they can produce excellent results and being so small and lightweight can easily be used handheld without affecting stability.

Extension tubes

Extension tubes are hollow rings that fit between the camera and lens. They work by increasing the distance between the sensor and lens, allowing the camera to focus closer than normal and increase magnification. They lack any optics and so do not affect the image quality of the lens they're coupled with, making the image quality superior to close-up filters. They can be purchased individually or in a set of three lengths: 12mm, 25mm and 36mm. Their level of magnification is calculated by dividing the amount of extension by the focal length of the lens being used. For example, 25mm of extension used with a 50mm standard lens results in a 1:2 reproduction – or half life-size. To achieve 1:1 life-size, the extension would need to equal the focal length of the lens attached. Therefore, they are most effective when combined with relatively short focal lengths.

Macro lens

A macro lens is optimised for close focusing. While they are highly corrected to give their best results at close range, they can also be for general use and are popular among portrait photographers. At its minimum focusing distance, a dedicated macro lens will normally produce 1:1 reproduction. They are available in a range of focal lengths: short macro lenses, in the region of 50mm to 70mm, are lightweight and compact, making them easy to use handheld. However, at their maximum magnification, they don't have a generous working distance. Therefore, this focal length is not the best if you wish to photograph subjects which are easily disturbed, such as butterflies. Generally speaking, focal lengths upwards of 90mm are a better choice. They provide a greater subject-to-camera distance and make it easier to isolate your subject.

5-in-1 reflector kits

A small circular silver/white reflector is the most affordable reflector and a useful aid when shooting close-ups. However, a 5-in-1 kit, which offers a silver, white, gold and (rarely used) black finish, along with a translucent panel, is the best choice. You can also use it to shade your subject, as well as use one of the reflective surfaces to provide additional light on your subject, They're also obviously ideal for other forms of photography, in particular portraits. The following three 5-in-1 kits are among the best value options on the market.

Elemental 5-in-1 (107cm)

www.studio-flash.com

GUIDE PRICE: £35
STREET PRICE: £35

Better known for their excellent range of budget studioflash, Elemental also offers a couple of 5-in-1 kits that both represent excellent value. This 107cm kit comes in its own black zip-up bag and once removed, the 5-in-1 reflector looks and handles much like the similarly-priced Interfit. The translucent panel is nicely manufactured and the coloured sleeve has a slot for the panel's tab to slip through when zipped up. The sleeve can be used to give a silver/black or gold/white effect and is thick and well put together. This is a great budget option and excellent value for money.

VERDICT **An excellent budget buy.**

Build quality (panel)	★★★★★
Build quality (sleeve)	★★★★½
Versatility	★★★★☆
Performance	★★★★★
Value for Money	★★★★★
OVERALL	★★★★★

Interfit 265 (107cm)

www.interfitphotographic.com

GUIDE PRICE: £44
STREET PRICE: £30

The white surface of the well-made translucent panel offers a ½-stop efficiency and has a thick black edge and small cloth tab for hanging off a hook. The sleeve is made from thick material and can be wrapped around to give silver/black or gold/white options. The zip has a smooth action and at its end, the sleeve has a gap for the tab to stick through. Interfit makes a large number of kits so you should have no trouble finding the most suitable size for you. Better still, they're available at an excellent price too. A nicely made and high quality kit, supplied in a zip-up black bag.

VERDICT **An excellent, affordable kit.**

Build quality (panel)	★★★★★
Build quality (sleeve)	★★★★½
Versatility	★★★★☆
Performance	★★★★★
Value for Money	★★★★★
OVERALL	★★★★★

Lastolite Bottletop 4896 (120cm)

www.lastolite.com

GUIDE PRICE: £85
STREET PRICE: £80

This 120cm kit is the largest in the range, and also the biggest and most expensive 5-in-1 in our test. It's also different in a number of ways. First, the 5-in-1 kit is made up of a panel and two reversible elasticated sleeves: a gold/white and a silver/sunfire. This has a number of benefits: it's quicker to change from one to another as there is no zip, and you can fit one over each side of the panel, allowing you to have different combinations to suit your liking. The build quality is first-rate, and spare panels are available so you can place a sleeve on each and have two reflectors at the ready.

VERDICT **Versatile and made to last.**

Build quality (panel)	★★★★★
Build quality (sleeve)	★★★★★
Versatility	★★★★★
Performance	★★★★★
Value for Money	★★★★☆
OVERALL	★★★★★

Gadget bags and backpacks

YOUR MAIN CONSIDERATIONS should be how much kit can it hold and whether to go for a bag that hangs over the shoulder or a backpack. Most outdoor photographers prefer backpacks as they distribute weight over your shoulders and back, making it far easier to carry gear over long distances. The daypack holds photo gear in the bottom section and general items in the top compartment, while dedicated photo backpacks are designed with larger kits in mind. Consider the following:

Comfort: As you carry more kit, the weight increases, so shoulder straps are important. The wider and more padded they are, the less they dig into your shoulders. Waist straps are useful, as they relieve tension from the lumbar region and help keep your back straight. Another important factor is the bag's frame. Some are sturdier than others, which may seem uncomfortable at first, but can help keep your back straight on long treks.

Capacity: Think about how much kit you plan to carry. This will ultimately determine the size of bag you need. All the bags in this test have adjustable compartments, so they are quite versatile. We also list internal dimensions, so you can see exactly how much space they offer.

Features (see panel below): Some photographers just want a bag with lots of space, others are more demanding over specific features. Most have have front pockets, designed to help you organise your memory cards and batteries into used and unused. Many of the bags have water bottle holders, tripod clips or pouches and rain covers.

Build Quality: How well the backpack is put together, including the stitching, zippers and weatherproofing, determines how long it ought to last, how strong it is and how well it protects your equipment.

Price: We've stated average street prices at time of publication.

Features

1) STRAPS Check to see if the straps are adjustable, padded and wide, to stop them from cutting into your shoulders on long journeys. Also look for waist straps.

2) PADDING Some bags have pressure pads on the back, which will take a lot of the strain out of long journeys and spread the weight of the gear over a larger area.

3) STORAGE/CAPACITY Does the bag hold all the equipment you will need for your photography? If there is too much empty space, the bag will be unbalanced, which can be bad for your back. All the bags in this test feature adjustable dividers and offer quite a bit of versatility.

4) WEATHERPROOFING/ RAIN COVER Most bags are weather resistant. Some are weather proof, and others have all-weather covers that can be pulled out from a hidden compartment, usually on the base.

5) LAPTOP COMPARTMENT Make sure that the laptop compartment is big enough for your computer, as they vary in size. The padding is also important here.

6) ACCESSORY CLIPS Some bags allow you to attach further bags, tripods and monopods, but some are only compatible with the manufacturer's own clip systems.

7) ZIPS If you go out a lot in bad weather or near water, make sure that the zips are up to it. Wildlife photographers should also consider the noise made by the zips, as animals can be easily frightened off.

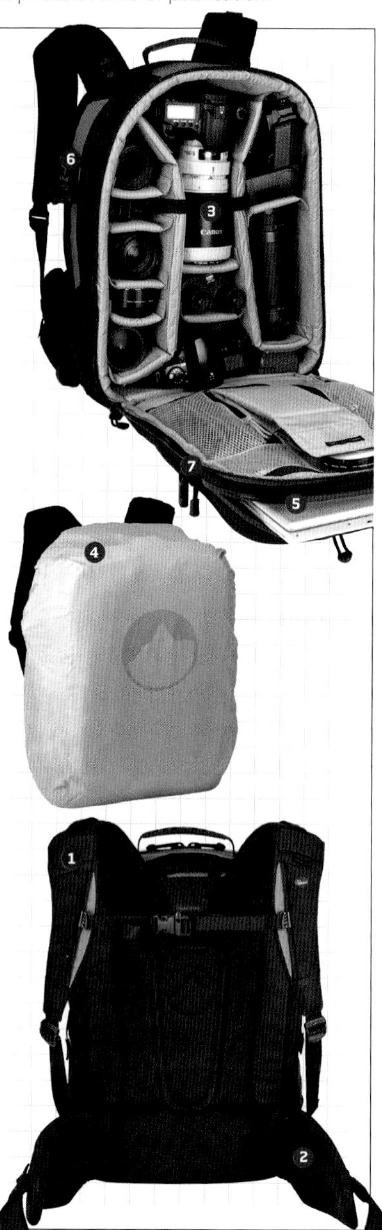

Kit watch!

Fitting and wearing a bag properly

If you're carrying a lot of heavy kit, it's important that your bag sits correctly on your back or at your side. This advice can prevent all kinds of back and posture problems. With a backpack, ensure that both straps are over your shoulders and tightened so that the bag sits in the centre of your back. If it has waist and chest straps, make sure you use them to distribute the weight evenly across your back, rather than just your shoulders. For shoulder bags, pull the strap over your head to the opposite shoulder. This will distribute the weight better than if it were on the closest shoulder and stops it from slipping off your shoulder, or being easily snatched.

Gadget bag

Backpack

Tamrac Adventure Messenger 5

DIMENSIONS: 37x30x22cm
WEIGHT: 1.07kg
WARRANTY: Five years
CONTACT: 01628 674411
WEBSITE: www.intro2020.co.uk

If you want to carry a laptop with you, then this is a good budget choice, as it has a well-padded, laptop compartment at the rear. There is lots of internal space and comfortably holds a large DSLR, like a Nikon D700 with 24-70mm lens attached, a 70-200mm f/2.8 zoom lens and flashgun. There are four dividers to change the layout, so you could easily keep a smaller body, extra lenses, and other accessories in there too. It's not short on features either, with a padded non-slip strap, a carry handle and slots to add on components from the Tamrac Strap Accessory System. A large pocket at the front has sections for pens, stationery or note pads, a pocket in the lid for smaller items and a dedicated mobile phone pocket. If you have a medium or large DSLR, extra lenses and a laptop, this is a great buy.

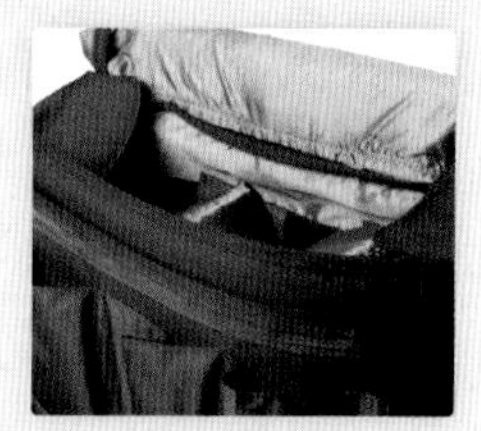

£45

Lowepro Classified 250 AW

DIMENSIONS (OUTER): 46.5x28x35.5cm
WEIGHT: 1.9kg
WARRANTY: Lifetime
CONTACT: 01902 864646
WEBSITE: www.daymen.co.uk

A discreet camera bag with room for lots of camera gear as well as a laptop. The interior of the bag is very deep, so you can double-up on storage by stacking items on top of each other. The bag's depth also makes it very suitable for cameras with long lenses. A padded section provides storage for a 15in laptop. Leather is used to good effect throughout the bag and the grab handles and shoulder strap are very well designed. Entry into the main section of the bag is through a clever roof zip that is easy to access on the move and is protected by the handle buckling over it. You'll be able to fit at least two DSLRs with an additional two or three lenses in the spacious main section. A luggage sleeve means that you can attach this bag to the handles of a wheelie case. The bag is hand-luggage friendly too.

£110

Lowepro Fastpack 250

DIMENSIONS: 31.5x24x46cm
WEIGHT: 1.6kg
WARRANTY: Lifetime
CONTACT: 01902 864646
WEBSITE: www.daymen.co.uk

Available in black, blue or red trim, the Fastpack 250 features two compartments and is ideal for travelling light. The camera compartment is well padded, holds a large DSLR with zoom attached, along with one or two small lenses and flash. There's no room for a second body or larger lenses though, but the rear padded pocket does hold a 15in laptop. The side entry compartment helps you get at your gear quickly, but you do need to take it off to get gear out safely. The top compartment isn't as well padded, so is not designed for camera gear, but it does include two pockets for memory cards and pens. Thanks to the generous padding on the shoulder straps and back, the Fastpack 250 is comfortable to carry, the sternum and back support straps hold it nicely in place and there's a carry handle to boot.

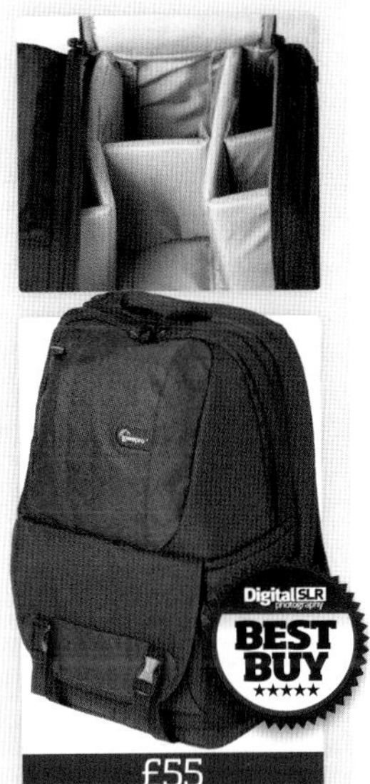

£55

Tamrac Aero Speed 85

DIMENSIONS: 36x23x50cm
WEIGHT: 1.6kg
WARRANTY: Five years
CONTACT: 01628 674411
WEBSITE: www.intro2020.co.uk

With space to hold personal and camera gear, the Aero Speed Pack 85 is similar to the Adventure 7, but a bit bigger, and the alternate layout allows you to carry more gear. It can hold a large DSLR, at least three lenses and it's also compatible with Tamrac's SAS system to slip on extra pouches. There's both side and front entry access, which makes getting gear out a little quicker, although you still need to take this backpack off first. The top of the bag has room for a light coat, lunch and a few other essentials, but there's no laptop compartment. Other pockets are limited too, there are a couple of side mesh pockets, and Velcro and zipped pouches for storing memory cards and batteries. Padding on the rear and non-slip straps is thin and there's no sternum strap, waist belt or rain cover either.

£80

Hama Defender 170 Pro

DIMENSIONS: 40x26x45cm
WEIGHT: 2.8kg
WARRANTY: 30 years
CONTACT: 0845 2304262
WEBSITE: www.hama.co.uk

This large backpack has two compartments, both of which feature generous space. The lower compartment fits a large DSLR with 24-70mm f/2.8 attached, a long zoom, flashgun, two small primes and even a second body. The flexible dividers make it versatile too, as the whole padded section can also be removed, and there's a large 17in laptop compartment. The construction is robust with Ultra Dobby Nylon, protected zips, tough belts, strong metal hooks and a rubber base that covers the bottom, so no problems leaving it on wet ground. The shoulder straps are adjustable, but not very well padded, and there's a waist belt, lumber support and padding on the rear for improved comfort. Features are good too, with a detachable microfibre cloth, memory card wallet, rain cover and several pockets.

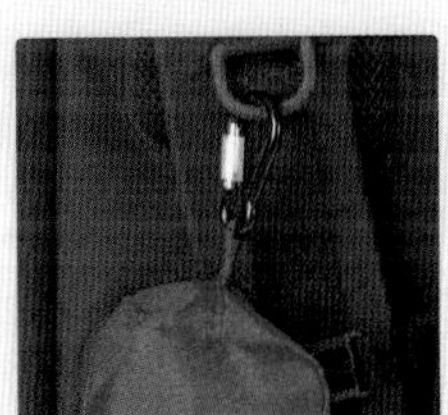

£80

Lowepro Vertex 100 AW

DIMENSIONS: 30x25x42cm
WEIGHT: 2.3kg
WARRANTY: Lifetime
CONTACT: 01902 864646
WEBSITE: www.daymen.co.uk

This is a traditional photo backpack designed predominantly for carrying camera gear. It has water-resistant zippers, a seam-sealed All Weather finish and dedicated rain cover. The adjustable harness makes it very comfortable to carry, and there's sternum and waist support belts to help spread the load. Internal space makes it possible to squeeze in two DSLRs with lenses attached and at least three more lenses too, and there are plenty of dividers to alter the layout. There is also a 13in laptop compartment, not to mention a detachable tripod foot, and the exterior dimensions conform to the maximum hand luggage specifications for airlines too. The front pockets feature pouches for spare batteries and memory cards, there are a couple of mesh pockets for other essentials and a documents pocket, too.

£100

Lowepro Pro Runner 450 AW

DIMENSIONS: 34x29x50.5cm
WEIGHT: 2.7kg
WARRANTY: Lifetime
CONTACT: 01902 864646
WEBSITE: www.daymen.co.uk

The Pro Runner 450 AW holds a lot of gear, with room for two large DSLRs with zooms attached, and space for several extra lenses, flashguns, a third body and a 17in laptop too. The shoulder straps are thickly padded and adjustable, and the waist belt and carry handle will be appreciated when carting about all that weight. The compression straps help reduce the bulk on the 450AW for easier transportation, there's a built-in All Weather cover and you can carry a tripod using the loops and tripod foot. The front pocket will hold a few personal items, the three internal pockets feature windowpane panels to help keep things like filters on display, and there are two dedicated memory card pouches, too. This bag is a great option for carrying a large outfit as well as personal gear.

£120

Tamrac Expedition 7x

DIMENSIONS: 33x34x50cm
WEIGHT: 2.9kg
WARRANTY: Five years (limited)
CONTACT: 01628 674411
WEBSITE: www.intro2020.co.uk

The Expedition 7x boasts lots of room and a comfortable harness system. There's loads of padding on the shoulder straps, lumber support and waist belt, together with airflow channels to keep you cool. There's no rain cover, but water-resistant zips and a lock-down rain flap help protect your gear. The dual hinge divider system helps you carry one or two DSLRs, with zooms attached; with room to spare for other lenses, and and you can boost capacity with Tamrac's Modular Accessory System and Strap Accessory System. There's a 15in laptop compartment and two 'wing' accessory pockets with Tamrac's Memory and Battery Management System for organising those essentials. There's also a plastic reinforced pocket, which provides protection for fragile accessories and acts as a tripod footrest.

£135

Tripods for outdoor use

A TRIPOD SHOULD BE viewed as an essential part of your outfit. When shooting landscapes, you'll usually be using a small aperture setting to maximise depth-of-field, along with a low ISO rating to give the highest quality results, which will result in long shutter speeds. Hand-holding might be feasible with some shots but with a tripod you never need to worry about the shakes. You'll also find that by placing the camera on a support, you can spend more time and attention on fine-tuning the framing of the scene to get the best possible composition. It's also an essential aid when shooting in low light and at night and is very useful for close-ups too. You'll find a huge variety of tripods on offer, so choosing one isn't straightforward, but there are two key factors to consider. The first is stability – while cheaper models may be tempting, the fact is if a tripod doesn't provide a stable platform, it fails. So ensure you pick a model that is sturdy enough to keep your camera kit totally still when shooting. The second factor to think about is how much a tripod weighs, which is important as you'll be carrying it, along with the rest of your gear, for considerable distances. Most tripods are made from aluminium, which is very sturdy and fairly lightweight, although you're looking at tripods weighing around 2kg or more for decent models. If you want a tripod that's just as sturdy but far lighter, you'll want to check out tripods made from carbon-fibre, although you'll have to be prepared to pay a premium for one.

The selection of tripods here have all received the highest ratings in *Digital SLR Photography* magazine. We've chosen examples that cover various price ranges to ensure you find a model that suits your budget. Bear in mind that with the more expensive models, you buy the tripod and the head separately, so you can mix and match to suit your needs.

Kit watch!

Interchangeable tripod heads

Most high-end tripods aren't supplied with a head. This allows users to choose their preferred legs and a specialist or general-purpose head. The two most common types of heads are as follows:

Ball and socket: These range from very simple heads with one control to complex units with panoramic locks and gauges, grip-locks, and hydraulic ball-locking systems. Usually stronger and quicker to adjust than pan and tilt heads, they allow free movement in all directions. 'Slipping' used to be a problem, not so much now, though.

Three-way heads: Commonly available as pan and tilt heads, these are good for precision work like macro photography, but are great for all types of photography. Panning gauges, showing the shooting angle, are useful for panoramic shots, although there are specialised heads made for this too. Fluid heads have the smoothest panning motion, making them ideal for sports photographers.

Ball & socket

Three-way

Features

1) HEAD There are various types of tripod head available, from ball and socket to three-way pan and tilt. Some have interchangeable heads. We have tested all the tripods here with three-way pan and tilt heads, which are the most popular for general use. When choosing a tripod, attach your DSLR securely and ensure the head is free from movement.

2) QUICK RELEASE PLATE These allow you to quickly attach and detach your DSLR to/from the tripod. All of the tripods in this review have one.

3) LEG LOCKS Most of the tripods in this test feature 'clip' locks, which are easy to use and provide a firm lock.

4) LEG SECTIONS Tripods with three leg sections or less tend to be the most sturdy, as the more sections you have, the less stable they can become.

5) SPIRIT LEVELS Useful for landscape photography in particular, many tripods feature built-in spirit levels, but if not, you your local photo store should sell one that slots on to your hotshoe.

6) BAG HOOK Some tripods have hooks on the central column, from which a bag can be hung, using its weight to add stability to the tripod in windy conditions.

7) TRIPOD FEET Spikes are good for grip outdoors but will scratch flooring. Rubber feet offer good grip indoors and outside and are the best choice for general use.

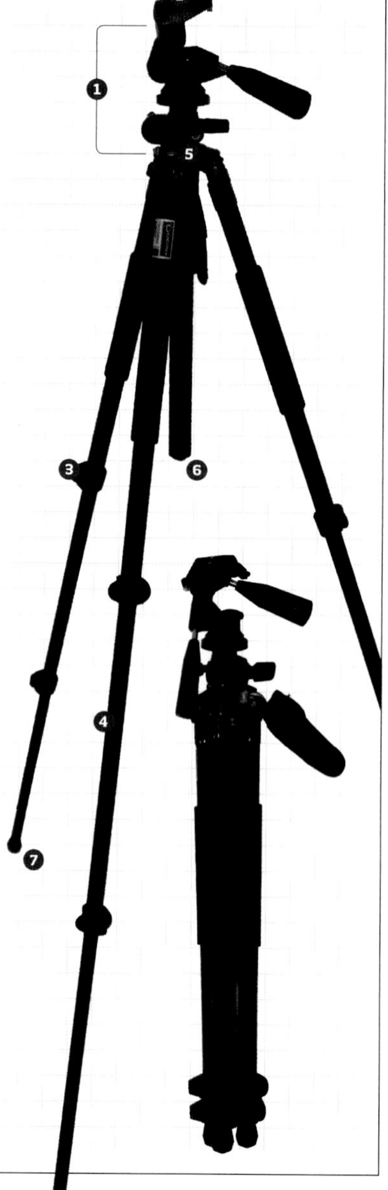

Giottos MTL9351B + MH5011 head

LENGTH (CLOSED): 64cm
NUMBER OF LEG SECTIONS: 3
HEIGHT (LEGS EXTENDED): 159cm
TYPE OF HEAD: Three-way pan and tilt
WEIGHT: 2.1kg
WEBSITE: www.daymen.co.uk

The Giottos has very solid aluminium legs with foam insulators, to keep' hands from freezing to them on cold days. The nuts and locks are a combination of plastic and die-cast aluminium, and are as solid as could be hoped for at this price. The three-way head is easily controllable and features three spirit levels in addition to the one on the legs, so there's no excuse for wonky horizons! It has a lockable rotational central column, which can be removed and re-inserted horizontally or inverted for macro or copy work. The tripod is very sturdy for the price, and comes with its own tool kit in case you need to make any adjustments. There is also a hidden bag hook underneath the central column. The MTL9351B had absolutely no problems coping with our test camera (Nikon D80) and would provide a very suitable platform on which the amateur landscaper could mount his DSLR.

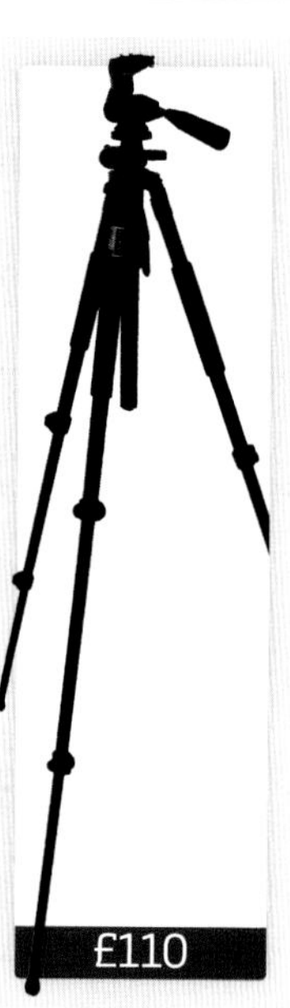
£110

Giottos MTL3361B + MH5001 head

LENGTH (CLOSED): 68cm
HEIGHT (LEGS EXTENDED): 165cm
NUMBER OF LEG SECTIONS: 3
MAXIMUM LOAD: 8kg
WEIGHT: 3.3kg
WEBSITE: www.daymen.co.uk

The build quality of the Giottos is very good. It's heavy, but very solid. The thick aluminium legs offer good stability, even in strong winds. The joints and locks are built to a high quality, and come with a tool kit should they need adjusting. At its maximum height with the central column extended, it still feels stable, and kept our test camera very steady. The tripod has rubber feet, which are slightly pointy, making it perfect for beaches and fields, but it takes a bit longer to stabilise on tarmac or hard surfaces; although once it is set up, it is perfectly steady. The central column can be removed and replaced horizontally, which, when combined with the three-position lockable legs (and they open really wide), allows the camera to get down really low for macro work. With this head fitted, there are three spirit levels to keep your shots straight, and panning is a breeze. There is also a bag hook.

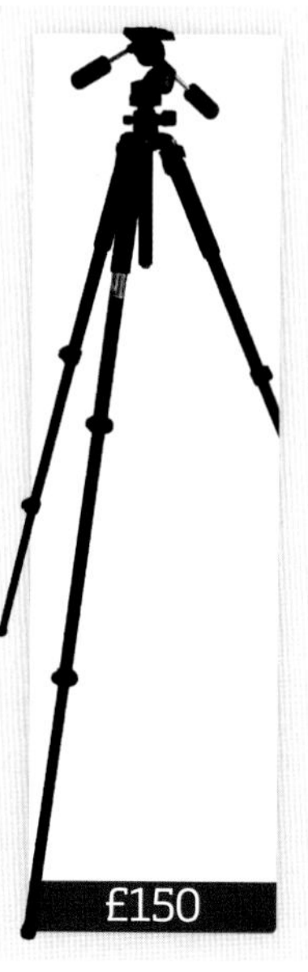
£150

Giottos MT8246B + MH1302-652 head

LENGTH (CLOSED): 51cm
HEIGHT (LEGS EXTENDED): 148cm
NUMBER OF LEG SECTIONS: 4
MAXIMUM LOAD: 3kg
WEIGHT: 1.375kg
WEBSITE: www.daymen.co.uk

This tripod is exceptionally light, especially for its size, yet it is sturdy, although the maximum load may prove restrictive for some. The rubberised twist locks are secure and comfortable to use and foam leg grips give a comfortable grip in cold weather. The three-position angle locks ensure that the legs don't slip, which is reassuring to those using expensive kit. The central column is reversible for low level and macro shots, and has a bag hook. The ball and socket head is also very secure, and it is easy to manoeuvre the head into just about any position. It has a variable friction control, allowing the user a great deal of control, which means that precision adjustments are quick and easy to implement. The three spirit levels help to ensure that horizontals and verticals are perfectly aligned, making this a great all round tripod for almost any type of photography, not least landscapes.

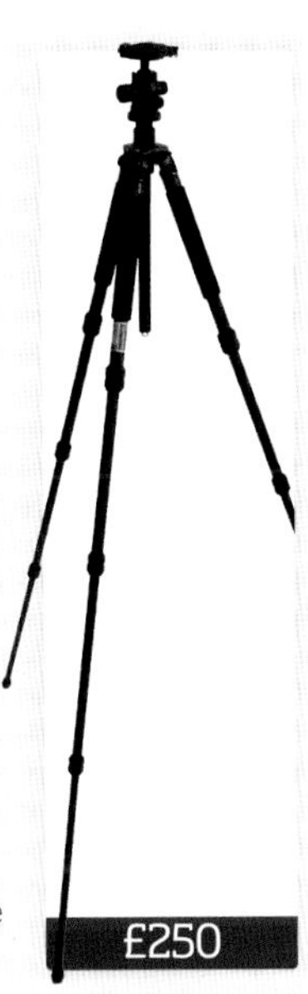

Manfrotto 190CXPRO3 + 484RC2 head

LENGTH (CLOSED): 58cm
HEIGHT (LEGS EXTENDED): 146cm
NUMBER OF LEG SECTIONS: 3
MAXIMUM LOAD: 5kg
WEIGHT: 1.62kg
WEBSITE: www.manfrotto.com

This Manfrotto is exceptionally light, and its sleek design looks fantastic. Despite its thin legs, it was sturdy and supported our test camera with ease. The twist locks are very strong and prove quick to use. The central column can be raised and moved into horizontal position without removing it from the legs, making the tripod perfect for macro and low level shots, and very easy to use. The multi-position leg locks have a depressable button, making them much easier and nicer to use than those that have clips that must be lifted. The ball and socket head is very smooth and easy to use, as one switch controls everything. This is ideal for quick positioning, but not as precise as some of the other heads in the test. There is a spirit level, to ensure that your tripod is level, and the centre column boasts a bag hook, allowing extra weight to be attached for stability in high winds.

Manfrotto 190XPROB + 460MG head

LENGTH (CLOSED): 57cm
HEIGHT (LEGS EXTENDED): 146cm
NUMBER OF LEG SECTIONS: 3
MAXIMUM LOAD: 5kg
WEIGHT: 2.25kg
WEBSITE: www.manfrotto.com

This aluminium tripod from Manfrotto is one of the lightest in this price category. The legs are very sturdy and supports the camera perfectly well in all positions. The flip locks are easy to open and close and very secure, and there are vari-position locks to keep the legs secure at different settings. Perhaps the most interesting feature of the legs, is that the central column can be switched to horizontal position, for macro shots, without removing it from the legs. This is an excellent feature, as it makes the process very easy and fast to carry out. The head is very versatile, as it can pan, tilt and swivel in just about any direction, and is very easy to operate. The lack of panning handles may not be to everyone's taste, but the head is so versatile that it more than makes up for it. Spirit levels can be found on the head and central column brace, and a bag hook is located on the legs.

Velbon Sherpa 435 With PHD-41Q head

LENGTH (CLOSED): 53cm
HEIGHT (OPEN): 161cm
NUMBER OF LEG SECTIONS: 3
WEIGHT: 1.49kg
MAX LOAD: 3kg
WEBSITE: www.intro2020.co.uk

At the more affordable end of the market is this combined head and legs set from Velbon. The tripod's black aluminium legs have three sections, locked in place with easy-to-open clip-style locks. The centre column is adjustable and reversible for low-angle shooting. For an entry-level model, the PHD-41Q head is a good buy too. It's bigger and more sturdy than others in this bracket and will take loads of up to 3kg with no problem. We like the head's relative simplicity: using it quickly becomes second nature. Two padded handles control movement and one of these unscrews and fits inside the other when the tripod is stored. A well-designed quick-release plate completes the package. This is a cracking buy for the beginner or intermediate photographer who wants a general purpose tripod to improve their images and open more options.

Manfrotto 055XPROB + 322RC2 head

LENGTH (CLOSED): 65.5cm
HEIGHT (LEGS EXTENDED): 178.5cm
NUMBER OF LEG SECTIONS: 3
MAXIMUM LOAD: 7kg
WEIGHT: 3.15kg
WEBSITE: www.manfrotto.com

The build quality of this die-cast aluminium tripod is excellent. It is very sturdy, and very reassuring. The 055XPROB features the same dual positioning central column as the 190XPROB, as well as a spirit level, bag hook and foam leg grips, which help to protect the user's hands when using the tripod in cold weather. The legs each have a four-position lock, which makes it versatile and secure. You'll either love or hate the trigger-style grip head, but we found it incredibly quick and easy to adjust, getting your camera into just the right position with the minimum of fuss. Not having to tighten levers also saves time, and reduces the risk of knocking the head out of place. The head has its own spirit level, allowing you to make sure that your camera is level. This head is particularly useful when combined with the versatility of the central column of the tripod and when shooting

Slik Pro 700DX with 700DX pan & tilt head

LENGTH (CLOSED): 76cm
HEIGHT (LEGS EXTENDED): 190cm
NUMBER OF LEG SECTIONS: 3
MAXIMUM LOAD: 6.8kg
WEIGHT: 3.2kg
WEBSITE: www.intro2020.co.uk

The largest tripod in this category is very sturdy and feels as though it could withstand any treatment. The design is simple but stylish, and it certainly looks like a tripod for serious use. Although it is quite heavy, it is still very portable for its size. The locks are strong and secure, yet easy to open, while the reversible central column allows users to take low level and macro shots with ease. This is particularly effective when used with the legs open wide, which can be done easily using the three-position locks, which hold them firmly in position. The pan and tilt head features a panning lock, and has a very smooth panning motion. The quick release plate is circular, which makes it very easy to attach and detach the camera. There are two spirit levels, which help to keep horizontals and verticals straight. Although there is no bag hook, the tripod is so sturdy you are unlikely to miss it.

Ultimate tripods

Any sturdy, lightweight tripod is suitable for outdoor photography, but a number of models have been made for those looking for the most compact possible design. Often termed travel tripods, these have an innovative design that allows them to take up less storage space and are worth looking at if you plan to head out on trips on a regular basis.

Giottos Vitruvian VGR8255 kit

www.giottos-tripods.co.uk

GUIDE PRICE: £260
STREET PRICE: £290

Supplied head: MH5310-630
Material: Carbon-fibre
Folded Height: 40cm
Minimum Height: 39cm
Max Height without Centre Column: 136cm
Max Height with Centre Column: 157cm
Weight: 1.28kg
Maximum load: 4kg
Number of Leg Sections: Five
Case Supplied: Yes

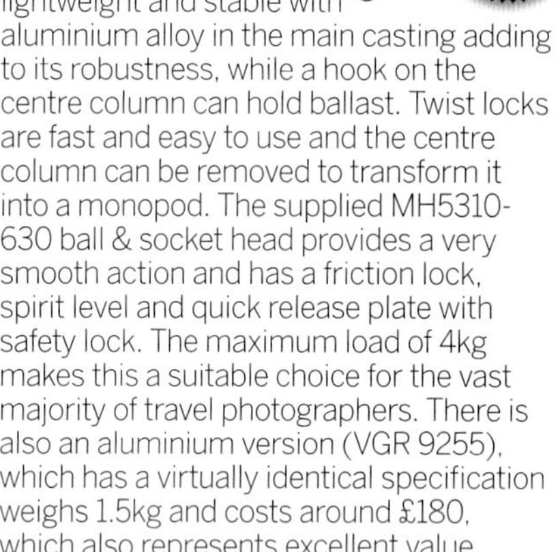

Boasting the 'reverse technology' design, the legs of the Vitruvian VGR 8255 folds 180° to surround the centre column, reducing the length to only 40cm. Open the five-section legs (shoulder locks provide two splay settings) and you can extend it to an impressive 1.36m (1.57m with centre column raised too). Made from six-layer carbon-fibre, it's lightweight and stable with aluminium alloy in the main casting adding to its robustness, while a hook on the centre column can hold ballast. Twist locks are fast and easy to use and the centre column can be removed to transform it into a monopod. The supplied MH5310-630 ball & socket head provides a very smooth action and has a friction lock, spirit level and quick release plate with safety lock. The maximum load of 4kg makes this a suitable choice for the vast majority of travel photographers. There is also an aluminium version (VGR 9255), which has a virtually identical specification weighs 1.5kg and costs around £180, which also represents excellent value.

VERDICT An innovative and high quality tripod. For most, the aluminium Vitruvian 9255 is a more realistic buy, but this carbon-fibre model represents great value.

Build quality	★★★★½
Versatility	★★★★½
Stability	★★★★★
Value for Money	★★★★★
OVERALL	★★★★★

Gitzo Traveler GT1550T kit

www.gitzo.co.uk

GUIDE PRICE: £490
STREET PRICE: £499

Supplied head: G1077M
Material: Carbon-fibre
Folded Height: 35.5cm
Minimum Height: 22cm
Max Height without Centre Column: 125cm
Max Height with Centre Column: 146cm
Weight: 1kg
Maximum load: 2kg
Number of Leg Sections: Five
Case Supplied: Yes

The Traveler series by Gitzo was the first to offer tripods with the 180° leg storage design. There are currently three in the range, with this being the mid-range model (the GT1541T costs around £430 while the GK2580TQR costs around £600). The Gitzo is the smallest model when stored of the tripods on test and when extended, its maximum height is slightly less than the Giottos. Like the Vitruvian, the centre column has a hook for a stabilising weight and can be removed to allow for low-level photography. This works in combination with the four-section legs, which can be splayed wide to allow for shooting close to ground level. The twist locks work well, allowing for legs to be extended or closed down quickly, but we're a little concerned by how thin the lower leg section is – it's the same width as a Biro – so stability may be compromised in windy conditions. The ball & socket head has a single friction lock control and is very fluid in use. The Gitzo is beautifully made but the current price is way too high.

VERDICT This compact and well-made tripod should last for years. However, the Giottos represents far better value and we doubt you'd note any real difference in use.

Build quality	★★★★½
Versatility	★★★★☆
Stability	★★★★☆
Value for Money	★★½☆☆
OVERALL	★★★½☆

Benro Travel Angel C-268M8

www.kenro.co.uk

GUIDE PRICE: £370
STREET PRICE: £370

Supplied head: Optional. (B-1: £160)
Material: Carbon-fibre
Folded Height: 41cm
Minimum Height: 41cm
Max Height without Centre Column: 121cm
Max Height with Centre Column: 151cm
Weight: 1.26kg
Maximum load: 12kg
Number of Leg Sections: Four
Case Supplied: Yes

Benro is a relatively new brand in the UK but has an extensive range of tripods, including six in its Travel Angel series: three carbon-fibre and three aluminium. The Benros use eight-layer carbon-fibre tubing, as opposed to the six-layer tubing used by Giottos and Gitzo, and claims it is 60 percent stronger. The C-268 is the premium model in the range and offers an advantage over rivals of a far superior maximum load of 12kg when used with the optional B-1 head, although this will set you back a further £160. It's a versatile tripod: as well as the 180° storage option, the legs can be locked at a number of angles, including low-level, although this process isn't as slick as with its rivals. The centre column is reversible and the main body is made from durable magnesium. The twist locks are water and dust-resistant and the rubber feet can be replaced with spikes. The B-1 head is very sturdy and has friction and panning locks and a quick release plate. It's a great tripod but unless you use a very heavy outfit, look at alternative Benros or go for the Giottos.

VERDICT The Benro is sturdy and a good choice if you use a heavy outfit. Otherwise, check out the other models in the range as they'll be far cheaper.

Build quality	★★★★½
Versatility	★★★★☆
Stability	★★★★☆
Value for Money	★★½☆☆
OVERALL	★★★½☆

Essential accessories

1) MEMORY CARDS Take enough cards so you aren't forced to delete images to free up space while away. We'd suggest going for 4Gb, 8Gb or 16Gb capacities from reputable brands like SanDisk, Lexar, Samsung or Kingston.
Lexar: www.lexar.com
Kingston: www.kingston.com
Samsung: www.samsung.com/memorycard
SanDisk: www.sandisk.co.uk

2) MEMORY CARD CASES Ensure that your cards are safely stored away when not in use to prevent them being lost or damaged. Our favourite cases are the Lowepro PixelPak and the Gepe CardSafe, which are extremely tough and durable with prices starting at around £5. Both come in a variety of options so you can choose the one suited for the types of cards you use. Even more handy is the OpTech Media Keeper (£8), which can be attached to a camera strap for fast access to spare cards.
Gepe: www.johnsons-photopia.co.uk
Lowepro: www.lowepro.com

3) PORTABLE STORAGE DEVICE (PSD)
The safest way to back-up images while away is to copy them to a PSD, which also allows you to edit and review images too. Epson's range of photo viewers is by far the most popular, proving easy to use, fast and reliable. We'd recommend the top-end P-7000, which boasts a massive 160GB capacity, boasts a 4in screen and has slots for CF and SD cards. It's great value to at around £400 or less.
Epson: www.epson.co.uk

4) SENSOR CLEANING There is always a risk of dust getting inside the camera body when the lens is removed. A variety of options are available to help remove any that has settled on the sensor that your camera's anti-dust system has failed to shift. There are a number of leading brands in this area and a variety of anti-dust solutions. Green Clean are one of the market leaders and make a large number of cleaning kits, many of which are based around a compressed air duster or mini-vacuum. For outdoor photographers, we'd recommend the LC-7000 Optic Cleaning Kit and SC-5200 After Shake Sensor Cleaner kit, as they're very portable and easy to pack away. Dust Aid are another brand you can trust, making swab and brush-based kits that are easy to stash away in your bag. Finally, there are the Arctic Butterfly sensor brushes from Visible Dust, which have built up an enviable reputation for easy, fuss-free sensor cleaning. All these brands are reputable so visit their websites and choose the best kit for your needs.
Arctic Butterfly: www.visibledust.com
Dust Aid: www.dust-aid.com
GreenClean: www.flaghead.co.uk
Lenspen: www.newprouk.co.uk

5) LENS CLEANING Cleaning accessories are cheap, take up hardly any room in your gadget bag and weigh virtually nothing, so be sure to take some when you head outdoors. A £3 microfibre cloth is ideal for removing fingerprints and dirt from optics and can be washed and reused. A £10 Lenspen is another option to consider. It has a brush at one end to wipe away dust and dirt, and a small pad at the other to clean away smears, so take one of these too. You may also want to invest in a small lens cleaning kit, which costs around £10 from most photo dealers and has swabs and cleaning fluid to help remove more stubborn marks.

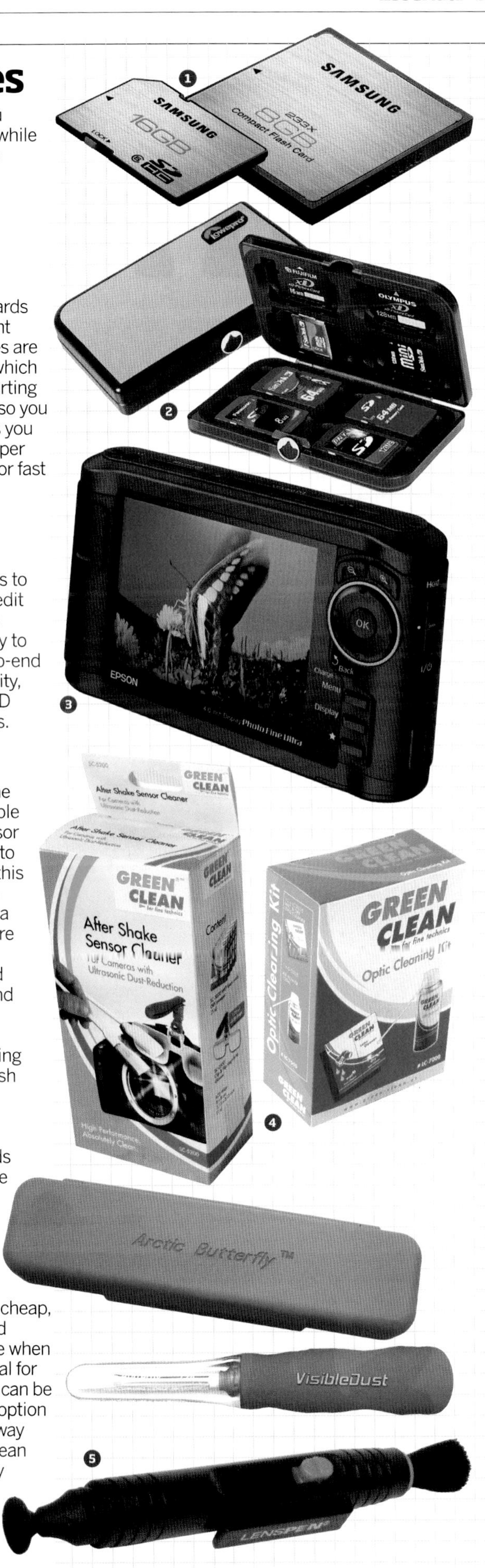

Useful aids

LCD COVERS
You use the LCD monitor for reviewing images, shooting with LiveView and accessing functions via the menu system, so it's worth spending a little to protect it and get the best from it. LCD protectors are thin sheets of film that are carefully placed over the screen's surface to protect it from scratches and damage. They come in different sizes, cost under £10 and once carefully attached last for years. The other useful LCD accessory is the shade, which allows the monitor to be viewed more easily in bright light. Look for shades by Delkin and Hoodman.
Delkin: www.delkin.com
digiCover: www.flaghead.co.uk
Hoodman: www.flaghead.co.uk

STRAPS
The vast majority of photographers use the wide strap supplied with their camera without any problem. But if you're carrying a heavy outfit or have the camera hanging off your shoulder for extended periods of time, then you should consider buying a thick, padded strap. We'd strongly recommend one of the many produced by OpTech. The £18 Pro Strap is a classic, a tough non-slip strap that is far more comfortable than your standard strap.
Optech: www.newprouk.co.uk

REMOTE RELEASE
A remote release is lightweight, inexpensive, small and helps minimise shake, so buy one.
Hama and Hahnel make the best value remotes, compatible with all major camera brands.
Hahnel: www.hahnel.ie
Hama: www.hama.co.uk

Clothing accessories

DEDICATED OUTDOOR PHOTOGRAPHERS are often shooting from before dawn until after dusk and you'll find them dressed accordingly. As well as thick clothing to deal with cold temperatures and high winds, you should also consider breathable garments to allow perspiration to evaporate in the heat and comfortable footwear that can handle hours of trudging along green countryside, rocky mountains and wet bogs. Ensure you're protected from the elements by following our guide to the best.

1) KEEP YOUR HEAD WARM WITH A BEANIE HAT! You lose close to a third of your body heat through your head and so it's important to wear a hat or cap in cold conditions. While baseball caps are OK, their peak will get in the way when you hold the camera to your eye. You can always spin it round but maybe opt for a beanie hat instead, which will help keep your head warm and won't take up much space when you take it off. You'll find them available in plain or patterned designs to suit your fashion sense (or lack of it!).

2) KEEP YOUR FINGERS NIMBLE! Cold winds can really freeze up your fingers and make it more difficult to press buttons and tweak controls on your DSLR. The easiest solution is to wear gloves, although standard types are quite thick and still make it difficult to operate your camera. Our favourites are both made by Outdoor Designs (www.outdoordesigns.co.uk) and are well worth trying out. The Takustretch has a grip palm and is made from wind-resistant materials to keep your hands warm. Better still is the Konagrip convertible, a windproof fleece glove with leather grip palm and flip-over finger mitt.

3) WEAR GOOD FOOTWEAR! You're more than likely going to cover miles in pursuit of stunning landscapes, so your average trainers aren't the best choice. Depending on how far you plan to walk, the type of terrain and time of year, you should look to wear shoes that are comfortable, hard-wearing and practical. Walking boots are best for serious treks and the likes of the £90 Berghaus Explorer (www.berghaus.com) are ideal, offering comfort, durability and support. You'll find them available for men and women in various colours. Another great option is Patagonia's Thatcher hiking shoes (www.patagonia.com), which are extremely comfortable and lightweight and incredibly durable. They're fashionable too and very well priced at around £60.

4) DON'T FORGET YOUR SOCKS! Cold or wet feet make walking around a real misery, as can wearing too thick a sock in warmer conditions. It's worth buying a couple of pairs of decent socks to suit the season and type of shoe you wear. Bridgedale (www.bridgedale.com) are leaders in this department, offering socks to suit cold weather, light treks or longer walks where comfort is essential. They've a bewildering choice on offer, but we'd recommend the Endurance Trekker and Comfort Trekker for longer walks, and the lightweight Bamboo Crew in warmer weather.

5) KEEP YOUR BODY WARM AND DRY! The humble fleece is an unsung hero in outdoor clothing, proving relatively lightweight, incredibly warm and very hard-wearing. They're also available in various designs and colours too, so are as fashionable as they are practical. You'll find all high street fashion stores stock their own brands, but we'd really recommend you check out those from outdoor specialists like Patagonia, Paramo and Berghaus as they're generally made from better quality materials. In cold weather the general rule is wear one or two thinner layers as opposed to one thick layer as the air between each layer is warmed up. So a fleece top with an outer fleece is a good option to consider. If it's especially cold or windy, a windproof jacket adds an extra layer of protection. For this guide, we tried out a number of fleeces and found the Patagonia R1 Pullover and Berghaus Arana to be excellent choices as a fleece top. The Berghaus Aura is a decent choice as an outer layer, while we found when shooting by the coast that Paramo's Pajaro and Cascada (www.paramo.co.uk) offered superb protection from the wind and sea-spray and are well worth investing in. Incidentally, when choosing colours, bear in mind right reds are great for visibility, so perfect when heading to remote locations, but not such a good choice if you ever plan on stalking wildlife!

6) PROTECT YOUR LEGS! In truth, few amateur photographers head outdoors in anything other than a pair of jeans and while they're comfortable, they're not ideal when the going gets wet. If the weather is unpredictable or you know you'll be shooting near the coast, consider a pair of waterproof trousers. Again, outdoor specialists are best, with Paramo's Cascada trousers generally considered to be one of the best.

ADAM BURTON

Be sure to bracket!

Whether you use the grey card or not, in tricky lighting conditions, bracket your exposure by +/-1 stops using your camera's exposure compensation or AEB functions to ensure you get the shot

Metered to perfection!

Scenes with bright skies can lead to exposure error. Use a grey card and you should have no problems.

How to use your free exposure metering and WB cards

The 18% grey card can be used to ensure perfect exposures when shooting in tricky lighting conditions (see below). Both reference cards can also be used to set a custom White Balance. Depending on the camera you use, you need to take a White Balance reading off the grey or the white card (your camera's instructions will show you how)

DIGITAL SLRS USE sophisticated exposure systems and all work using the same assumption that the average of the scene that is being metered from is a mid-tone, or 18% grey to be exact; i.e. the average of all dark, light and mid-tones mixed together is 18% grey. It's the basis of all metering patterns and works surprisingly well but while it's fine for the majority of shooting situations, it can lead to incorrect exposures when the scene or subject is considerably lighter or darker in tone than 18% grey. For example, very dark areas can fool the metering system into overexposing the image. Similarly, very light subjects, such as a snow scene, can fool the camera into underexposing them – making them appear darker than they are – as the light meter will take a reading designed to render them as a mid-tone. As a camera is trying to render an image 'grey', it's your job to ensure you compensate to keep the tones true to life. You can do this by either using one of your camera's exposure override facilities, such as exposure compensation or the AE-Lock button, or by metering from an area of the scene that has a mid-tone. And that's where our grey card comes in. Using it is very simple as our step by step guide below illustrates. The key thing to remember is that you need to place the grey card in similar lighting to your scene, for instance, don't place it in a shaded area if your scene is bathed in sunlight. Also, make sure that the card fills the metering area – we'd recommend you use spot or partial metering as the card won't need to fill the entire image area – but any is suitable. You can either lock the exposure using your camera's AE-Lock facility or note the aperture and shutter speed and then switch to Manual mode and set these, although this method isn't suitable to days here lighting is variable. The card has AF reference lines to help your camera's autofocus lock on to it. However, you don't necessarily need it to be in focus to work correctly. The grey card (as well as the white card) can also be used to take a custom White Balance reading from too.

1 GETTING STARTED Place your grey card on the ground angled towards you and ensure it's located in a spot that is bathed in the same light as the majority of your scene you plan to shoot.

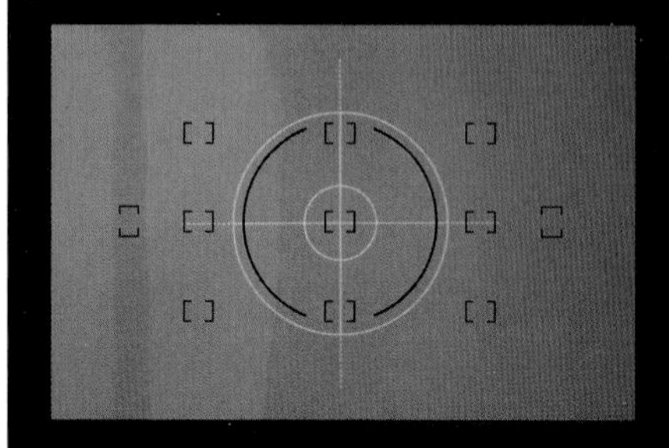

2 TAKE A METER READING Ensure that the entire metering area is filled by the grey card (in this instance we're using multi-zone metering) and lock the exposure with the AE-Lock button.

3 COMPOSE & SHOOT With this exposure locked, you can compose your scene and take your shots. When you check it on your LCD monitor, the exposure should be perfect.